UPSTART EMPIRE

PARIS DURING THE BRILLIANT YEARS OF LOUIS NAPOLEON

S. C. BURCHELL

UPSTART EMPIRE

PARIS DURING THE BRILLIANT
YEARS OF LOUIS NAPOLEON

MACDONALD · LONDON

The author wishes to thank the following for permission to quote from copyrighted works: FABER AND FABER LTD. and HARCOURT BRACE JOVANOVICH, INC. for "The Waste Land" from *Collected Poems 1909–1962* by T. S. Eliot; FARRAR, STRAUS & GIROUX, INC. for *Imitations* by Robert Lowell, copyright © 1961 by Robert Lowell; THE HARVILL PRESS LTD. for Roy Campbell's translation of *The Flowers of Evil* by Charles Baudelaire, published in England by THE HARVILL PRESS LTD. 1952; Norma Millay Ellis for Edna St. Vincent Millay's translation, "Parisian Dream" from *The Flowers of Evil* by Charles Baudelaire, HARPER & ROW, PUBLISHERS, copyright 1936, 1963, by Edna St. Vincent Millay and Norma Millay Ellis; and David Paul for his translation of Charles Baudelaire's "Morning Twilight," © David Paul, 1954.

First published in Great Britain in 1971 by
Macdonald and Company (Publishers) Ltd.,
St. Giles House, 49 Poland Street, London W.1.

SBN 356 03801 7

Reproduced and printed in Great Britain by
Redwood Press Limited
Trowbridge & London

FOR

KATHERINE

AND

ALEXANDER

Ce n'était pas un empire comme il faut, mais nous nous sommes diablement bien amusés.

COLONEL FLEURY

CONTENTS

The illustrations are between
pages 166 and 167.

UPSTART EMPIRE

PARIS DURING THE BRILLIANT
YEARS OF LOUIS NAPOLEON

PROLOGUE

1840

A T FIVE O'CLOCK on the morning of November 30, 1840, the frigate *Belle Poule,* under the command of the Prince de Joinville, dropped anchor in the waters off Cherbourg. The ship was back from the island of St. Helena, and on board were the remains of Napoleon Bonaparte. The emperor's final wish had been explicit: "I desire my ashes to rest on the banks of the Seine in the midst of the French people whom I have loved so well."

For a long time no one paid a great deal of attention to this last testament. But now, nearly twenty years after his death, Napoleon was on the final stage of the long journey back to Paris. The French of late, bored with the colorless monarchy of Louis Philippe and nostalgic for vanished glory, had begun to regild the Napoleonic Legend. The presence of veterans of the Grande Armée at every level of society and the popularity of such books as the *Mémorial de Sainte-Hélène* by the Comte de Las Cases served to feed the flame. The bourgeois king, astute and pear-shaped, succumbed to the delusion that he could control the opposition by joining it. So he had dispatched his third son, a naval officer, to collect what remained of the fallen emperor. At Cherbourg the remains were transferred to a steamer and carried to the mouth of the Seine between Le Havre and Rouen where a flotilla of ten small vessels was waiting. The cortège began the voyage upriver, the ship carrying Napoleon's coffin painted entirely black and flying the imperial standard. By December 14, 1840, the little fleet had reached Neuilly, and in the evening the coffin was placed at the foot of the Arc de Triomphe.

The next day was dark and cold with flurries of snow and a bitter wind. Nevertheless, it seemed as if every person in Paris had gathered along the Champs Elysées to watch the funeral procession. Victor Hugo, then an enthusiastic Bonapartist, wrote down a description of that memorable day: the winter sky and the gusts of wind and the muffled drums and the double rank of soldiers at attention all along the avenue. With the others he waited in silence, until a horseman came riding down from the direction of the Arc de Triomphe and the procession began.

Suddenly the sun appeared from behind the dark December clouds and sparkled on the weapons and helmets of the soldiers passing by: the Gendarmerie de la Seine and the Garde Municipale and the Lancers with their tricolor pennants snapping in the winter wind. Then cannon sounded and the sunlight grew more intense and a single white horse appeared. It was covered with a violet cloth and led by two grooms in green and gold. These were Napoleon's colors, and Victor Hugo reported that this was Napoleon's old battle horse. Cries of *"Vive l'Empereur!"* came from both sides of the avenue, and then the elaborate hearse containing the body had passed by. At a few minutes before two o'clock the procession crossed the river and reached the chapel of the Invalides, where Louis Philippe was waiting to place the sword of Austerlitz on the coffin.

4

Later that afternoon Victor Hugo mingled with the crowd which still filled the Boulevard in spite of the numbing cold. At one point he came across a magnificent and nostalgic sight: a towering hussar of the old Garde Impériale in full uniform. A sky-blue dolman hung from his shoulder, his busby was rich with colored silk and gold cord, there was a saber at his side and on the leather pouch swinging near his thigh a gleaming imperial eagle. The crowd made a path for him and children ran around and around the splendid figure, clapping their hands and shouting: *"Vive l'Empereur! Vive l'Empereur!"*

At this moment, in a medieval château in the marshes of northern France, a young man of thirty-two was enduring the first months of a sentence of perpetual imprisonment. For the second time he had made an unsuccessful attempt to overthrow Louis Philippe's government—a somewhat eccentric adventure, considering the means at his disposal. He had little more than his name—Louis Napoleon Bonaparte—and he was the nephew of the dead emperor who had finally come back to the French people. The life sentence in the fortress of Ham did not seem to worry him.

"Is anything in France perpetual?" he asked in his mild and enigmatic way.

In the end, of course, he was right. And he never lost confidence in the certainty of his imperial destiny. The Napoleonic Legend, gaining new strength after 1840, at last carried him into the palace of the Tuileries. And into a gaudy age of paradox and masquerade, to some measure an age of his own making—a time of false dawns and unexpected sunsets, of glorious springtimes and fearful winters, of bright surfaces and unbearable truths. A time of misery and a time of splendor.

PART ONE

THE GARDEN OF THE TUILERIES

There was much of the beautiful, much of the wanton, much of the *bizarre,* something of the terrible, and not a little of that which might have excited disgust.

EDGAR ALLAN POE
The Masque of the Red Death

CHAPTER ONE

The Garden of the Tuileries

Open now to every wind, a phantom palace at its eastern limit, the garden of the Tuileries occupies today an enigmatic and uncertain place on the Right Bank of the Seine. True, children still play beneath its trees and sail toy boats in the great octagonal pool. There is a puppet theater and a merry-go-round, the Impressionist painters have left the record of an era in the Jeu de Paume and the Orangerie, and old men with time on their hands stroll the terrace at the river's edge, looking down into the water. But the garden is no longer the focus of Parisian life, and it is surely not a stage for the dramas of republican France. The royal vista designed by Le Nôtre, which began at the palace of the Tuileries and extended down the central allée across the octagonal pool and along the Champs Elysées past the Arc de Triomphe, has no present meaning. The aureole is gone, leaving behind little more than a windy open space—nostalgic and inexplicable and vaguely embarrassing. The garden of the Tuileries lacks all identity, now that the actors have gone and the play is over.

The play, while it lasted, was superb. For three hundred

years the garden filled a compelling rôle in the life of the capital. At first the scenes were sovereign and particular: Louis XIII riding out to the hunt with a falcon at his wrist, Anne of Austria strolling among the flowers with her ladies-in-waiting, the infant King of Rome playing with his nurses. Later the cast was extended and other Parisians found their way into the enchanted garden. This was especially true of the last and most brilliant act of all, the act which began in 1852 and had as its background the extravagant springtime of the Second Empire.

These years have often been described but never more concisely than in a painting which can be seen today in the National Gallery in London: *La Musique aux Tuileries*. In the spring of 1863 an art dealer named Louis Martinet had responded to the demands of a new season and the mood of an adventurous era by presenting an exhibition of modern painting. On view in his gallery at 26 boulevard des Italiens were fourteen canvases by a controversial artist, Edouard Manet. One among them was the essence of spring: all light and color and movement and elegance and novelty. Manet had created an image of contemporary life, evoking not only the season itself but much of the sparkling atmosphere of Louis Napoleon's Paris as well. Like most of his other work, the painting was received with displeasure and disgust. One influential critic, an intimate of the Goncourt brothers, wrote in *La Presse* that the canvas "scorches one's eyes as the music at fairs makes one's ears bleed." Certainly—this was the point.

La Musique aux Tuileries does scorch the eyes, much as the Second Empire scorches the imagination, with violent color and the excitement of a new age. The painting was one of the first impressions of modern urban life and well in advance of its day. Surely it is appropriate that the whole should have been conceived while Manet walked with Charles Baudelaire in the garden on spring afternoons—two intellectual dandies in the Second Empire's great open-air salon, discussing the rôle of the artist in the middle of the nineteenth century. The tensions and paradoxes of modern life are favorite themes with both of them, keeping their work fresh and their insights rewarding to the present day.

Manet's impression of the garden of the Tuileries is a compelling example. The scene is one of lively confusion, the sunlight is strong, and the blues and yellows and reds of the ladies' bonnets provide sharp accents of color. The atmosphere is urban and elegant, charged with movement and anticipation. Like his friend Baudelaire, Manet had committed himself to a diagnosis of modern life. And the fact that the painting was such an accurate presentation of the contemporary scene explains to some degree the antagonism it generated in a middle-class society. Parisians of the Second Empire were not interested in self-analysis or the literal record of their daily lives. They were far more interested in entertainment: an amusing evening at the Bouffes Parisiens or a cancan at the Bal Mabille or the pretty picture of some voluptuous dryad. To a contemporary, *La Musique aux Tuileries* might well have seemed shocking—and disturbingly modern. In a very real sense it was an act of rebellion, the unwanted acknowledgment that Europe was at the beginning of a new era. Unexpected patterns in life and art and social relationships were developing: first in England and in France, later in Germany and Russia and the Austro-Hungarian Empire. Western civilization was moving toward the threshold of the twentieth century and poised now, in a new world of science and technology and improved transportation, at a moment of transition. It was an inevitable commitment which only the most avant-garde painters and writers and musicians could comprehend.

Though Baudelaire describes Constantin Guys as "the painter of modern life," the phrase can apply equally well to Manet. Like Baudelaire, he had an eye for the modern urban environment and the splendor and misery it engendered. This tendency led his art instructor Thomas Couture to remark sadly: "My poor boy, you will never be more than the Daumier of your day." A magnificent, if unintentional, compliment—for, like Daumier, he was content to move among the realities of his own time and give back to the public, not chubby angels and nymphs and classical heroes, but men and women as they existed in a particular time and in a particular place—specifically, as they existed in those adventurous, contradictory and materialistic years of the Second Empire. For this truth Manet was marked as a failure, and 1863 saw not only the disappointment of *La Musique aux Tuileries* but the Salon critics' rejection of *Le Bain,* more familiar today as *Le Déjeuner sur l'herbe*. Undaunted, Manet began work on his *Olympia* in the same year. It was to create a major scandal.

In the two decades during which Louis Napoleon imposed his régime on a far from unwilling nation, the garden described by Manet exercised an enormous appeal. When spring came, Parisians of every kind—though we must except the majority of the working class—hurried there in the afternoons. At least twice a week, and sometimes more often, the military band of the Garde Impériale gave a concert. Such an occasion is described in the painting: the men in top hats and frock coats and light trousers, the women in billowing crinolines, privileged children at play, here and there the flash of a uniform. This elegant audience came from all the frothy layers of

Second Empire society: from the court and the international set, from the military and the demimonde, from the Boulevard and the Bourse. Even the most presentable of the Bohemians were on hand.

There were aristocrats, businessmen, writers, painters, politicians, journalists, financiers, wits and dandies and fashionable idlers. There were beautiful young women of varying degrees of morality, though the *haute bicherie* was far more comfortable in the Bois de Boulogne. M. Graindorge, Hippolyte Taine's mythical pork merchant from Cincinnati, noticed with approval that the garden afforded young ladies with proper chaperones (we are still in the Age of Victoria) the opportunity to learn the first intricacies of social intercourse. Taine's comments on the urban scene had begun to appear in *La Vie parisienne,* a journal of humor and manners founded in the spring of 1863.

Then, as now, children came to the garden with their governesses, carrying hoops and balloons and dressed in the latest fashion: in kilts and glengarries and Scottish tartans. Style was of the first importance and anything vaguely English much admired. Political content had been severely limited by the government, and newspapers and magazines of the day devoted an enormous amount of space to the subject of fashion. The number of words written about the crinoline passes human understanding, and matters of style grew subtle and complex. There was, for example, a popular color known as Bismarck brown. The color itself was simply—brown. But the arbiters of fashion insisted on dividing it into a number of different shades corresponding, we may suppose, to the mercurial moods of the future Iron Chancellor: *malade, content, en colère, glacé.* Nestor Roqueplan, Parisian wit and well-known patron of the Maison Dorée, took time to codify

13

some of the more mysterious gradations of chic. After writing about clothes and the theater and food ("It is impossible to eat a meal outside of France"), he came to an exhilarating conclusion not peculiar to the Second Empire. "Money," he pointed out, "is always chic."

On these spring afternoons the whole glittering cast assembled under Louis Napoleon and his Spanish empress came to stroll through the garden of the Tuileries. Some came after lunch at the Café Anglais or the Café de Bade. They came to gossip, to admire, to criticize. They came for assignations, for music, for fresh air, for intellectual and social stimulation. Briefly, they came to be amused. It is no accident that one of the popular musical revues of the 1863 season was *Paris s'amuse* (*Paris at Play*). Its songs were heard everywhere:

> Sans la toilette,
> Et le plaisir,
> Faut en convenir,
> La vie est bête.*

Frivolous and superficial the concept may be, but it was one of the basic beliefs of a number of Frenchmen who lived during the Second Empire: life, without money and finery and pleasure, was rather ridiculous. If there were harsher facts, one did not have to face them—not at the theater nor here in the garden of the Tuileries.

Manet came with the others, though his interests rested far less on the surface than theirs. After leaving the Café Tortoni he would walk from the rue Taitbout with Baudelaire. Together they would wander through the garden, the one talking and the other sketching. About five o'clock they would return to Tortoni's for the absinthe

---

* "Without finery and pleasure, we must agree, life is just a stupidity."

hour, when Manet showed his latest drawings to an admiring circle. Baudelaire, in fact, appears in the completed painting (though, oddly, he did not like it), as do many other contemporaries. We find Manet himself and Théophile Gautier and the painter Fantin-Latour. Here Aurélien Scholl, journalist and brilliant raconteur of the Boulevard; Champfleury, writer and friend of Murger and Courbet; old Baron Taylor, patron of the arts and producer of Hugo's play *Hernani*. And there, sitting on an iron chair beneath a tree, the magnificent and ungainly Jacques Offenbach, whose music will forever call back those baroque and vanished years.

Manet's realism, however, is curious. There is a strange duplicity about this scene in the garden of the Tuileries, a confusing double image. The people in the painting seem to be playing two parts at the same time: they are at once the audience and the performance itself. Clearly, these elegant men and women are waiting for something to happen, whether to be amused or to play a part we cannot say. Perhaps it is enough to know that we are at the theater. Manet has captured the atmosphere of that electric moment before the curtain rises, a moment heavy with impatience and anticipation.

Appropriately, the theater took a central, if not brilliant, rôle throughout the period. Performances at the Bouffes Parisiens and the Variétés and the Comédie Française were oversubscribed, and the Opéra in the rue Le Peletier was one of the great social facts of the city's life. Amateur theatricals were given in many of the sumptuous mansions of the faubourg Saint Germain as well as in the imperial residences at Compiègne and Saint Cloud and even at the Villa Eugénie in Biarritz. On Napoleon Bonaparte's birthday in August the theaters were open to the poor without charge, and every prospective father-in-law was the stage manager of a comedy of manners in his own house. Make-up and clothes and décor were serious matters, and much of the talent of the day gravitated to the arts of the theater and of adornment. There were many superb craftsmen who provided the masks and painted backdrops of the Second Empire. Their skills were far from negligible: scenarios by Dumas *fils,* music by Offenbach, scenery by Viollet-le-Duc, photographs by Nadar and paintings by Winterhalter, jewelry by Froment-Meurice, costumes by Worth—the revels directed by the Princess Metternich and the whole in honor of the stars themselves: Louis Napoleon and his empress, Queen Crinoline and the Man of December. People were content with the magnificent spectacle, pleased with the outer surfaces of life and the gay vulgarity of crimson velvet and gold leaf. True to the world which he had created, Louis Napoleon in the last days at Sedan put on make-up to hide his illness and pain.

If the garden of the Tuileries was one of the great theaters of the day, it was an image in miniature of a larger world surrounding it. That larger world was Paris, and to a great extent the lovely city we know today is the creation of Louis Napoleon and his aggressive prefect of the Seine, Baron Haussmann. Haussmann extended the rue de Rivoli, completed the Louvre and cleared away much of the débris—and charm—of medieval Paris. He supervised the construction of innumerable churches as well as the building of Les Halles, the central market near the Palais Royal with its airy glass-and-iron structures reminiscent of London's Crystal Palace of 1851. He built wide new boulevards and sewers and brought an increased supply of water into the city. With a group of engineers and landscape gardeners he carved the Bois de Boulogne from a ruined forest and created a splendid

English park, a park dear to the anglophiles of the Jockey Club and the gentlemen riders of Longchamp. The afternoon drive around the lake in the Bois was to become one of the great spectacles of the Second Empire. Calèches and daumonts and phaetons crowded one another, as harlots and duchesses rode past with their gleaming carriages and pure-blood English horses. Often the empress came, preceded and followed by grooms in imperial livery, with a handsome equerry circling her carriage on horseback.

There were other, less elegant, activities on every street corner. The boulevards were full of singers and organists with costumed monkeys, jugglers and saltimbanques, magicians and sword-swallowers and itinerant peddlers of every description. The clatter of carriage wheels and the ring of iron horseshoes were insistent, and the shrill voice of the street crier filled the air. Throughout the city the movement and color seen in the garden of the Tuileries were duplicated a thousandfold.

The great city was rich with façades and diversions and factitious splendor. Like the cancan and the Folies Bergère and the tunes of Offenbach, the eagles and the trumpets and the golden bees symbolized the compulsions of an era when no excess was too great. An Englishman named Charles Oman remembered seeing some of the endless parades as a boy: the Orphéonistes with gorgeous lyres on their standards, the firemen in gleaming brass helmets, little girls in blue sashes carrying statues of the Virgin Mary, the white breeches and black gaiters of Napoleonic veterans, and the Zouaves with their tasseled hats and their dogs and birds and goats and camp followers— the "Zouzous" from Algeria so dearly loved by the children of Paris. At every turning you came upon another glamorous sight: here the young Prince Impérial, Louis Napoleon's son, riding out of the Tuileries at the center of his guard of Arab horsemen; there the Cent Gardes going by on a spring morning in their sky-blue tunics and glistening jackboots with the sunlight reflected in their plumed helmets and golden cuirasses; and the aristocratic officers of the Guides swaggering along the boulevard toward the Café du Helder. In every way these scenes suggest a masquerade.

The Second Empire was a time of flamboyance and extravagance, and Guizot's motto of the previous generation was much in vogue: *Enrichissez-vous.* Make money and more money and spend it. Foreigners in particular took the advice to heart. Eager to trade gold francs for experience, they crowded into the magic city. They came to enjoy themselves, and the Goncourt brothers[1] complained that Paris had become the brothel of Europe and that foreigners had taken all the women. 1863, they said gloomily, was the Waterloo of French manhood, *"le 1815 du phallus."* But the foreigner came—Italian and Dutchman and Brazilian and Spaniard—not alone for the women, but for those diversions and spectacles which made even cities like London and Vienna seem dull and gray. Some of this enthusiasm was communicated by Offenbach in his operetta of 1866, *La Vie parisienne.* The happy invaders sing:

> Nous allons envahir
> La cité souveraine,
> Le séjour du plaisir . . .
> Oh, mon Dieu! nous allons tous
> Nous amuser comme des fous.*

So they came to the great capital of pleasure in search of one unrestrained amusement after the other. The Gon-

* "We're off to invade the royal city . . . Oh, Lord, we're going to have a mad amusing time."

18

courts noticed that every face in Paris had the unwholesome look of the morning after a masked ball. Daily the pleasure-hungry arrived, and during the Second Empire the city entertained some spectacular *viveurs*—among them, the Sultan Abdul Aziz and his countrymen Murad the Madman and Abdul the Damned. A mania for amusement characterized the whole period, lasting through the Belle Epoque and spilling over into the years following the First World War. It is still a part of the myth of Paris, and that myth is very largely the creation of the Second Empire. Its comedies and tragedies were played against a lavish background of music and uniforms and *fêtes impériales*.

The surface splendor of the Second Empire was marvelously appealing. It was a tonic for all those industrialists and financiers, for all those dandies and *cocottes* who led the careless saraband, sharing the first gaiety and wonder in the face of all that was new and enjoying the laughter and the music and the money—until, at last, a glimpse of reality at Sedan and during the Commune of Paris. But for a long moment the bread and circuses had been enough: the diamonds and the black lace and the stock certificates, the scent of Parma violets and the Bengal lights and the uniforms, the melodies of Strauss and Offenbach and the martial strains of *Partant pour la Syrie* —if no longer the *Marseillaise*. It was not to every taste, but it was a glorious world of show and tinsel and veneer.

A world, to be sure, with a darker side. It was a time of ostentation and vulgarity and overwhelming materialism. Corruption and scandal and sensuality mark it as one of the least noble periods of French history. Behind the masquerades of the court and the elaborate façades of Baron Haussmann's Paris were many unpleasant truths. There was poverty, of course, and all the various pressures of a new industrial society. But the failures and darknesses of the day came perhaps less from these directions than from an inherent weakness in the national character. Often before, and often since, the French have suffered from the paralyzing disease of ennui. In particular, the people of Paris have had an infinite capacity for boredom—boredom which can be blunted momentarily with food and sex and money and novel diversions. Perhaps above all, it can be blunted with wit and irony, and a perverse love of paradox. In the tapestry of the European nineteenth century, paradox is one of the recurring designs, and it is the obsessive central fact of the French Second Empire.

Manet saw it in his painting of the garden of the Tuileries. Though he acknowledged with skill the brilliance and color and movement of Louis Napoleon's Paris, he did suggest something far more somber. Consciously or not, he saw a disturbing play of light and shadow in the dark overhead foliage and the black forbidding tree trunks. Such strokes add another dimension to a scene that is otherwise gay and charming and full of sunny confidence. *La Musique aux Tuileries* is a miniature of the Second Empire, and the darker palette is there for all to see. It is a palette calling to mind some of the more unhappy contrasts of modern life: the façades and the slums, the desire for peace and the presence of war, the distance between dream and reality.

The darker vision of sadness and decay and ennui is insistent. It is there in Manet's painting of the garden of the Tuileries. It is there in the melancholy message scratched with a diamond on the mirror of a private room in the Maison Dorée: "Where do we dine tomorrow?" It was nothing new, and in earlier years Nicolas Chamfort had sensed the sadness all around him: "Paris is a city of gaieties and pleasures where four-fifths of the inhabitants die of grief."

During the Second Empire there were difficulties both foreign and domestic, though business in general was flourishing and money circulating and stores and theaters and restaurants filled to the bursting point. No one gave a great deal of thought to these difficulties (unless it was Louis Napoleon himself) or to the fact that the average workingman earned a little over three francs for an eleven- or twelve-hour day.[2] The range of compensation was wide: the delectable Contessa di Castiglione was rumored to have received a million francs for surrendering herself briefly to an English milord. The poor lived—even more so after the rebuilding of Paris—in the most appalling of conditions. Haussmann's façades hid from the general view an underworld of slums and tenements and drinking dens more terrible than anything seen in the worst days of Liverpool and Manchester, an inferno of impoverished workers and twelve-year-old prostitutes darting in and out among the carriage wheels of the newly rich. In Rouen the cotton workers lived on colza leaves, and the dreadful caves of Lille were notorious. Surely some pretty fairy tale was needed to obscure the truth.

Sated with pleasure, foreign visitors were quick to see the contradictions and absurdities of Louis Napoleon's régime. In particular the Second Empire did not appeal—unless furtively—to Germans. Karl Marx inevitably regarded it as a "ferocious farce." And Bismarck, so delighted to have chosen himself as one of its executioners, was more explicit. "From a distance it's stunning," he said. "When you get closer, however, there's nothing there at all."

The end, if not merciful, was quick. In the September of 1870—only a few years after Manet had set down his impression of the garden of the Tuileries, so gay and sunny and confident—the lovely party was over. One could have looked through the locked gates of the garden and seen defeated soldiers moving about under the trees and troopers washing their clothes in the octagonal pool. On the wall facing the place de la Concorde were obscene posters: Napoleon III balanced on a chamber pot, Napoleon III licking the boots of King Wilhelm of Prussia, Napoleon III leading a moth-eaten eagle across the French frontier. In those same September days Dr. Evans, the American who was to help Eugénie escape from the country, turned into the rue Castiglione and came upon a curious sight: a man in a tall silk hat standing on a ladder with a hammer in his hand. He was smashing the sign above the store which read: "Purveyors to His Majesty the Emperor"—a sign he had surely spent much effort to obtain. The scene was repeated in the place Vendôme and all along the rue de la Paix. The ship was sinking, and those who could were abandoning it. When spring came, there was more dramatic evidence of the fall of an empire, and the garden of the Tuileries lay under the smoke and firelight of a burning palace.

Inevitably, one is tempted to collect all the broken images of success and defeat, of sunlight and darkness, of order and disorder: to wonder what took place between the April of the Second Empire and the dark spring of the Commune, to explain the enigma of those gorgeous and disastrous intervening years. Was the Second Empire no more than a distraction conceived by an adventurer in ghostly imitation of the past and dominated by spendthrifts and prostitutes and cynical politicians? Does it mark an interruption in the course of French history? Or was it a giant step into the twentieth century?

PART TWO

MASQUERADE

The French take the shadow for the substance, the word for the thing, the appearance for the reality. . . . Their gold is fool's gold and their diamonds paste. The artificial and the conventional are enough for them.

HENRI-FRÉDÉRIC AMIEL

CHAPTER TWO

An Evening at the Theater

THE beginning came in winter. With a fine sense of
fitness the Comte de Morny spent the early part of
the evening of December 1, 1851 at the Opéra Comique,
costumed well before time in his conspirator's uniform of
tail coat and white gloves. An elegant and shrewd oppor-
tunist, a lover of horses and women and fine art, Morny
was a man born squarely and accurately in the right time
and in the right place. Far more so than his half-brother
Louis Napoleon Bonaparte, he was at home in that new
and intricate world of speculation and finance and self-
seeking which began to flourish toward the middle of the
nineteenth century.

During the intermission Morny stopped to chat with a
fashionable lady of his acquaintance. Like many others on
that December night, she sensed that some important
change was in the air. For months the rumor of a coup
d'état had been going around the city. In fact, it had been
predicted on a dozen different occasions. There was no
secret that Louis Napoleon, now President of the Second
Republic, wished for a more permanent arrangement.
The lady told Morny that she had heard they were going

25

to make a clean sweep of the Assemblée Nationale before very long. "I don't know what's going to happen," said Morny. "But if there is a clean sweep, madame, rest assured that I will try to be on the side of the broom handle."

Then he exchanged pleasantries with other friends, tactfully avoiding two important generals in the audience, Cavaignac and Lamoricière. To their surprise, they were to find themselves swept into jail the following day. Morny, it so happened, would be holding the broom.

This suave and self-appointed aristocrat was born in 1811 as plain Auguste Demorny. He had chosen to rearrange his name and elevate himself to the nobility on the strength of some rather unusual relatives, however unacknowledged they must remain. He was the illegitimate grandson of Talleyrand and, more spectacularly, the illegitimate son of Hortense Beauharnais, daughter of the Empress Josephine. The latter relationship suggested his coat of arms, which features a hydrangea, and to the wits on the Boulevard he was forever known as the Comte Hortensia.[1] There was almost no pleasure or luxury (or woman) he had not enjoyed, and his rise in the world had been rapid during the reign of Louis Philippe. He possessed an enviable talent for knowing the right people at the right time: surely it did him no harm to include among his best friends the king's son, the Duc d'Orléans. In addition, he had a gambler's instinct for leaping from high places and landing squarely on his two feet. He used friends and relatives and mistresses without compunction and in return allowed them to enjoy the warmth of his extraordinary charm and worldliness. He was not always honest or particularly loyal, but he cannot be dismissed simply as a dandy and gentleman jockey and seducer of women. Morny became, next to Louis Napoleon, the most important figure in the Second Empire and remained so until his death in 1865.

As a young man with social connections and no money, he turned naturally to a career in the army. He joined the fashionable First Regiment of Lancers and was sent out to Algeria, where the French government was engaged in subduing Abd-el-Kader and laying the foundations of a colonial empire. Morny's two tours of duty were mildly distinguished, and he was decorated for saving the life of a general. By 1835 he had returned from Africa and resigned his commission. The next ten years were spent in leading the careless life of a Parisian man-about-town. He rode in the steeplechase newly brought over from England, gambled with his aristocratic friends in the Jockey Club and dined at the Café de Paris, one of Europe's most glamorous restaurants. He had a stable of English horses and the exquisite wardrobe of a dandy: beautifully fitted redingotes, black vests with gold piping and hats *à la Morny*. It was all very expensive, and the young man had no apparent source of income. At this time, however, he began a long and comfortable affair with the Comtesse Le Hon, wife of the Belgian ambassador. The daughter of a wealthy banker, she provided Morny over the years with some of the money he needed to indulge his extravagant tastes. Later, deciding to marry the young Russian Princess Troubetskoi, he left her easily and without regret. It is some indication of Morny's charm that the countess was not overly bitter. But she could not resist a final remark: "I found him a lieutenant and left him a minister of state."

During those early days his life was not all idleness and dissipation and self-indulgence. He had begun speculating in the stock market, and he interested himself in various business enterprises. When he came to power during the

Second Empire, the knowledge that he had a hand in some financial venture was enough to guarantee its success. *"Morny est dans l'affaire,"* they would say, and there would be a wise nodding of heads. Along with his talent for attracting money, he was beginning to learn the art of politics. At one stage in his career he had bought a sugar-beet factory near Clermont-Ferrand, a provincial city south of Paris and capital of the Department of Puy-de-Dôme. In 1842, having waged a vigorous and witty campaign, he was elected to represent the department in the Chamber of Deputies. He continued to be re-elected for the rest of his life.

Six years later, after the February Revolution and the pathetic flight of Louis Philippe, Morny took time to consider which way the wind was blowing. It was quite apparent that his connections with the House of Orléans could be of little use at the moment. By 1848 the French political scene was in one of its periodic states of convulsion. When the July Monarchy of Louis Philippe came to an end, a shaky provisional government had taken control. Under the direction of such idealists as the romantic poet Lamartine it planned in all good faith to proclaim a republic. But there was wild disagreement about the form it should take. On the left there were radical socialists, Jacobin democrats and liberal republicans maneuvering for power—and, on the right, bourgeois and Bonapartist and monarchist joining in the search for stability and moral order. On top of this confusion the nation's finances, already burdened by the unbalanced budgets of Louis Philippe's reign and the poor harvests of 1846, were at the edge of disaster. In March government bonds were down almost fifty points, and stocks and other bonds quickly followed suit. There was widespread unemployment, a disturbing number of businesses were bankrupt and many factories had closed. Money was in short supply, and real-estate values were falling. The majority of workingmen faced poverty and starvation. Clearly, some immediate action was necessary.

In June, the workman of Paris himself took that action and mounted the barricades once more. His breaking point had been reached when the National Workshops were abolished. Ineffectual as these may have been, they at least provided some form of employment and financial aid. Now they were gone and bread was gone and revolution seemed to be the only answer. The June Days of 1848 were some of the bloodiest in the history of Paris, and the city was long in a state of siege. At last the insurrection was put down with impartial brutality by General Cavaignac, who had at his disposal the army and the Garde Mobile and the Garde Nationale. For a time Cavaignac was virtually dictator of France. The revolt served no other purpose than to point to a widening rift in nineteenth-century society—a rift unhappily emphasized by technological progress. In the industrialized countries of western Europe two nations faced each other with new antagonism; the Rich and the Poor. Three years earlier, in his novel *Sybil,* Benjamin Disraeli had described the phenomenon as it appeared in England. Now in France the June Days were leaving a legacy of class hatred that was to shape much of the nation's future history. In particular, it prepared the way for the authoritarian régime of Louis Napoleon. The revolt had served to discredit the radicals, and members of the middle and upper classes—more fearful than ever of the Red Menace—looked for law and order and waited hopefully for a strong man on horseback to appear.

The men on horseback came soon enough: General Cavaignac and Prince Louis Napoleon Bonaparte. When the constitution was finally drafted and the Second Republic proclaimed, the choice for president lay between the two of them. The people quickly rejected idealists like Lamartine and socialists like Louis Blanc and Ledru-Rollin. Of the two major candidates Louis Napoleon was the lesser known, although his exile had come to an end after the flight of Louis Philippe and he had been in and out of Paris since the February Revolution. He had managed to get himself elected to the Chamber of Deputies, and his agents were everywhere—trying to convince the middle class that he stood for law and order, the army that he would revive the glories of the past, and the workers that he was practically a socialist. Oddly enough, all of these representations were quite true. In the end it was his magic name alone which won the election and gave him five and a half million votes out of seven million cast. On December 20, 1848, he took an oath to defend the new constitution and became President of the Second Republic. It was an oath he did not honor for long.

The step from president to emperor, however, was a giant one and needed endless skill and preparation to accomplish. From his first days at the Elysée Palace a group of aggressive and dedicated Bonapartists grew up around the prince-president. One of the first among them was Auguste de Morny, deputy and man of fashion. That both he and Louis Napoleon were the sons of Queen Hortense was really no more than a happy—or unhappy—coincidence. Morny's intelligence and shrewd love of self would have led him to the sources of power in any case. For the moment, power lay in the hands of his half-brother, and he turned his considerable skills to the task of bringing that power to full maturity. Morny spent long hours in a mysterious house on the rue du Faubourg Saint Honoré near the presidential palace. The house, haunted by the

Praslin murder which had taken place there a few years earlier, was now headquarters of the Bonapartist conspirators. The Comte Bacciochi lived in it and the faithful Persigny and Jean Constant Mocquard, the prince-president's secretary and once secretary to Queen Hortense.[2] Morny was a faithful visitor, laying plans for the coup d'état which would make Louis Napoleon, like his uncle, emperor.

There is little doubt that Morny was responsible for most of the work involved and the majority of the decisions made. He was cool and arrogant with a gambler's sense of timing, and surely the high stakes must have appealed to him. He was never modest about his own part in it: "I believe I can say that without me there could have been no coup d'état." Many years later, when she was an old lady and the Second Empire quite forgotten, the Empress Eugénie acknowledged that Morny had been the architect of her husband's rise to imperial power. Moral considerations aside, she said, the accomplishment was a masterpiece and "Machiavelli himself . . . would have had nothing but praise for the Second of December."

While Morny was at the theater on the evening of December 1, 1851, Louis Napoleon was giving his Monday-night reception at the Elysée Palace. Nothing was out of the ordinary: on hand were the usual diplomats, officers, deputies, French and foreign noblemen. Only the most clairvoyant of observers could have made something of the fact that Louis Napoleon stopped to talk in a low voice with a Colonel Vieyra of the Garde Nationale. The party continued uneventfully, and at around ten o'clock the prince-president excused himself and retired to his study.

The time had come to set the machinery of the coup d'état in motion. Louis Napoleon sat at his desk under a portrait of Queen Hortense and, one by one, greeted his fellow conspirators as they came into the room. When everyone was assembled, he reached for a bundle of papers tied with a ribbon. It was marked with the single code word: RUBICON. The moment was openly theatrical and more than a little self-conscious. The atmosphere of make-believe was entirely appropriate, however, when one considered the odd group gathered here in the president's study. They might easily have been mistaken for the cast of some imperfect melodrama: Prince Louis, an adventurer; Morny, a bastard; Persigny, a false nobleman; Saint Arnaud, a soldier; Maupas, a conspirator; Mocquard, another conspirator. It was a shady group by any standard. Three of its members had false names, and all were gamblers and opportunists and parvenus. Surely this tawdry general staff was perfect to command the followers of Louis Napoleon—whom Karl Marx, at least, characterized as a collection of "vagabonds, disbanded soldiers, discharged prisoners, fugitives from the galleys, sharpers, jugglers, professional beggars, pickpockets, conjurers, gamesters, pimps, brothel-keepers" and so forth.

Debonair in the black and white of their evening clothes (Saint Arnaud was in uniform), the conspirators understood the desperate change they were taking. Most of them were in debt, especially Morny, and none of them had a great deal to lose. Mocquard was loyal and Maupas ambitious, Persigny would have followed Louis Napoleon into a volcano and General de Saint Arnaud had spent some years in Africa perfecting the *razzia,* a murderous raid on defenseless villages. All of them were ready for the next throw of the dice. Money was distributed and final instructions given. On leaving, Morny turned to Louis Napoleon.

"Whatever happens," he said, "there'll be a guard outside your door tomorrow morning."

Then he hurried off for a rubber of whist at the Jockey Club, and Mocquard was late for a party. Louis Napoleon went to bed.

The first workmen out in the morning saw white proclamations posted at every street corner. Standing in the freezing rain, they listened as the more literate among them read the notices aloud. There were three, and it was no accident that they were dated December 2, 1851: the anniversary of the battle of Austerlitz as well as of the coronation of the first Napoleon. All of them were signed by the prince-president—one explaining that the Assemblée Nationale had become a center of subversion, another appealing to the army to maintain law and order, and a third indicating some of the drastic changes that had taken place while Paris slept:

I   The National Assembly is dissolved.
II   Universal suffrage is restored.
III   The French people is summoned to the polls between December 14th and 21st.
IV   Martial Law is declared throughout the 1st Military Division.
V   The Conseil d'Etat is dismissed.

Silently and efficiently during the night the proclamations had been printed and the drums of the Garde Nationale slashed (Colonel Vieyra had done his job well). Maupas had assembled over eight hundred policemen, and in the early hours of the morning they arrested a large group of parliamentary deputies, army officers and republican journalists. These were taken without a struggle to temporary jails at Vincennes, the boulevard Mazas, Mont Valérien and the cavalry barracks on the quai d'Orsay. Morny himself awakened the Minister of the Interior and announced suavely that he was taking his place. The operation was smooth and, for the moment, bloodless. A strong man had imposed his will on the French people, and Louis Napoleon—though still president and not yet emperor—was certainly dictator.

As the morning progressed, the city of Paris began to learn what had happened during the night. At ten o'clock Louis Napoleon himself rode out from the Elysée Palace to test the temper of the public. With him were his uncle, old King Jérôme of Westphalia, and the sunburned African generals Magnan and Saint Arnaud. Louis Napoleon's reception in the streets of Paris was not precisely enthusiastic, but neither was it hostile. More and more people, in fact, were welcoming the news of the coup d'état. That morning the elegant Englishman Captain Gronow was being shaved, and his barber talked of nothing but the virtues of the prince-president. From the window of her apartment at 138 avenue des Champs Elysées the well-known poetess Elizabeth Barrett Browning could see troops marching into the city. She had watched the president ride by and had heard the shouts of *Vive Napoléon!* In a letter to an English friend she remarked on his popularity: "All our tradespeople, for instance, milkman, breadman, wine merchant, and the rest, yes, even the shrewd old washerwoman, and the concierge, and our little lively servant were in a glow of sympathy and admiration." There were many Frenchmen (particularly outside of Paris) who made no great distinction between the Bonapartes, uncle and nephew. And not a few peasants thought that the First Consul himself had returned. The name was enough and the promise of discipline and glory it carried with it. Mrs. Browning did mention, however, that the wits on the Boulevard thought the slogan LIBERTY! EQUALITY! FRATERNITY! might well be changed to INFANTRY! CAVALRY! ARTILLERY!

The coup d'état was not without its brutal side. The trouble began, as Morny said it would, on the third day. Returning from a visit to his banker, Captain Gronow and a friend from the British Embassy saw a brigade of lancers charge into a crowd. Victor Hugo (whose new and violent bias as an anti-Bonapartist must not be overlooked) witnessed a number of atrocities: a thirteen-year-old child slaughtered by soldiers who laughed as they enlarged his wounds with their sabers; a harmless pedestrian shot down simply for saying he was on his way home; a pregnant woman slipping in the street and troopers finishing her with the butt ends of their muskets. There is little way to confirm these gruesome details, but the fact remains that the results of the coup d'état were drastic enough. In the neighborhood of the boulevard des Italiens, and in many other parts of the city, soldiers had fired on crowds and stores and theaters. Nearly thirty thousand prisoners were taken: almost ten thousand of them were transported to Algeria, a few hundred to Cayenne and others expelled either from the country or from the towns in which they lived. The harshness of those days was to haunt Louis Napoleon for the rest of his life.[3]

Unlike Morny and the African generals, he was not comfortable in the face of violence. There was in his nature something of the feminine, and with it came a large measure of human sympathy. History has delivered to us a very imperfect portrait of the strange and contradictory man who became Napoleon III. He is remembered only for the brutality of his coup d'état and the ignominy of his defeat at Sedan. It has been the fashion to think of him as the first of the modern dictators—to compare him, in fact, to Adolf Hitler, finding clever parallels for the shabby belted trenchcoat and the beer-hall putsch. At best the comparison is forced and has little relation to the facts either of the Second Empire or of the oddly attractive personality of the man himself.

His coup d'état was no isolated phenomenon: it conformed to a resurgence of strong government found throughout Europe in reaction to the revolutions of 1848. That resurgence was to be seen in Italy and Hungary and in the German states. Many people, especially those in the middle and even in the working class, felt that they had been betrayed by radical idealists and longed for order and security. In France, on December 21, 1851, a plebiscite—conducted largely without coercion and in a democratic spirit[4]—approved Louis Napoleon's seizure of power by an astounding majority: seven and a half million affirmative votes as against 640,000 opposed. Three days after the plebiscite the Paris correspondent of the *Illustrated London News* could report that the stock market was rising and that satisfaction glowed on every face. Paris, if anything, was gayer than usual. The reason for this almost universal joy among Frenchmen was not difficult to understand. "Liberty has disappointed them," said the English reporter, "interfered with their business, led to nothing but bloodshed, and just for the novelty they are quite willing to try what the strong hand will do, and to leave theories alone." Certainly this was to gloss over a number of unpleasant facts and to ignore the bitterness that was present, and would continue to be present, in many quarters. Essential liberties were lost and, at the beginning at least, opposition tolerated not at all. But the gray tensions of a police state did not exist in those first days, nor did they exist later. It simply was not the style of the Second Empire. A few nights after the coup d'état Captain Gronow saw Louis Napoleon at a ball given by the Duchess of Hamilton. He was accompanied only by his friend Bacciochi and left the party without an escort, returning to the Elysée Palace in a one-horse brougham. These were not the actions of an uncertain tyrant like the Emperor Soulouque of Haiti, with whom clever journalists like Rochefort were always pleased to compare him—however obliquely.

In spite of the panache of his régime there was a disarming simplicity about Louis Napoleon himself. It was a quality which made many otherwise intelligent people quick to underestimate his capabilities. On the face of it, he was an unlikely surrogate for his uncle. When he came back to Paris in 1848 a few days after the flight of Louis Philippe, he took modest rooms at the Hôtel du Rhin. From his window he could see Napoleon's statue on top of the column in the place Vendôme, a circumstance which the wits on the Boulevard found wildly amusing. They came around to have a look at the Bonaparte pretender and found him wanting in every way. He was a gauche enough little man with a large nose and a lusterless expression about the eyes. He seemed languid (although at least *that* could be attributed to his well-known sexual excesses), but he spoke French—and this was unforgivable —with a German accent. "He looks," said Théophile Gautier, "like a ring-master who has been sacked for getting drunk." To General Changarnier (who may have had cause to regret the witticism as he sat in jail after the coup d'état) he seemed more like a "melancholy parrot." And the elastic M. Thiers, less metaphorical, simply dismissed him as a cretin. The first impression was not a good one, and nothing about Louis Napoleon seemed to reflect the imperial image.

He was born in Paris in 1808, the son of Louis Bonaparte, King of Holland and the first Napoleon's brother. His mother was Hortense Beauharnais, Napoleon's stepdaughter. The greater part of his life had been spent out of the country, and he was in many respects a European rather than a Frenchman—a fact explaining some of the future enigmas of the Second Empire. Actually, he did speak French with a German accent and German, it must be said, with a Swiss accent. An election song, popular in 1848, pointed to his internationalism:

> Je suis Corse d'origine,
> Je suis Anglais pour le ton,
> Suisse d'éducation
> Et Cosaque pour la mine;
> Je suis Arlequin-le-Grand;
> Je veux être président.*

After the birth of L'Aiglon, Napoleon Bonaparte's son, in 1811 there seemed little chance that Louis Napoleon would play any significant part in the First Empire. And the defeat of Napoleon at Waterloo made dreams of a fabulous destiny rather more remote. Nevertheless, even as a schoolboy in Switzerland, young Louis Napoleon was convinced that fate had chosen him for a unique and imperial rôle. Surprisingly enough, as the years passed, his dream became less and less unreasonable. Fate was more than co-operative: L'Aiglon, then Duc de Reichstadt, died in Vienna in 1832. Louis Napoleon's older brothers were already dead, and by 1846 so were his father and his uncle, the King of Naples. Finally the unexpected had taken place: he was now the only legitimate pretender to the Napoleonic Dynasty. The trick, of course, would be to restore the empire.

He made two gallant and absurd attempts to do so. In 1836 he chose to invade France through the half-German

---

* "I am Corsican by origin, English in manner, Swiss by education and a Cossack in looks. My name is Harlequin the Great, and I want to be president."

frontier town of Strasbourg. He hoped to win over the
military garrison and lead the population, already hostile
to Louis Philippe, in a general uprising. Unhappily,
within two hours he found himself under arrest and the
great invasion was over. The French government, with
tolerance and not a little amusement, put him on a ship
bound for the Americas, certain that it had seen the last of
him.

Four years later he was in England with a larger group
of followers and an even more elaborate plan. He proposed to make a landing at Boulogne on the Channel
coast and march from there to Paris, taking the garrison
along with him. The invaders sailed down the Thames on
August 4, 1840, in a pleasure boat hired for the occasion.
The *Edinburgh Castle* carried some fifty men, two carriages and nine horses, an assortment of muskets and pis-
tols and French uniforms along with a number of cases of
wine and other spirits. At Gravesend Colonel Parquin
went ashore to buy some cigars and came across a young
boy with an eagle. The symbolism did not escape the colonel, and he bought the bird for a pound, securing it to the
mainmast of the *Edinburgh Castle*. There the creature remained until the adventure was over, in spite of a rumor
circulated along the Boulevard that it had come to France
crouched on the imperial shoulder. Be that as it may, the
invaders finally landed on the French coast some twenty-
four hours behind schedule. The crossing had been rough,
and they landed a little to the north of Boulogne, coming
onto the beach in the dark in open boats. Shortly before
sunrise they began the march to Boulogne, one of them
carrying a tricolor banner inscribed with the great victories of Marengo and Austerlitz and Moscow, and Louis
Napoleon leading the way in a general's uniform. The
fiasco was even more conclusive than it had been at Stras-

bourg: within three hours the ragged band was back on the beach, wading toward the boats under the fire of the Garde Nationale. Louis Napoleon was wounded and two of his followers killed.

This time Louis Philippe's government decided to take the Bonaparte pretender seriously. Perhaps they took him too seriously, for he was given a public trial that allowed him notoriety and the chance to indulge in a good deal of propaganda. He described himself as "a French prince in exile" and appeared in court dressed in black and wearing no decoration but the Légion d'Honneur. When asked by what right he wore it, he announced imperiously: "I found it in my cradle." His moment in the limelight, however, was soon over, and he was sentenced to a term of perpetual imprisonment in the fortress of Ham in northern France.

Still they had not heard the last of him: in 1846 he escaped from prison disguised as a workman, carrying a plank over his shoulder and wearing a blue apron and a black wig. Tradition holds that the workman was called Badinguet, and this was to become Louis Napoleon's nickname in popular mythology. He crossed the border into Belgium and from there took a Channel boat to England. In London he resumed his exile and took up again the life of an English gentleman. He dined out among the aristocracy, and he was a familiar figure in the clubs along St. James's as well as a member of Lady Blessington's circle at Gore House. His mistress was the sumptuous Miss Howard, whom he had appropriated from a certain Major Mountjoy Martyn of the Life Guards, and he drove around the West End in a carriage with the imperial eagle emblazoned on the door. Everyone found him charming: Lord Malmesbury spoke of his "remarkable smile." And even Queen Victoria, a few years later, had to admit that there was something "fascinating, melancholy and engaging" about him. The English admired him for his coldness and correctness and reserve—for all those Anglo-Saxon qualities he possessed in such abundance. He was content to wait in London, certain that the day of his destiny was near. Even in prison he had never lost faith in his star. "My power," he told Lord Malmesbury at Ham, "is in an immortal name."

The immortal name had sustained him through many long years of scorn and exile. Until 1848 he lived as an outcast and counted himself among the disinherited of the world. Those lonely years, however, had not been wasted. They taught him silence and the unusual ability to listen: Mocquard could say that next to him "William the Silent would have been a garrulous fool." They taught him self-sufficiency: did he not refer to the prison of Ham as his university, where he read and studied and learned alone? Most important of all, they taught him sympathy for the poor and outcast like himself. But that sympathy never prevented him from having at the same time a singular mistrust of humanity.

Nevertheless, he developed a feeling for his fellow man and a sense of the future almost unique among his contemporaries and certainly unique among the European rulers of the day. His vision was a simple one: he saw with clarity that the future belonged not to the Few but to the Many. Intellectually a Saint-Simonian socialist, he was on surer ground emotionally.[5] All his life he had had a great concern for the sick and the poor and for those who suffered social injustice. His views were expressed in a number of books, the most important being *Des Idées napoléoniennes* (1839) and *L'Extinction du paupérisme* (1844). In them he put forward his interpretation of the ideals of the First Empire (for the most part, generously wrong) as well as his own conceptions of social justice. During his reign as emperor he tried in every way to give substance to these conceptions. He believed in universal suffrage, an end to feudalism and the reward of talent. He worked for international peace, the integrity of individual nations and the development of liberal institutions for the benefit of all. In spite of inevitable extremes and final disaster he did bring many of these remarkably modern concepts to fruition. And they served to carry his own country —and much of Europe—into the twentieth century. It may be that in the larger book of history the Second Empire warrants a more important place than its predecessor, which created a number of glorious legends but left few tangible results. Mountebank and seedy conspirator he may have been, but Louis Napoleon had gifts of intelligence and compassion unhappily not found in the opportunists with whom he surrounded himself.

By 1852 the dangerous gamble of the coup d'état had been won, and he set about to play his destined rôle at last. He swiftly began the transition to empire which he felt necessary for the inauguration of his social programs. In the fall of the year he went on a tour, courageously going into those parts of central France where his seizure of power had been most violently opposed. He traveled along the valley of the Rhône and visited the turbulent cities of Lyon and Marseille. His trip came to an end in the seaport of Bordeaux, where he gave a memorable speech to the Chamber of Commerce. Its theme was peace, and in it he outlined an imperial program:[6]

We have immense uncultivated lands to reclaim, roads to open, ports to build, rivers to make navigable, canals to finish and railroads to complete. Across from Marseille we have a great territory to assimilate to France. . . . Above all, we have ruins to rebuild everywhere, false gods to put down and truth to make triumphant. . . . These are the conquests I have in mind and if, like me, you wish only for the good of the nation, then you are my soldiers.

The speech called for prosperity and progress, and the country in general accepted it with wild enthusiasm. On the afternoon of October 16, 1852, Louis Napoleon returned to Paris in triumph. He was surrounded by squadrons of cavalry, and workmen in the streets greeted him with banners flying: "To Napoleon III, Emperor and Savior of Modern Civilization, Protector of Art, Science, Agriculture, Industry and Commerce." All through the city, church bells tolled and cannon sounded. The music of military bands filled the air, and imperial symbols decorated theaters and stores and public buildings. Along the boulevard, vendors sold shiny new medallions marked with the words: *Napoléon III Empereur*. The inscription may have been a month premature, but that afternoon was clearly the beginning of empire.[7] Even the petulant Comte de Viel Castel felt obliged to end his diary for the day with a resounding "HAIL CAESAR!"

CHAPTER THREE

Imperial Saraband

Most Parisians were delighted to turn their backs on the republican simplicity of earlier days. And perhaps some antidote was needed to counteract the drab and stingy grayness of the July Monarchy and of the confused régime which followed it. Louis Philippe, the citizen king, had carried an umbrella and worn the colorless clothes of a businessman, while the honest radicals of Lamartine's government had been plebeian in dress. Now everything was changing: the people of Paris longed for uniforms and ball gowns, for the sparkle of diamonds and military decorations, for a return to the grandeur of the First Empire. The temper of the times was insistent, and Louis Napoleon hurried to provide his countrymen with the splendor they wanted. Among other advantages, it would serve as a welcome distraction and allow people to forget essential liberties that had been lost. The creation of an imperial court became the new régime's first concern.

Above all, it was necessary to restore the palace of the Tuileries. After the flight of Louis Philippe in 1848 the Paris mob had swarmed into the palace with republican fervor—its custom in periods of change ever since the

Great Revolution. Windows and mirrors and crystal chandeliers were broken, paintings slashed, statues pulled down, books and papers burned. In the confusion everything movable disappeared, and some three thousand bottles of wine and several barrels of rum were drained on the spot. The thirst for destruction grew: Louis Philippe's throne was hurled from an upper window and carried over to the place de la Bastille, where it was burned with enthusiasm.

Though still prince-president, Louis Napoleon moved into the palace within a month of the coup d'état. Even while living at the Elysée Palace, however, he had entertained at the Tuileries and begun the restoration of the building. The work was supervised by Visconti and Eugène Lecroix, among others, and an army of masons and carpenters and painters labored on the probject. By spring the great reception rooms were virtually finished, and they were to form—the salon des Maréchaux and the salon d'Apollon and the others—an imposing setting for the entertainments of the Second Empire. On May 12, 1852, Louis Napoleon was able to give a magnificent dinner for some eight hundred officers in the galerie de Diane. The return to an imperial dispensation demanded more parades and more uniforms, and these officers had recently taken part in the ceremony of distributing the eagle standards to the army on the Champ de Mars. By the time the empire was inaugurated on December 2, 1852, the restoration of the palace was complete and a rich background for the imperial masquerade had been provided.[1]

The palace of the Tuileries was coming to life again, and it was being furnished with proper servants and an imperial staff. Soon the only thing lacking was a mistress of the house. In 1852 Louis Napoleon was forty-four years old, and he knew that the time had come for him to find a suitable wife. His English friend Miss Howard, who had been with him openly since his arrival in Paris during the February Revolution, was out of the question.[2] He needed a wife not only to supervise the imperial household and to act as his hostess but, most important of all, to provide him with a son. It was more than disturbing that his cousin Prince Napoleon—the quarrelsome and republican and atheistic Plon-Plon—was presently the only legitimate heir to the Napoleonic Dynasty.[3] French diplomats began to look for a possible empress among the royal families of Europe. A Swedish princess was considered, as well as Adelaide of Hohenlohe, one of Queen Victoria's German nieces. Whatever the young ladies may have felt at the prospect of living in Paris as an empress, their families were not enthusiastic. Louis Napoleon was, among other things, an adventurer, a Catholic and—a Bonaparte. At the Congress of Vienna in 1815 the rulers of Europe had made it clear that no Bonaparte would ever sit on the throne of France again. The event was coming to pass, but surely that was no reason to sacrifice any of their daughters.

The rebuffs failed to offend Louis Napoleon, since he had taken arrangements into his own hands. And how different the Second Empire would have been had he married some shy princess from Saxe-Coburg-Gotha. He chose instead a gay and accomplished sophisticate well known in the international circles of Paris and Madrid. She was Eugenia de Montijo, Condesa de Teba. And she was to become, as Nestor Roqueplan put it, "the best kept kept-woman in France." Perhaps this was an unfair description, but the Spanish countess was twenty-six years old and not without experience or ambition when she caught Louis Napoleon's eye.

Though he had seen her briefly on several occasions, he

first met her at a party given by his cousin Princess Mathilde.[4] Later he invited Eugenia and her raffish mother to many of the presidential receptions at the Elysée Palace. It was Louis Napoleon's compulsion—often gratified—to possess every attractive woman he met, and the Spanish beauty was no exception. What was exceptional, of course, was that she consistently refused him. This was a point of view he had not encountered in some years, and he grew desperate. During the fall of 1852 he asked her to a succession of house parties at Compiègne and Saint Cloud and Fontainebleau. At every opportunity he gave her expensive gifts: on one morning walk, for example, she admired a clover leaf sparkling with dewdrops. Bacciochi was dispatched to Paris immediately, returning next day with a gold leaf covered with diamonds. No matter, Eugenia's defenses remained as impregnable as ever. Once, during a game of hide and seek at Compiègne, Louis Napoleon took the opportunity of stepping behind a curtain in one of the empty rooms of the château and throwing himself upon her when she appeared. The rumor around the Boulevard had it that she pushed him away with the chilling words: "Not until I'm empress." Often accused of being empty-headed and interested only in clothes, Eugenia seems to have had a remarkable grasp of what it was she wanted from life. Her sister had married a grandee of Spain, and Eugenia was not to be outdone.

When she became Empress of the French, there were many who felt that she was a vain and silly woman—and others who thought she was an astute politician and gracious ruler. But no one seriously disagreed about her looks: her blue eyes and infinite grace and magnificent auburn hair were immediately striking. Even Winterhalter's portraits of her were not so far removed from the truth as those he habitually did of others. Friends and courtiers alike were lavish in their praise, and not all of it was flattery. Mme. Carette, a lady-in-waiting, spoke of her lovely smile and of her arms and shoulders which looked as if they belonged to a statue. Lady Augusta Bruce saw her wedding at Notre Dame and remarked on her "beautifully chiseled features and marble complexion." She went on to say that "her exquisitely proportioned figure and graceful carriage were most striking and the whole was like a Poet's Vision!" The highest praise of all came from the Princess Metternich, though it must be said that she was one of Eugénie's best friends. The unusual point about these descriptions of the empress and her "incomparable grace" is not only their unanimity but the fact that they came from other women. Men were inclined to find her cold and forbidding. And surely this is the way she must have seemed to Louis Napoleon in those first days. Much to the surprise—and annoyance—of his friends and relatives and advisers, he came to the conclusion that the only way he could have this tantalizing Spaniard was to marry her.

"One makes love to women like Mlle. de Montijo," said Plon-Plon, who had had a good deal of experience in matters of the kind. "One doesn't marry them." Morny and King Jérôme also were strongly opposed to the idea, as were others who felt that the emperor's wife should be above reproach. In the eyes of European royalty Louis Napoleon was still a parvenu with an unsavory reputation. It could bring no great credit to the régime for him to make some foreign adventuress his consort, no matter how attractive she might be. Nevertheless, the emperor had made a decision: on January 22, 1853, he summoned his deputies and senators and counselors of state and announced that he was going to marry Mlle. de Montijo. It seemed appropriate that he had asked her to become his wife some ten days earlier at a ball given in the palace of the Tuileries. He pointed out that he was placing domestic happiness above dynastic interests: "I have chosen a woman whom I love and respect rather than one unknown to me." Emperor at last, he anticipated no objections. There were none. The announcement was received with little enthusiasm, however, although Dupin, a former president of the Assemblée Nationale, expressed the secret feelings of many of those present. They were, after all, Frenchmen. He said he was delighted that the emperor had not chosen to marry some scrofulous German princess "with feet as big as my own."

By imperial order, the wedding was quickly solemnified, first at a civil ceremony in the palace attended by a more than usually surly Plon-Plon and then, on January 30, 1853, at a religious ceremony in the cathedral of Notre Dame. The marriage was performed by the Archbishop of Paris and conducted with all pomp and circumstance. There had not been a pageant like it since the time of the First Empire. Persigny, in charge of the arrangements, was careful to reproduce every possible aspect of more glamorous days. The couple rode to the church in the same glass-and-gilt carriage which had taken Napoleon Bonaparte and Marie Louise of Austria to their wedding. Even accident contributed to the evocation of the First Empire: as the carriage left the courtyard of the Tuileries, the golden crown on top of it was shaken loose and clattered to the ground. The same ominous incident had taken place in 1810. Nevertheless, Eugénie was radiant with orange blossoms, her coiffure created by the fashionable hairdresser Félix and her bridal gown of white silk and velvet and Alençon lace designed by Mme. Vignon. On her head was Marie Louise's diamond coronet, and Louis Napoleon wore his uncle's Légion d'Honneur. Preceded by a squadron of the new regiment of Guides and followed by a division of heavy cavalry, the carriage passed down the rue de Rivoli—the great street decorated with colored streamers and flowers and triumphal arches. From balconies along the way hung green velvet banners embroidered with golden bees and eagles. The weather was clear and cold, an enormous crowd waited in the square in front of Notre Dame, and five hundred musicians played the march from Meyerbeer's opera *Le Prophète.* The people of Paris were curious, though by no means enthusiastic. As one observer noted, "coarse jests passed from mouth to mouth." [5]

However, Louis Napoleon now had the woman he desired, and the nation had a beautiful woman who, as much as anyone else, set the tone of the Second Empire. For this gift the French were not grateful, and Eugénie was never loved—in spite of her charm and piety and many charities. Like Marie Antoinette, for whom she felt a strange kinship, she was regarded always as a foreigner: *L'Espagnole,* as her idol had been *L'Autrichienne.* And it was true enough that the stunning court over which she came to preside was largely foreign in character.

This was the result not only of hasty improvisation but also of the unwillingness of many French aristocrats to recognize the court. Both Louis Napoleon and Eugénie had lived their lives as cosmopolitans and were acquainted with a wide range of Europeans. Unlike older and more formal courts of the continent, the Tuileries was basically democratic and frankly international. It encouraged a mixed society and was open to money and talent as well as to noble birth. Eugénie's Monday-evening receptions were filled with foreigners: from wealthy South Americans like the Errazu sisters, whose father had married *"une sorte de négresse,"* to Italian women like the Comtesse Walewska,

whose husband was a Pole and the illegitimate son of the
first Napoleon. The Duchesse de Persigny was a German,
the Duchesse de Morny a Russian and the Duchesse de
Malakoff a Spaniard, the Marchionesse de Chasseloup-
Laubat a Creole and the Maréchale Canrobert a Scots-
woman. And of all the foreigners at home in the new imperial court, the most at home and the most influential
was the Princess Pauline Metternich: Hungarian by birth,
Austrian by marriage and —Parisian by adoption.

"Two parts whore and one part great lady," in Prosper
Mérimée's words, she was the daughter of Count Sandor,
a famous Hungarian horseman. Mad Moritz, as he was
called with good reason, had fallen on his head an incal-
culable number of times and enjoyed some minor notoriety in 1850 by attempting to smash all the furniture in a
Viennese club while suffering from a fit of insanity.
Though a good deal less violent than her father, Pauline
was quite as erratic. She established her social position by
being at once the granddaughter and the daughter-in-law
of the great chancellor. Her husband, Richard Metternich,
was Austrian ambassador in Paris during the Second Empire, and the embassy in the rue de Varennes was the
scene of many of the splendid parties of the era. Unlike
most of the other ladies of the court, Pauline was known
more for her wit than for her beauty. She was, in fact,
remarkably ugly and had the presence of mind to describe
herself as looking like a "rather chic monkey." For the
entertainment of the court she learned to dance the cancan
and to sing the off-color ballads made famous by Thérésa
in cafés-concerts like the Alcazar. Prince Poniatowski remembered visiting her at the embassy one Mardi Gras
when he was a boy: she was upstairs in her room, lying in
bed with a cold and smoking a huge cigar. In spite of—or
because of—these eccentricities, she became one of Eugé-

nie's best friends and served for years as the Second Empire's unofficial mistress of ceremonies. It was she who discovered the English couturier Worth and organized the amateur theatricals which became such a popular feature of court life at Compiègne and elsewhere. On a higher level, she was one of the few who encouraged Richard Wagner to produce *Tannhäuser* in Paris in 1861. She is as much a part of the mythology of the Second Empire as Eugénie herself. And surely her years of happiness and glamour must have ended on the day her husband, Richard, and the Italian ambassador escorted the empress out of the Tuileries for the last time.

An enormous staff was required to produce the pageants of the imperial court. These pageants took place not only in the palace of the Tuileries, but in the great châteaus of Saint Cloud and Fontainebleau near Paris, at Compiègne in the north of France and at the Villa Eugénie, the summer retreat in Biarritz near the Spanish border. Louis Napoleon and the empress (and later their son, the Prince Impérial) had separate household staffs. There was a military flavor over all: the African generals Saint Arnaud and Magnan, now marshals of France, were *Grand Ecuyer* and *Grand Veneur,* respectively.[6] The protocol of the First Empire was re-established and much else borrowed from earlier periods of French history, particularly from the era of Louis XV. Courtiers with resounding titles and elaborate costumes crowded one another in the long corridors of Versailles and the Tuileries, of Saint Cloud and Fontainebleau and Compiègne.

Perhaps the most elegant courtier of all was the *Grand Chambellan* himself: the Duc de Bassano. In his rôle as principal chamberlain of Louis Napoleon's household he yielded place only to the military commander and to M. Achille Fould, who was in charge of finances. Tall and slim and worldly, the Duc de Bassano appeared in the magnificent reception rooms of the various palaces wearing a plumed hat and a richly embroidered scarlet coat. Around his neck hung the symbol of office: a great key on a chain of green-and-gold acorns. His wife was Eugénie's *Dame d'honneur* and Comte Bacciochi his first chamberlain. In addition, Bacciochi was the director of imperial theaters as well as a discreet stage manager for Louis Napoleon's frequent sexual adventures. And Colonel Fleury, aide-de-camp to the emperor and commandant of the Guides, was largely responsible for organizing the court along the lines laid down during the First Empire. All these officials, and others like them, moved with the imperial court as the change of season brought a welcome change of locale.

The spring and most of the summer were spent at Saint Cloud and Fontainebleau. Of the two, Saint Cloud was perhaps the more formal. Destroyed later during the Franco-Prussian War, it was a sumptuous château a few miles from Paris on the Left Bank of the Seine and often selected for entertaining foreign royalty. As the years passed and Louis Napoleon became more acceptable to the rulers of Europe, there were many elaborate state visits. One of the most memorable was made by Queen Victoria and Prince Albert during the course of the Crimean War. Their visit marked the first time that a reigning English monarch had been in the country since the time over four hundred years earlier when young Henry VI was crowned King of France in Notre Dame. In the spring of 1855 Louis Napoleon and Eugénie had visited England with great success, and now Victoria was returning the visit—ostensibly to see the Paris Exposition of that year, but actually to cement the new Anglo-French relationship as allies.

Victoria and Albert arrived in Saint Cloud on Saturday, August 18, 1855, after a torchlight procession through the streets of Paris. The English queen was enchanted. "It was like a fairy tale," she said, "and everything so beautiful!"

She woke in the morning to find that her suite looked out toward Paris across a lovely garden filled with fountains and long avenues of orange and beech trees. A week later a great ball was given in her honor at Versailles; the motif was taken from a print of the era of Louis XV, and the galerie des Glaces was ablaze with light. At the end of the evening there was a splendid display of fireworks, the finale being a representation of Windsor Castle. The queen was delighted with every minute of her visit and charmed by the French imperial couple. Even Prince Albert began to think that there was something to Louis Napoleon, after all.

In the latter part of the summer the court moved on to Fontainebleau, where the great pond and beautiful forest provided many mild diversions. The novelist Prosper Mérimée, an old friend of Eugénie's mother, was often on hand, and his complaints were constant: "Every day we eat too much, and I'm half dead." Eating and drinking and sleeping did seem to be major amusements, but there were other small excitements to vary the monotony of court life. On the famous fishpond, for example, a variety of boating was available, including a gondola for the empress complete with gondolier from the Piazza San Marco. Her son had his own little steamboat, and two sailors from the Imperial Navy were there to help him with it. Often exotic gifts arrived from faraway places: one July day a number of crates came for Louis Napoleon from the Emperor of Cochin China. Mérimée described the elephant tusks—"very yellow"—and the case of moldy cinnamon, which gave off an odor of decayed fish. That afternoon there was to be a picnic in the forest, and Mérimée, long familiar with things Spanish, was in charge of making the *gaspacho.*

In September the court moved on to Biarritz for a few weeks of informal life at the Villa Eugénie, a small retreat Louis Napoleon built for the empress.[7] Only the most intimate friends of the imperial family were to be found here, and Prosper Mérimée once more seemed to be a permanent guest. In Biarritz, so near to her native Spain, Eugénie was at ease and often organized outings for the amusement of her friends. Pauline Metternich describes one of them: a yachting party on the little steamer *Mouette,* which was to sail out into the Bay of Biscay and visit the picturesque Spanish town of Fuenterrabia. A number of elegant ladies came on board—the stunning Lisa Przezdziecka in a hat with blue feathers, the Comtesse Walewska all in mauve and a Miss Vaughan from London, who kept repeating how much the English loved the sea. Finally the empress herself arrived, wearing an Italian straw hat with white plumes and surrounded by handsome equerries and chamberlains. They settled into cane chairs on the rear deck as the yacht raised anchor and turned into the Bay of Biscay.

Before long the sea began to grow rough, and suddenly an Austrian count who had been talking to the empress put a handkerchief to his lips and ran in the direction of the railing. Others followed suit, and within a short time some fifty exquisitely dressed ladies and gentlemen were lying on the deck wrapped in plaid blankets. Some time later the servants made the mistake of appearing with trays of pastry and ices and babas au rhum. Cries of anguish were heard, and the sea was now so rough that the yacht could not enter the harbor of Fuenterrabia. By seven in the evening they had sailed back to Biarritz and found the

harbor closed there as well. The *Mouette* sailed back and
forth like a phantom ship along the French coast, and
finally at two o'clock in the morning the desperate travelers were returned to the Villa Eugénie. An unwanted
meal was served, and Pauline Metternich described the
guests as cadavers with their beautiful clothes in tatters.
They were, she added, "the flower of the court of Napoleon III, a court known for its elegance in every corner of
the world."

At the beginning of autumn it was the habit of curious
Parisians to spend certain afternoons at the gare du Nord
watching the emperor's guests leave for Compiègne on a
special train. The train was made up of six parlor cars for
guests, six first-class carriages for servants and a number
of baggage vans. The château of Compiègne was some
fifty miles north of Paris near a beautiful forest famous for
its game. Invitations to follow the court there during the
hunting season were highly prized. Punctually at three
o'clock in the afternoon the imperial train would steam
out of the gare du Nord, arriving at Compiègne a little
over an hour later. Horses and carriages were waiting at
the station with postillions in powdered wigs and green-
and-gold livery. There was always a great scene of confusion in the courtyard of the château when the baggage
finally arrived. Some days there were as many as nine
hundred trunks coming in at the same time, and servants
scurried back and forth looking for the proper luggage.
Adding to the chaos were piles of enormous wooden
boxes, each containing a single crinoline. Artists and writers and prominent businessmen were often asked to Compiègne, and their wives worried a great deal about status—
since there were several different series of guest lists. Princess Metternich describes a brief conversation on this important subject.

"Are you in the elegant series?" asked one lady of another.

"No, indeed, I'm in yours."

Because of fine hunting and shooting, Compiègne was one of the favorite locales of the imperial court. The forest teemed with stag and boar and fox, as well as with pheasant and partridge and rabbit. One of the great honors of the Second Empire was to be made a member of the imperial hunt and so allowed to wear the silver buttons with the gold stag on them. Among the "Buttons" were many prominent figures of the day: Prince Murat and Prince Plon-Plon, the foreign ambassadors Lord Cowley and Prince Metternich, Auguste de Morny and the handsome Count Nieuwerkerke, who was Princess Mathilde's lover, as well as important bankers like Achille Fould. Not everyone who came to Compiègne, of course, was a proficient sportsman: gamekeepers often hit rabbits over the head for the benefit of one Minister of Finance who could not kill them otherwise. And there was a certain Minister of Justice who panicked on the day he mistook a tame badger named Pablo for a wild boar. Such entire incompetence, however, was rare.

One of the great events of the season was the fox hunt on St. Hubert's Day. At three o'clock on the morning of the third of November the horns sounded and English foxhounds were brought into the courtyard of the château. Mass was celebrated at the old church of St. Jacques and a consecrated brioche offered to the emperor by the huntsmen and whippers-in. Then they would ride out into the dawn wearing Louis XV costumes of green-and-crimson velvet with lace at their cuffs and tricornered hats on their heads. The night of the hunt there was a more elaborate dinner than usual in the Great Hall—the enormous room blazing with light and the table dominated by

57

a silver centerpiece of finely chiseled hunting scenes.

Evening entertainments at Compiègne were mild enough: perhaps billiards or dancing the Sir Roger de Coverley, table quoits (Louis Napoleon's favorite game), spelling bees or blindman's buff. Some nights there would be a play in the five-hundred-seat theater given by members of the court or by a professional troupe from Paris—from the Odéon, perhaps, or the Gymnase or the Ambigu. On other occasions there might be a lecture by one of the guests, a chemist like Pasteur or an astronomer like Leverrier.

It was in Paris, however, that the new régime could be seen at its best. The imperial court created by Louis Napoleon and Eugénie soon emerged as the most splendid in Europe, if not the most splendid in French history. Much of the splendor was improvised, but it served to establish the atmosphere of an entire era and came to influence almost every level of society. Even the aristocrats of the old nobility, however they may have sneered and stayed away, took their cue willingly enough from the court.

The pale years of Louis Philippe were no more than a memory. Music was heard again in the great houses of the faubourg Saint Germain, and lights burned at night all along the chaussée d'Antin. Paris became a city of new and charming sights: in the dusk of a winter's day you could see elegant ice skaters in the Bois, torches all around the pond and the women wrapped in Russian sable. On a Wednesday or a Friday evening during the season you could see carriages gliding along the Champs Elysées through the soft snow toward the Opéra or to some fashionable masked ball. There were parties all the time now, and restaurants like the Café Anglais stayed open through the night to accommodate the careless revelers. Pursuit of pleasure became an obsession, and the happy few enjoyed

an abundance of food and wine and music. Every tempo
of the brilliant saraband was called from the palace of the
Tuileries.

Soon after the wedding of Louis Napoleon and Eugénie
the lovely evenings of empire began in earnest. While the
imperial court remained in Paris—from the middle of December until Easter—there were innumerable receptions,
banquets, concerts and ballets, and all were remarkable
for extravagance and luxury. The most extravagant were
four great balls given in winter between the first of January and the beginning of Lent. Four to five thousand
guests were invited to each, and for each occasion the palace was a blaze of light—the contours of both façades outlined by burning gas jets. As early as eight o'clock in the
evening a file of carriages could be seen in the rue de
Rivoli and all along the quai des Tuileries. One by one the
gleaming carriages drew near the palace, and guests
stepped down into the courtyard. Gentlemen wore knee
breeches and silk stockings or the richly embroidered uniform of French officers and foreign diplomats. Ladies
wore enormous crinolines, their breasts almost bare and
tiaras gleaming in their elaborate coiffures. Among the
clouds of colored silk and velvet and the glitter of diamonds and rubies and emeralds you would see splendid
international beauties like the Duchesse de Pourtalès and
the Duchess of Hamilton and the Marquesa de Contades.

After leaving their carriages, the elegant guests walked
under a marquee into the entrance hall of the pavillon de
l'Horloge. Here in an antichamber rows of footmen in
powdered wigs and sumptuous livery waited. Swiss
guards stood by, halberds at hand and plumed helmets on
their heads. Guests were escorted to the foot of the Fontaine staircase, which led to the wonderland above: the
vast salon des Maréchaux with portraits of the great sol-

diers of France lining the walls. Here Louis Napoleon and Eugénie waited in gilded armchairs set on a raised platform, and Johann Strauss himself might be poised in a gallery above, ready to begin the music of the first quadrille—music that would last until four in the morning.

The long staircase was lined from top to bottom with élite troopers of the Cent Gardes, standing tall and immobile on both sides of each step. Often on the way upstairs some lady would pause to study her make-up in a trooper's gleaming breastplate, and there can hardly have been a more vainglorious moment in any woman's life. It began to seem that the Goncourts were right when they said that only four things mattered at the Tuileries: youth, beauty, diamonds—and a dress.

CHAPTER FOUR

Hall of Mirrors

ON A DAY not long after the fall of the Second Empire one of the defeated emperor's more vulgar and more enduring mistresses was reminiscing with Arsène Houssaye. "You can still have a good time," said Marguerite Bellanger, "but it's not the same thing."

Houssaye, man of letters and former director of the Comédie Française, disagreed. But he must have remembered the masked balls at the Tuileries and the opening nights of the Bouffes Parisiens and the money and the stock certificates whirling like dead leaves and—the women.

A great deal about the Second Empire does seem to revolve around women, and there is a soft and feminine shading to the whole era. For many, sex was a compelling obsession: even at those famous intellectual dinners chez Magny, the Goncourts and Sainte Beuve and the others devoted much of their time to adolescent discussions of love. Emile Zola, writing his fictional history of the Second Empire, titled a novel in that cycle *Au Bonheur des dames (For the Happiness of Women)*.[1] And the title may stand as one of the epigraphs of twenty frantic years

—years devoted, among much else, to making people and events seem quite different from what they actually were.

Like the décor of the Second Empire, the women of the day were painted and gilded, and their allure was largely on the surface. Clothes and make-up were nothing new in the world, but they achieved an unexpected level of importance during the years of Louis Napoleon's masquerade. In every area of life, careful attention was paid to façades: like the furniture and the public buildings and the palace itself, women were first of all objects of decoration and then objects of pleasure. Lust was confused with love, and surface beauty came to be regarded as an ultimate value. Like so many other aspects of contemporary life, the example was set by the imperial court with its emphasis on outward splendor and its array of beautiful women. Reality was put to one side, and this stunning weakness in a nation's philosophy was often noted. Soon after the beginning of the empire the Goncourts could point to the great defect in French society: "Never have appearances been so important to people, so demanding, so destructive and demoralizing." Parisians, in particular, seemed to have lost faith in everything but the material world, and the blemish was obvious to a number of foreign visitors.

The Austrian Archduke Maximilian, who was, after all, a Habsburg and the brother of Franz Josef, could hardly have been expected to find the new imperial court of the Tuileries to his taste. And, indeed, he did not. He came to Paris in the spring of 1856, and his first reactions were not favorable. He quickly sensed the truth that lay beneath the surface: he thought the city unnecessarily grandiose and the court itself clumsy and vulgar, imperial only in a second-hand way. Like so many others, he was surprised to find Louis Napoleon far from imposing in appearance and far from regal in manner. The Empress Eugénie was attractive enough, but he did think she wore too much make-up. He found Princess Mathilde undistinguished and the emperor's other cousin, Plon-Plon, actually offensive, with the look of "a worn-out basso from some obscure Italian opera house." In a letter to Franz Josef the archduke complained that the first dinner at Saint Cloud was badly served and Louis Napoleon more than a little nervous. "It occurred to me," said Maximilian (who was a very young man), "that he still felt ill at ease in the presence of a prince of more ancient lineage."

Some days later a ball was given in honor of the Austrian visitor. He found himself surrounded by a motley group of adventurers and social climbers, a group "distinguished for its disgusting dress and tactless behavior." It was only necessary to look at the Contessa di Castiglione, done up like some trollop from the early days of Louis XV, to understand that the court lacked all tone. In the end Maximilian did begin to sense something of the emperor's charm, but he could hardly wait to board the French imperial yacht at Le Havre. On the way to Belgium he may have thought that he had seen the last of the Second Empire and its improvised noblemen.

At every level of Parisian society there were those who would have agreed with Maximilian. Perhaps sensing its basic unreality and its lack of values, most of the aristocrats of the faubourg Saint Germain carefully avoided the court. And intellectuals were ever delighted to point out its shortcomings—the Goncourts characterizing it as flashy and insecure, a court composed of newcomers with stolen titles and crude pretorians with clanking sabers. They found the atmosphere a comical mixture of Marie Antoinette and Rigolboche.[2] The aura of make-believe was pervasive: ushers with powdered hair and plumes in their hats stood at various doorways of the palace ready to call out: "The Emperor!" should Louis Napoleon choose to go by, perhaps carrying his favorite rhinoceros-hide walking stick with the golden eagle on top.

A confusing hall of mirrors, like so much else in the Second Empire, the Tuileries appeared to be far grander than it was. However splendid the décor and public rooms may have been, the palace itself was uncomfortable. Living quarters were dark and badly ventilated, and a constant stream of servants carried wood and water and coal up and down the interior staircases. Only the imperial apartments had any form of central heating, and gas jets flickered in the gloomy halls all during the day. Much of the attendant glamour was specious: the gold service, for example, had been electroplated in the interests of economy. And Eugénie's private suite was tasteless and pretentious: a vast expanse of white satin curtains and marquetry cabinets and quilted sofas, the walls generously decorated with gilt. Too, there was something faintly absurd about the imperial family dining in the Louis XIV salon, with the great Sèvres centerpiece on the table and a Nubian servant in Venetian costume standing behind the empress—a scene with many of the ingredients of an enormous joke. Like the era itself, the palace and its inhabitants were a trifle *louche:* shady and more than slightly ambiguous. "It was not exactly a proper empire," admitted Colonel Fleury, "but we did have a damn good time."

The good time took many different forms and ranged all the way from simple extravagance to complex perversion—the cue in most matters coming from above. Eugénie was obsessed with clothes and Louis Napoleon with women, and they were tireless arbiters in the areas of their individual interest. It is as reasonable to condemn the

64

empress for the vanity of the régime as it is to credit the emperor with its moral decadence. Neither of them did anything contrary to French tastes, however; they simply exaggerated prevailing tendencies. With characteristic generosity, the nation has always blamed them for its own weaknesses.

Immune to her beauty, unkind critics have dismissed the empress as a frivolous woman of mediocre intelligence who moved in a cloud of cold cream and patchouli. The Goncourts were disgusted to learn that even her hairdresser appeared in the palace to arrange her coiffure wearing knee breeches and a sword. And Princess Mathilde took delight in pointing to the disastrous consequences of her love of clothes and ostentation: "She undermined our Society by her excessive luxury, by setting the example of boundless coquetry, by constantly giving more importance to the outward appearance of men and things than she did to their essential qualities." Perhaps this is to overstate Eugénie's importance in the fabric of French history. It is certainly to overlook the nature of the French themselves, who very much shared her fascination with the outside of things. The imperial couple did not impose their weaknesses on a moral and unwilling nation, and, in spite of a certain foreign patina, there was something unmistakably French about Louis Napoleon and his Queen Crinoline.

In a time and in a great city devoted to clothes and decoration and pageantry Eugénie was a natural leader. It was appropriate that the emperor's wife should set the style, and she did, never once taking the women of Paris where they did not wish to go. The popularity of the crinoline—a fashion both expensive and uncomfortable—may be traced to Eugénie's desire to disguise her pregnancy. And, perhaps because of her own generous endowments, she favored the extreme décolletage of the day. So did an enormous number of Frenchwomen, and it was apparent that the higher one rose in society, the smaller the bodice became. A popular story of the era concerned the Papal Nuncio who had just arrived from Rome: at a ball in the Tuileries he found his path blocked by two ladies whose elaborate crinolines filled an entire doorway. They moved aside with apologies.

"Pardon, monseigneur, but there is so much material in our skirts . . ."

"That there is nothing left over to cover the top," finished His Eminence with a worldly bow.

News about clothes—or the lack of them—filled the journals and magazines of the day. And it is rather too easy to dismiss this interest in fashion simply as a substitute for the political commentary that had been so limited by the government. If anything, considerations of style and décor are perhaps as fundamental to the French sensibility as an interest in politics.

Paris soon emerged as the fashion center of the world, and women's clothes became wonderfully elaborate. There were designs and colors and fabrics for every taste. In harmony with the imperial masquerade, many of the fashions of the day had a military flavor: Zouave jackets, Garibaldi shirts, new colors like magenta and solferino from the Italian campaign, shades like Crimean green and Sebastopol blue—not to mention Bismarck brown. Innumerable luxury shops catered to extravagant tastes: one bought cashmere shawls at the Compagnie des Indes in the rue de Richelieu, cosmetics at Piver and shoes at Massez. Shoes, like everything else, came in a wild variety of colors—violet and bronze and scarlet—and Russian leather boots were especially popular, threaded with beads of jet and crystal and gold and decorated with tassels and colored silk. Gloves and parasols were covered with embroidery, and even garters became miniature works of art, made of gold and silver filigree and designed by jewelers like Froment-Meurice in the rue Saint Honoré.

Fashionable women changed their clothes six or seven times a day, and their closets were bursting with dressing gowns, négligés, toilettes de Bois for the afternoon drive around the lake, dinner dresses and ballgowns of every description. Marvelously rich and heavy fabrics were available: the famous brocade from Lyon, for example, embroidered with damask roses, bluebells, crimson carnations, lilacs and tulips. Dresses were adorned with tasseled points and fringes and feathers, with ribbons and flowers, with velvet and lace. No excess was too great, and most elaborate of all was the court gown itself: perhaps a billowing crinoline of white satin, trimmed with bands of green velvet edged in gold, meeting at the back to join a great train of Brussels lace.

During the gaudy days of the Second Empire there was only one accepted place to buy such clothes: the House of Worth at 7 rue de la Paix. They said that the staircase inside was like a Jacob's ladder with an angel on every step, and rich women came there from all over the world —from the rest of Europe and from South America and the United States. Inside there were handsome young men in bright cravats and tightly fitting frock coats waiting to greet you. They might take you to the Salon de Lumière where the windows were hermetically sealed and the walls mirrored from floor to ceiling and the gas jets burning brightly. Here you could see exactly how your ballgown was going to look later in the week at the Tuileries. More important clients were taken care of by the great couturier himself or by his assistants, Miss Mary and Miss Esther. Worth spoke French with a strong English accent, his coat was so tight that he could scarcely bow and his glance, when angered, was Napoleonic—First Empire, to be sure. He himself disliked the crinoline and the open bodice, and in the last years of the régime he succeeded in changing these prevailing fashions.

Charles Frederick Worth came to Paris in 1846 to make his fortune, and within a dozen years one of the great legends of the Second Empire had been created. In London he was an apprentice at Swan & Edgar, the well-known firm of drapers, and in Paris he found a similar position chez Gagelin. He rapidly advanced from shop assistant to associate of the firm, leaving in 1857 to open a house of haute couture in partnership with a Swede named Boberg. Soon, through the patronage of Princess Metternich, he became leading dress designer for the beautiful women of the court and the international set and, most important of all, for the empress herself. Naturally, he raised his prices, and Princess Metternich found that she could no longer buy a ballgown for three hundred francs: "He is expensive, horribly expensive, monstrously expensive!"

For more than thirty years Worth dictated the fashions of Paris, and his firm robustly survived the Franco-Prussian War and the fall of the Second Empire. He died in 1895 in his villa at Suresnes near Paris, the garden filled with marble and other remnants from the vanished palace of the Tuileries. He was not only an artist but also an innovator and shrewd businessman: he conceived the idea of live mannequins, so much a part of the Paris fashion houses of today, and he brought prosperity to the failing silk and cotton industries of Lyon. After one particularly splendid ball during the Paris Exposition of 1867, newspapers devoted a good deal of space to describing the gowns he had designed for it. Discussing the publicity with Pauline Metternich, he remarked on his rôle in French society: "Tell them it is I who have invented you"—an observation perilously close to the truth. Worth was a figure as central to the spirit of the Second Empire as, each in his different way, Offenbach and Manet and Baudelaire and Dumas *fils*.

The obsession with fashion and the adornment of women did not exist exclusively at the level of the court and the very rich. The Second Empire saw the flowering of the great department stores, many of which are still in business today: for example, Le Louvre (1855), Le Printemps (1865) and La Samaritaine (1865). Au Bon Marché was founded in 1852 by Aristide Boucicaut, who was one of the first businessmen to develop modern merchandising techniques appropriate to an expanding population and increased prosperity. He focused his attention primarily on women, encouraging them to browse and spend money freely. Everything was under one roof, and all the prices were fixed and clearly marked. By 1860 Boucicaut was doing five million francs' worth of business a year, compared with 500,000 francs in 1852. In design and quality the department store was far from being a House of Worth—but the customers were still women, and the working girl and the harlot and the duchess shared the same love of clothes. It was an obsession that sometimes led to an odd distortion of values. The Goncourts, for example, heard of one woman who had given explicit instructions to her dressmaker. "Make sure I always have something black on hand," she said. "You know I've got three sons at the Crimean front."

If the concern for clothes occasionally led to some difficulty in determining proper values, confusion could be seen more clearly in another area of fashionable life. This confusion grew up around the morality of the new imperial court. A rich mythology developed, and rumor

painted the court as the scene of bacchanalian revels and
unspeakable orgies. What was the truth? One night after
dinner at Compiègne Pauline Metternich was suddenly
overwhelmed by the absurdity of the popular image. She
had been watching the fatuous Comte Tascher de la Pa-
gerie cranking the handle of a barrel organ while two list-
less couples danced and spectators yawned openly. Turning to a friend, she whispered: "Sodom and Gomorrah!"
—and they both dissolved in laughter. Nevertheless, the
charge of immorality cannot be dismissed so lightly, particularly by Pauline Metternich, who often left some
private dining room at the Café Bignon with several of her
more liberated friends and walked with the prostitutes on
the boulevard des Italiens until finally asked by the police
for her permit.

As Eugénie set the tone in the world of fashion, so her
husband set the tone in another area of endeavor—an area
where the opportunities for moral ambiguity were even
greater. It was generally agreed among the wits of the
Boulevard that the only thing Louis Napoleon inherited
from his famous uncle was an insatiable sexual appetite.
The point is not capable of argument, but it is enough to
know that a discreet apparatus existed at court under the
direction of Comte Bacciochi for the relief of the emperor's more pressing needs. Many methods were developed to choose his companion of the moment, and his
sensuality was treated as a charming game. Often at Fontainebleau, for example, a straw basket was filled with
trinkets, one of which had been designated in secret as a
prize. Amid much giggling and merriment a number of
elegant countesses and duchesses would gather around the
basket and fight for the prize: the prize, of course, being
Louis Napoleon himself. "It must be said in defense of the
emperor," remarked one unfriendly observer, "that the

lucky winner did not ordinarily take off her clothes on the spot."

As a rule, the imperial approach was less subtle. The emperor would simply go up to a lady who had caught his fancy, twist the points of his mustache and murmur in her ear: "Until tonight." Immediately an elaborate chain of events would be set into motion. If the lady's husband were at court—generally the case—he was sent off on some mission or other a great distance away. As soon as he had left, his wife would find herself moved to another room. One marquise, a veteran of the imperial amours at Compiègne, took time to relate her experiences to a young friend who had just been selected by the emperor. She described the luxurious room in which she found herself at night: the walls hung with silk and the woodwork painted white and gold. There was an ormolu clock on the mantel over the fireplace and at one end of the room a small and unobtrusive door. The marquise undressed without taking her eyes from the "terrible door" and in a moment of panic determined to escape. All the doors to the room were locked from the outside, however, and she resigned herself to climbing into bed and waiting. As the clock on the mantel struck one-thirty, the terrible door slowly opened, and there was the emperor in a flowing nightshirt of mauve silk with a golden bee embroidered on the collar. Approaching the bed in the dim light, he held his hands in front of him in order not to stumble and at last bent down over the marquise.

"After a little while His Majesty got up," she told her friend. "He crossed the room with his hands outstretched, groping from one piece of furniture to the other. Then the little door opened, a bright light blinded my eyes and the emperor was gone." The clock struck two and, as she pointed out to her friend, "it had only taken a half hour to make me an empress."

In addition to these casual encounters Louis Napoleon had a succession of more or less permanent mistresses. Among the earliest, and most spectacular, was the Contessa di Castiglione, an Italian beauty who had briefly shared the bed of Victor Emmanuel, King of Piedmont and Sardinia. She had been sent from Turin to Paris by his prime minister, Camillo Cavour, in order to seduce Napoleon III and so kindle his interest in the unification of Italy. The first part of the assignment proved ridiculously easy, but Cavour underestimated the emperor. Louis Napoleon was not given to mixing business with pleasure, and he spent more time in bed with the countess than he did worrying about the problems of modern Italy —at least at that point. In Paris the Contessa di Castiglione was universally admired for her good looks and universally disliked for her personality, which, however, appeared to be nonexistent. She never spoke to other women and made her appearance in the French capital in 1856 during a masked ball at the Tuileries. She arrived on the arm of an old dandy whose nickname was "Chinchilla," and she wore the revealing costume of a Roman lady of the Decadence. Everyone noticed her extravagant figure, and it surely did not escape the attention of Louis Napoleon, standing by in the dress of a Venetian nobleman and surrounded by agents of the Sûreté in domino.

Before long the Duchesse de Dino could report that the emperor had given the Contessa di Castiglione an emerald worth some hundred thousand francs and his carriage often could be seen in the early-morning hours outside her apartment in the avenue Montaigne. Visits to the countess were not without danger: on one occasion, as he was driving away in the dawn, three men rushed from the shadows and seized the reins of the imperial horses. The coachman succeeded in striking them aside with his whip and driving off; no doubt, like her, they were intent on the liberation of Italy. But the young countess was primarily interested in herself: she is said to have slept in black satin sheets to accentuate the whiteness of her body and to have spent long hours every day naked in front of a mirror. Queen Victoria's minister to Paris, Lord Cowley, remarked that the emperor's relationship with La Castiglione could be of no benefit to him "either morally or physically." In any case, Louis Napoleon soon tired of her, and she ended her career behind closed shutters in an apartment on the place Vendôme, unable to accept the changes which time had made upon her beauty. The emperor moved on to other women, who varied in style and quality from court beauties like the Comtesse Walewska to vulgar circus riders like Marguerite Bellanger.

Moral ambiguity in the imperial court was by no means limited to the emperor. There is a story told about the Duc de Persigny, who one day complained to a group of friends on the subject of his wife's conduct.[3] The elegant Duc de Gramont-Caderousse was there, and he finally interrupted with irritation. *"Monsieur le duc,"* he said to Persigny, "I cannot allow you to criticize my mistress in this fashion."

It was inevitable that the careless morality of the imperial court should be duplicated at other levels of society. Imitation was one principal motive, since the elegance of court life served to obscure much that was sordid. More than this, in the rapid commercial and industrial expansion of the Second Empire's early years, money and leisure became available as never before. A number of bored Parisians, floating at the edges of the imperial court and of the glittering international set, longed for a life of gaiety and sensuality. Their number included newly rich businessmen, unhappily married women, curious journalists, imbecile men of the world and debauchees of one persuasion or another. No matter what its own moral defects, society in the traditional sense was not prepared to accept them, and they were forced to create a world of their own. It was a world very much on the model of the imperial court, with an elaborate hierarchy, a loose code of conduct and a frantic interest in clothes and ostentation. Like the imperial court, it had its own private language and its favored locales: for the most part near the boulevard des Italiens and including theaters like the Variétés and restaurants like the Maison Dorée and the Café Anglais—an area described by Lord Hertford as *"le clitoris de Paris."*

That world was the demimonde, a shadow world whose sexual activities lay somewhere between the glossy infidelities of the upper class and the brutal prostitution of the poor. Traffic moved easily in and out of these different worlds, and, indeed, they touched at many points. It was more than possible to be accepted at court and in the demimonde as well, and there was no limit to the heights a girl from the gutter could reach. Like so many other areas of Second Empire life, the half-world was dominated by women: in this case by *les filles,* who were certainly not ladies, though by no means common prostitutes. The extent of money and gifts received and the social status of the gentlemen involved determined their position in the hierarchy of the demimonde. Some of them were more acceptable than others, and they were divided with nicety into a number of different categories where they shared the same extravagance of dress and looseness of morals. Among others, there were *lionnes, lorettes, biches* (a term invented by Nestor Roqueplan), *comédiennes* and *cocottes.* Even the terminology of the railroad age was used, and farther down on the social scale there were *wagons* of first and third class. In editing the great dictionary that began to appear in the 1860's, Pierre Larousse pointed out under the definition of *cocotte* that the word was a new one and that it described women kept by "rich idiots bent on destroying themselves." He concluded his definition on a moral note: "This is the age of corruption, and the example comes from on high."

Mistresses and kept women, prostitution and depravity, however, were hardly new in French society or restricted to the Second Empire. It was a matter of degree, and the ambiguous atmosphere generated by Louis Napoleon and Eugénie called for a moment of synthesis and definition. To a large extent that synthesis was made by the novelist and playwright Alexandre Dumas *fils*.[4] His most famous play, *La Dame aux camélias,* was the sentimental story of a courtesan who flourished briefly in the time of Louis Philippe: Marguerite Gautier (Marie Duplessis in real life). Adapted from his own novel, the play had its première in Paris in 1852, and its appearance at the beginning of the Second Empire was perfectly timed. Although it dealt with French society under the July Monarchy, *La Dame aux camélias* crystallized much of the moral decadence of Louis Napoleon's régime. Within a few years Dumas *fils* went on to perfect his vision of the Second Empire and to define the unique nature of the society which it had created. A new word entered the French language when his play *Le Demi-monde* opened at the Gymnase on March 20, 1855. The demimonde will always be associated with the Second Empire, and Dumas *fils* described it on the stage with the same realism Constantin Guys used to present it in his paintings and drawings. This realism offended many, and Dumas' plays were often condemned on the grounds of lewdness and immorality. Such hypocrisy was consistent in a régime which would prosecute Flaubert for his novel *Madame Bovary* and Baudelaire for his poems *Les Fleurs du mal*. Among those who appreciated the accurate way in which Dumas *fils* had held a mirror to French society was his own famous father. "I find my subjects in my dreams," he said, "my son takes his from real life. I work with my eyes shut, he with his open. I draw, he photographs."

In spite of chic clothes and money and jewels, there was much that was ugly in the demimonde. Syphilis, for example, was rampant and incurable and may be considered one of the thematic diseases of the Second Empire.[5] In his office at 52 rue de Tournon, Dr. Ricord, the well-known specialist in venereal diseases, had more patients than he could handle. According to the diagnosis made by Dumas *fils,* the demimondaine was a woman outside the boundaries of normal society because of her marital infidelity or careless behavior: she did not necessarily take money from men. In reality, however, the demimonde soon came to include all the loose women of the day. The sordid truth was that the leaders in this new area of French society were crude and vulgar courtesans with little beauty or intelligence to recommend them. They were not without charm: Anna Deslions with her velvet eyes and Renaissance Italian head; Céleste Mogador, veteran of the Bal Mabille, ex-equestrienne of the Cirque Franconi and at last (through the idiocy of a young nobleman) Comtesse de Chabrillan; the lovely Giulia Barrucci, who treasured a memento from Louis Napoleon; and Léonide Leblanc, nicknamed Mademoiselle Maximum, whose lovers included Plon-Plon and the Duc d'Aumale, one of the sons of Louis Philippe. Stripped of all façade and decoration, the appeal these women exercised was purely and starkly sexual.

This was the reality which Emile Zola came to understand when he wrote *Nana* (1880), one of his many novels dealing with life during the Second Empire. In part, Nana was modeled after Blanche d'Antigny, a well-known courtesan of the day who died of smallpox penni-less and alone in the Hôtel du Louvre in 1874. Zola did his research well, choosing as authorities in matters of the demimonde two literary men-about-town—Edmond de Goncourt, who with his brother, Jules, had ventured into every level of contemporary society, and Ludovic Halévy, who had helped provide Offenbach with many a spar-kling libretto. In Zola's novel the beautiful Nana makes her debut in an operetta at the Théâtre des Variétés just before the Paris Exposition of 1867. In the rôle of the Blond Venus she appears on the stage almost naked, and Zola sets down the immediacy of the moment:

> And when Nana lifted her arms, the golden hairs in her armpits were observable in the glare of the foot-lights. There was no applause. Nobody laughed any more. The men strained forward with serious faces, sharp features, mouths irritated and parched. . . . "By God," said Fauchery, quite simply, to la Faloise. . . . the Count was sitting straight upright, with mouth agape and face mottled with red, while close by him, in the shadow, the restless eyes of the Mar-quis de Chouard had become cat-like, phosphorescent, full of golden sparkles. The house was suffocating, people's very hair grew heavy on their perspiring heads.

For this kind of stimulation the courtesans of the Sec-ond Empire were rewarded lavishly, and none more so than the famous La Païva. In the later stages of her career she came to have one of the most luxurious houses in Paris, paid for by an indulgent German named Henckel von Donnersmarck, whose Silesian miners worked many long hours underground to provide him with the money he needed for his insatiable mistress. Her name was Thérèse Lachman, and she was a Russian Jewess who had been born in Moscow. Her house, the fabulous Hôtel de Païva, had a staircase made entirely of onyx, and Baudry painted a ceiling of naked nymphs which included the mistress of the house herself.[6] The walls of her bathroom were covered with mirrors and agate and ceramic tile, the tub was made of marble and silvered bronze and each faucet was encrusted with jewels. Her bed alone was said to have cost a hundred thousand francs. In the days when she conducted a salon for writers, the Goncourts could complain of the insolent luxury of her table, where even the wine carafes were "cathedrals of crystal." She had once been married to the Marquis de Païva, a Portuguese nobleman whose name (and title) she kept, although she had sent him away after the wedding night—saying she was content to be a whore and he had been amused sufficiently. She took delight in wearing cheap clothes and covering her neck and arms with jewels worth half a million francs. For all her vulgarity, however, she was no match for Cora Pearl.

"If the Frères Provençaux served an omelette with diamonds in it," said the Duc de Gramont-Caderousse, "Cora would be there every night."[7] Born in England with the unfortunate name of Emma Crouch, Cora quickly changed it and sought her fortune across the Channel. Once in France, she appealed hugely to the Second Empire's fascination with vulgarity: she spoke French like a stable boy and never lost her strong Cockney accent. Though she had a splendid figure, she was far from being beautiful. Nevertheless, she soon came to command five or ten thousand francs for a night (the average worker was earning three francs a day) and included among her regular patrons Achille Murat, the tireless Plon-Plon and the young Prince of Orange, who was known to the wits along the Boulevard as Citron. Cora, portrayed in *Nana* as Lucy Stewart, changed the color of her hair and her carriage and her servants' livery as the mood struck her. During dinners in her luxurious house she is said to have danced the cancan in the nude on a carpet of orchids and to have bathed before her guests in a silver tub full of champagne. A number of plaster casts of her breasts were found after she died, and something of her compassionate nature can be sensed in the words she spoke when one of her lovers shot himself in her living room: "The pig has ruined my beautiful carpet."

It may be difficult to believe, but these were some of the rich and powerful and influential women of the Second Empire. They were everywhere: in all the best shops and restaurants and cafés, gambling on the Bourse, creating manners and styles and—so the Goncourts complained—eating *marrons glacés* next to your wife at the theater. They had wealthy and important friends, ranging from Louis Napoleon himself down through all the upper levels of contemporary society. Their protectors were bankers, financiers, senators, army officers, aristocrats from the Jockey Club and foreign noblemen. The Prince of Wales, later Edward VII and appearing in *Nana* as the Prince of Scots, was a devoted member of the demimonde who came to Paris whenever he could escape from his mother. The Duc de Morny was well known among the little ballet girls of the Opéra: there was a rumor after his death that a mysterious casket had disappeared from his bedside table. It was said to have contained nude photographs of his many conquests, the ladies interestingly decorated with flowers.

The rich patrons of the demimonde—among them, Russian grand dukes, Turkish pashas, South American millionaires and all varieties of local men-about-town— spent unbelievable sums of money on women and pleasure. No gesture was too extravagant: one Easter Day the madcap Duc de Gramont-Caderousse gave his mistress a giant egg containing a horse and carriage. Fortunes were dissipated with rare speed, and many joined the Second Empire's growing company of *viveurs* and *mangeurs:* wastrels and spendthrifts. Young Arthur de Lauriston, for example, awoke one morning to find everything gone. He took the news casually enough. Putting on his most elegant clothes, he summoned his phaeton and drove over to the gare de Lyon, where he boarded a train for the south. Eventually he ended up in Algeria as an officer in the army. Others, with less faith in the future, simply threw themselves into the Seine.

For all its waste and debauchery, the Second Empire often appears in a haze of nostalgia, and it is difficult to separate the dream from the reality. To some it has come to mean what the Habsburg Empire symbolizes for certain eastern Europeans: the good old days, when splendor was not an embarrassment and no indulgence was forbidden. In retrospect, there is a tantalizing ambiguity about the Second Empire, for it is a period at once appealing and repellent. Hardly anything was what it seemed to be, and the imperial court and the demimonde were quite as sordid and decadent as they were elegant and amusing. A number of realities existed side by side, and many reflections could be seen in the same mirror. Everything was touched by paradox, and ugliness and poverty were hidden just beneath the imperial façade. Nevertheless, sleight of hand was the Second Empire's great talent, and persistent images of splendor and magnificence do brighten the whole era.

They are reflected in one gaudy surface after another: in the glass walls of Worth's Salon de Lumière, in the footlights of the Variétés, in the mirrors of the Maison Dorée, in the crystal of the chandeliers illuminating the long staircase of the Tuileries. They are reflected in the gleaming white buildings and golden eagles of the new imperial city. Little has survived the insubstantial pageant of the Second Empire, but that magic city remains. Paris was then, and is now, one of the loveliest capitals in the world and Louis Napoleon's most lavish gift to the future.

CHAPTER FIVE

The Splendid City

IN DESCRIBING Louis Napoleon's transformation of Paris from a half-medieval city of slums and narrow streets into a modern metropolis, contemporaries often found themselves at a loss for words. They repeated the metaphor of the magician-emperor: no other image came to mind to characterize the remarkable alterations that had been made.

"The day will come," said the author of a guidebook in the 1860s, "when history will call the capital of France, changed as if by magic in less than a quarter of a century, THE PARIS OF NAPOLEON III as it has called the Eternal City THE ROME OF AUGUSTUS CAESAR."

Captain Gronow, an Englishman familiar with Paris since the days of Waterloo, was enchanted by the new Bois de Boulogne, once the haunt of footpads and gypsies. He found the flowers and lawns and waterfalls and winding streams superb and could only say that the change had been accomplished "by the hand of an enchanter." After his visit to Saint Cloud in the summer of 1855, Prince Albert wrote that "Paris is signally transfigured." Like Captain Gronow, he was much taken with the grounds of the

Bois. "How all this could have been done in so short a time," said Albert, "no one comprehends."

Long before he came to power Louis Napoleon had dreamed of remaking the capital of France. He was strongly influenced by the Saint-Simonians, who had proposed a complete rebuilding of Paris after the cholera epidemic of 1831. As early as 1842, while still a prisoner in the fortress of Ham, he expressed the desire to be like the Emperor Augustus, who had turned Rome into a city of marble. Once elected President of the Second Republic, he began almost immediately and in the face of considerable opposition to build a modern city appropriate to the needs of French society at the middle of the nineteenth century.

In 1850 Paris was still partly medieval. Captain Gronow saw it as a place of patchwork magnificence: many of its streets were clogged with mud and garbage and paved, if at all, with crumbling blocks of sandstone. The central city, lying behind the barrier of the Fermiers Généraux, was a labyrinth of tenements and small shops.[1] There were elegant sections, of course: in the neighborhood of the rue de la Paix and the rue Saint Honoré on the Right Bank of the Seine and in the faubourg Saint Germain on the Left Bank. But these were exceptions. The Ile de la Cité, for instance, while containing the Palais de Justice and the cathedral of Notre Dame, was otherwise filled with dirty narrow streets.[2] Much of Paris belonged to the poor, to the outcast and the disinherited, to the thief and the prostitute. Near the rue Montmartre there were rows of decaying houses with open sewers running in front of them, and in the vicinity of the rue Saint Denis piece-workers crowded into miserable little rooms where they made jewelry and artificial flowers and bronze doré for the few who could afford them. Unbelievably, in the space between the Louvre and the courtyard of the

Tuileries, there was a vile little slum.

At the half-century few buildings in Paris had running water, and what there was came from wells and nearby rivers. Napoleon Bonaparte brought the waters of the Ourcq into the city, and other sources of supply were the Bièvre and the stream of Ménilmontant and the Seine itself. The Seine, it must be added, also served as a sewer. Water was delivered from house to house and from floor to floor on the backs of porters, often sturdy peasants from the Auvergne. Most buildings had an adjoining cesspool, and in the early hours of the morning great dripping wagons could be seen as they lumbered through the streets carting human waste off to the Forest of Bondy east of the city. This rudimentary system of sanitation aggravated the cholera epidemics of 1831 and 1848, and in the latter year almost twenty thousand Parisians died. Street lighting was sporadic and varied with the season: thieves and darkness made it unsafe to walk at night even in the rich quarters of the Right Bank. Most depressing of all was the fact that no more than fifty acres of public park could be found in the entire city. Only the dusty gardens of the Champs Elysées and the small place des Vosges in the Marais offered the citizens of Paris sunlight or fresh air. Other gardens—the Tuileries, the Palais Royal, the Luxembourg and the Jardin des Plantes—were grudgingly opened to the public during certain hours. The French capital was in no way prepared to meet the demands of a new industrial civilization expanding in all directions, nor was it splendid enough to contain the pageantry of the Second Empire.

Captain Gronow realized that the "melancholy, gloomy, miserable portions of the city" held charms for the artist and the archaeologist but were impossible to live in. And surely, no matter what sacrilege the sentimental antiquarian may see in Louis Napoleon's razing of old Paris, the benefits derived from it far outweigh the loss of picturesque hovels. When the Second Empire came to an end in 1870, Paris could boast of almost five thousand acres of public park in place of a pathetic forty-seven. This accomplishment alone is enough to justify the building program—and it does not take into account the magnificent sewers and bridges and aqueducts, the tree-lined boulevards and railroad stations, the new Théâtre de l'Opéra and the great reading room of the Bibliothèque Nationale, the completion of the Louvre after seven hundred years, the renovation of the Hôtel Dieu and the building of other hospitals, the seventy schools and more than a dozen churches and synagogues, the military barracks and new markets including the modern glass-and-iron pavilions of Les Halles. Today, with the exception of the basilica of Sacré Coeur and the Palais de Chaillot and the Eiffel Tower, the city is still the Paris of the Second Empire.[3]

For better or worse, like so much else in the history of the period, the reconstruction of the capital must be credited almost entirely to Louis Napoleon. In his first days as prince-president he was often found with a map in front of him and a colored crayon in his hand, sketching out improvements for the modernization of the city. He had three compelling motives: to provide health and comfort for the people of Paris, to create the most splendid background possible for his régime and to generate economic prosperity through extensive public works. It would be unrealistic to deny his success in these areas, whatever aesthetic judgment may be made about the involved eclecticism of the city he created.

The vision of a new capital was his alone, but he had exceptional help in its realization. Georges Eugène Haussmann, like the Duc de Morny, was a man born precisely at the right time and in the right place—a man with his spirit turned toward the future, materialistic and aggressive and interested only in results. For almost the whole of the Second Empire he served as prefect of the Department of the Seine, and he was the administrator responsible for turning the emperor's dream of a new Paris into reality.

From the beginning the Duc de Persigny, not generally remarkable for his intellect, understood the nature of Haussmann's genius. As Minister of the Interior he came to interview the new prefect in the early years of the empire. "I had before me," said Persigny, "one of the most extraordinary products of our day: a large, strong, vigorous and energetic man who was at the same time subtle, clever and resourceful. This daring individual did not hesitate to reveal frankly the kind of person he was."

The kind of person he was offended many people, and the story of the rebuilding of Paris is largely the story of Haussmann's impatient and arrogant attacks on various vested interests. Even today his reputation is not a happy one and—in spite of his contributions to slum clearance and sanitation and urban growth—he is remembered only for having disemboweled a charming and perhaps mythical city known as "Old Paris" and for having put in its place a garish and pretentious stage set. Haussmann was a career civil servant and in 1852, when Louis Napoleon gave his famous speech of empire at Bordeaux, he was prefect of the Department of the Gironde, a little-known public official. The prince-president met him at the time and did not fail to notice the enthusiasm of the welcoming ceremonies he had staged. Soon after becoming emperor and in order to speed the rebuilding of Paris, Louis Napoleon decided to dismiss the timid and unsympathetic prefect of the Seine he had inherited from the July Monarchy. Looking through a list of candidates for the position, he came across Haussmann's name. "Useless to go farther," he said. "There's the man I need.

Certainly other régimes had tried to deal with the city's problems, and over the years many splendid improvements had been made—notably during the First Empire. But by the mid-nineteenth century the pressures of a new industrial civilization and of a growing population were enormous.[4] Temporary measures were no longer enough, and a master plan was needed to create a metropolis in harmony with the times. There were many ways in which Paris was deficient: in housing and sanitation, for example, in the control of traffic and in the suppression of crime in the streets. Working closely with the emperor, Haussmann approached each of these problems with the same direct pragmatism. Little precedent existed, since few attempts had been made in the past to refashion an entire city. On the very day he became prefect of the Seine (June 29, 1853) the emperor handed him a map of Paris on which he had drawn in four colors some of the changes he wanted. In spite of the impression Haussmann gave in later years, many of these changes had been initiated long before he took office. The rue de Rivoli, begun during the First Empire and extended by Louis Philippe, was being completed before he was appointed prefect. The rebuilding of Les Halles was under way, and landscape gardeners were carving out the Bois de Boulogne in a forest east of the city which once had been the hunting ground of the Valois kings.

Haussmann's first months as prefect were devoted to organization and planning. He was fortunate in having around him a group of brilliant engineers: among them, Adolphe Alphand, builder of the Bois and other parks, and Eugène Belgrand, responsible for the network of sewers and underground installations. At the beginning there were many technical problems, all made more difficult by the fact that no accurate map of the city existed. During the fall and winter of 1854 you would have seen a number of odd-looking wooden towers in the streets of Paris. From the platforms on top of them, surveyors were making triangulations within the limits of the *octroi* wall. The result was an exact relief map of the city as well as a detailed plan of streets and buildings. Throughout the years of construction a small scale copy of the street plan hung on the wall of the prefect's office in the Hôtel de Ville.

By 1854 Haussmann was ready to undertake a systematic reconstruction of Paris, and the demolition of many older quarters was begun in earnest. There were bitter opponents: poor people evicted from their homes to make way for parks and boulevards, provincial deputies annoyed by the amount of money lavished on the capital, members of the middle class afraid of the thousands of laborers brought into the city, and conservative bankers like Achille Fould and Baron de Rothschild horrified by the prefect's reckless spending and unorthodox financial methods.

In the end an adventurous approach to money did lead to his undoing, although he managed to complete or initiate most of the improvements planned by the emperor before he was forced to resign. It must be said in Haussmann's defense that he built his splendid city without levying any new taxes. He found money in a variety of other ways: through the resale of condemned property, through public loans and subsidies from the national government. Under the influence of Saint-Simonians like the Péreire brothers, he relied on inflationary finance and the extension of credit.[5] Long-term borrowing against future income did, in fact, keep funds available throughout the building of the imperial city. And Haussmann, in defiance of the cautious bankers of the Haute Banque, sold city bonds directly to the public, issuing them in five-hundred-franc denominations to encourage the small investor.

The first issue was for sixty million francs: shares went on sale at the Hôtel de Ville and other locations on June 14, 1855. The public responded enthusiastically, and the issue was oversubscribed by twenty million francs when the sale came to an end in the afternoon. It was fortunate for Haussmann that the early years of the Second Empire saw a resurgence of the French economy. The coup d'état had restored the confidence of the middle class, and 1852 itself was one of the great boom years. The stock market rose daily, and many railway shares doubled within six months of Louis Napoleon's seizure of power. Most important of all, capital was readily available for investment.

There was nothing illegal about floating bond issues, but over the years Haussmann engaged in more questionable procedures. He managed to create a hidden debt of some half-billion francs, based on an involved system of deferred payments, and he encouraged builders and contractors to issue their own bonds. Surely some unorthodox approach was called for, however, since he reported that between 1851 and 1867 construction had cost two and a half billion francs—an enormous sum for the time.[6]

By the final years of the Second Empire many of the prefect's cavalier methods were being brought to light, and in 1867 the republican deputy Jules Ferry wrote a series of exposés in the newspaper *Le Temps*. The following year the articles were published in book form as *Les Comptes fantastiques d'Haussmann*. A great deal of scandal had attended the reconstruction of Paris, and it was common gossip that some members of the imperial court had made fortunes in real estate on the strength of privileged information. But Haussmann's financial vagaries were the last straw. In 1869, hoping to shore up a crumbling régime, Louis Napoleon asked for his resignation. Years later, however, one of the prefect's bitterest opponents had a change of heart. "It is of little importance to us today that the accounts of Haussmann were fantastic," said Jules Simon in 1882. "He had undertaken to make Paris a magnificent city, and he completely succeeded."

The accomplishment was a magnificent one, and Paris benefits from it still. For half a century the city created by Louis Napoleon and his prefect of the Seine served as a model for urban planners in other parts of France and throughout the world. Echoes of Second Empire architecture and engineering are to be found in a variety of places: in Lyon, Marseille, Toulon; in Rome, Brussels, Stockholm, Barcelona, Madrid; and in many of the capitals of the New World. The Paseo de la Reforma in Mexico City, for example, was built by the Emperor Maximilian in clear imitation of the Parisian boulevards.

Certainly Haussmann's boulevards were among the most enchanting features of the new imperial city, and their long straight lines cut lovely vistas in every direction. Some of the ones most familiar today date from the era of the Second Empire: the avenue de l'Opéra (completed after 1870), the boulevard de Strasbourg, the boulevard de Sébastopol and streets like the avenue Foch (then avenue de l'Impératrice) radiating in splendor from the place de l'Etoile. Too much emphasis has been placed on the fact that they were designed for cavalry charges and troop deployment against the rising of a hostile population. In reality, the boulevards were as much for civilian as for military traffic, and they were quite as decorative as they were functional. The population as a whole was far from hostile and the emperor a long way from being a brutal dictator. In any case, the boulevards form only a small part of the wonders of Louis Napoleon's Paris.

When renovated, Les Halles—the central meat-and-produce market near the Palais Royal—constituted one of the most modern groups of buildings in the world. The market, referred to by Zola as "the stomach of Paris," [7] dated from the twelfth century and was in desperate need of modernization when the Second Empire began. The architect Baltard designed a heavy stone building. Louis Napoleon was displeased and, having admired the new train shed of the Strasbourg Railway (the present gare de l'Est), he suggested as an alternative a glass structure supported by "umbrellas" of iron. Taking his cue from the emperor, Haussmann gave the architect explicit instructions. "Iron! Iron!" he shouted. "Nothing but iron!" And by 1866 ten airy and functional pavilions had been built in the manner proposed by the emperor. They were constructed entirely of glass and iron, materials which formerly had been expensive and rarely used in any great quantity. Like the Crystal Palace in London, constructed in a similar way and put up for the Great Exhibition of 1851, the buildings of Les Halles influenced architectural design for years to come. Like so much else in a period often considered no more than a pallid imitation of the past, the new market looked directly and firmly into the future.

Of all the far-sighted accomplishments associated with Louis Napoleon's rebuilding of Paris, the one which has given the most pleasure to the most people is the Bois de Boulogne. For this gift the emperor was entirely responsible, since he not only conceived the idea himself but presented what had originally been government property to the people of Paris. It was only one of the splendid parks he provided: on the Right Bank of the Seine we find the

Bois de Vincennes and the Buttes Chaumont and the Parc Monceau, and on the Left Bank the Parc de Montsouris. Nevertheless, the Bois de Boulogne is the masterpiece—over two thousand acres of lakes and waterfalls and gardens and footpaths (some of them staked out by the emperor himself), a controlled wilderness in which four hundred thousand trees were planted and cafés and restaurants and grottos built, a stunning *parc à l'anglaise* calling to mind London's Hyde Park so much admired by Louis Napoleon in his days of exile. Today, a century later, it still provides endless pleasure and recreation for Parisians and for visitors from all over the world.

When the Bois was new, Paris found itself in the golden age of the horse and carriage, and consequently some forty miles of bridle paths and curving carriage roads were laid out in the park. In the 1920s an old lady recalled the riding lessons she had taken as a child during the early years of the empire. They were given by a Mr. Mackenzie Grieves, the "gentleman-centaur," and she remembered galloping through the Bois on spring mornings and stopping in the Pré Catalan for a glass of fresh milk and a slice of brown bread. On other days in the Bois you might have gone to the racetrack at Longchamp, a project promoted by the Duc de Morny and inaugurated in 1857 with the Grand Duke Constantine of Russia on hand for the opening ceremonies. Or daily you might have watched the *tour du lac,* the afternoon promenade around the lake. All along the avenue de l'Impératrice leading into the park there would be gentlemen riders—often the Duc de Morny or the emperor himself—and their ladies, "amazons" in elegant riding habits. Then gleaming carriages, some with two and some with four horses, would begin the drive around the lake: there Cora Pearl and La Païva, here Comtesse Walewska and the Empress Eugénie. This fashionable procession, one of the great pageants of the Second Empire, was often recalled in later years by those who had seen it. For Prince Poniatowski it was always the compelling image of a long-vanished and happy childhood. Like the garden of the Tuileries, the Bois de Boulogne became one of the lovely gathering places of the city.

However, the most revolutionary achievements of Haussmann's engineers and architects were less beautiful than the new park and were to be encountered, more often than not, underground. The sewers and aqueducts and gas mains of the Second Empire mark a giant step into the future and give some of the first evidence that Paris was approaching the twentieth century. On a visit to France the English reformer Edwin Chadwick remarked to Louis Napoleon: "May it be said of you that you found Paris stinking and left it sweet." And stinking he had found it: in 1851 there were only eighty miles of underground sewers to accommodate the city, and sanitary conditions were generally medieval. During the reign of Louis Philippe the first great collector sewers had been built under the rue de Rivoli and under some of the quais of the Left Bank. By 1857 Belgrand had begun the construction of the General Collector of Asnières under the rue Royale. When opened ten years later, it was one of the marvels of the contemporary world. During the Paris Exposition of 1867 its galleries were visited by innumerable foreigners, and today they are still open for inspection. When the Third Republic began in 1870, Paris could boast of nearly four hundred miles of underground sewers. And in the sewers were gas mains supplying the fifteen thousand new lights which Haussmann had added to the city.

For centuries one of the most common sounds in the

streets of Paris had been: *"A l'eau! à l'eau, oh!"*—the cry of the water carriers with their yokes and wooden buckets. Soon after he took office, Louis Napoleon's prefect continued the unending struggle to bring fresh water into the city. He did succeed in increasing the supply and piping water directly into more buildings, although during the Second Empire it was common enough to see porters carrying full bathtubs into private houses. In their first great project Haussmann's engineers had found a group of springs near Châlons, some hundred miles from Paris. They constructed a magnificent aqueduct which carried water by gravity along eighty miles of the valley of the Marne and through a complex of bridges and tunnels and siphons. On October 1, 1865, five million gallons of spring water poured into Paris. The amount, however, was far short of what was needed, and after Haussmann's resignation, work continued on the Aqueduct of the Vanne and other systems he had initiated. When the Second Empire came to an end, the water supply was still inadequate, but a hopeful beginning had been made.

Few of Louis Napoleon's critics have ever objected to these technological improvements in sanitation and water supply and comfort—unless for reasons of money. But they have objected violently to the architecture of the Second Empire, finding it tasteless and unnecessarily derivative. It is true that all the new buildings, with the exception of Les Halles, were imitative and eclectic. One perhaps could forgive Plon-Plon for his grotesque Pompeian mansion on the avenue Montaigne. But it was more difficult to excuse gaudy public buildings in a variety of antique styles: Romanesque and Gothic and Renaissance. In his indictment of Baron Haussmann, Jules Ferry mourned the loss of the Paris known to Voltaire and Diderot and denounced the "triumphant vulgarity and appalling materialism" of the imperial capital.

The charge was not without foundation, and among the most vulgar and materialistic public buildings of the day was the Théâtre de l'Opéra in the present place de l'Opéra. Though not completed until after the Franco-Prussian War, it may stand as a convenient symbol of all that was splendid and absurd in the Second Empire. Like the era which produced it, the building is at once a triumph and a disaster. During the whole of Louis Napoleon's régime the Opéra remained in its old quarters on the rue Le Peletier, communicating with the boulevard des Italiens through a covered passageway. Stage facilities and seating capacity were far from adequate, although the company itself was considered one of the best in the world and attracted composers like Verdi and Wagner and Meyerbeer. As a ceremonial gesture the emperor often attended, but he was not fond of music. However, he soon realized that a more splendid opera house would increase national prestige and enhance the lovely city he was building. In 1860 a competition was held for the design of a new house, and it was won by a young architect named Charles Garnier. He went on to create what is perhaps the most perfect example of the baroque style he christened "Napoleon III"—a gay and careless mixture of periods in which form has nothing whatever to do with function. Elaboration grew from elaboration, and critics have often equated Garnier's work with the confections of a pastry cook. The resulting mélange is an expression of Second Empire materialism in its purest form. The Opéra is, and was surely meant to be, a superb background for newly rich industrialists and *cocodettes* and imitation noblemen —for all the ambiguous supernumeraries of the age. Ironically, when the Palais Garnier was finally inaugurated by the President of the Third Republic on January 5, 1875, it brought back all the lovely vanished evenings of the Tuileries. Glowing under the gaslights, the Grand Staircase was crowded with beautiful women and elegant men, and troopers of the Cent Gardes lined the steps—though now they were called with less glamour the Gardes Républicaines. Only Louis Napoleon and Eugénie were missing: surely they would have approved this voluptuous gathering together of rare stones and precious marbles, of paintings and statues, of tapestries and mosaics. For all its ostentation, however, there is a nostalgic charm about Garnier's opera house, and it has come to symbolize Paris to the rest of the world as much as the Eiffel Tower or the Louvre or the cathedral of Notre Dame.

The reconstructions of the Second Empire had seen the passing of a smaller and more tranquil city. Under the direction of Baron Haussmann, modern Paris was born, a city appropriate to an age of technology and increased prosperity and mass population. The urban dweller of today would be at home in Louis Napoleon's Paris, for it soon became a crowded metropolitan complex rich in the delights and discomforts and problems of the modern city. Only London had preceded Paris in facing the unfamiliar environment of a new civilization. Second Empire Paris, in fact, was to provide endless material for students of Europe at the threshold of the twentieth century. The Impressionist painters found their inspiration in the urban scene, and so did poets like Baudelaire and Rimbaud. At first the painters (though we must make an exception of Honoré Daumier) were inclined to see it as a beautiful landscape filled with people and new activity, while only the poets sensed the growing horror of its aggressive materialism. In the beginning however, Louis Napoleon's Paris was new and fresh and vital, and it appeared an enchanting place of excitement and beauty and movement. With its dazzling white buildings and gilded iron railings and gaily striped awnings, the imperial city formed the exuberant background of a modern age. For the moment there were no hints of grime or rust or decay, and everything was unused: the age and the régime and the splendid city. Enthusiastic crowds moved along the boulevards with twentieth-century speed and noise.

In Second Empire Paris you could have heard the unfamiliar sounds of a new era: the iron carriage wheels and the first mechanical sweepers and the omnibuses rattling by with their colored lights blazing at night. Mingling with these new sounds were the sounds of an older city. There were the street criers: the sellers of sugar and soap and mussels; the egg merchants shouting *"A la coque!"*; the oystermen calling out *"A la barque!"*; the flower girls chanting *"Fleurissez vos amours!"* * There were wandering musicians with flutes and violins and the newly invented saxophone. Along the boulevard du Temple there were organ grinders, street singers, magicians, saltimbanques, jugglers and trained rats and dogs. There was Duchesne, the open-air dentist, in his white tie and black frock coat and the hand organ drowning out the cries of his patients. There was *l'homme-orchestre,* the popular one-man band, and along the Grands Boulevards were noisy salesmen of everything under the sun. There was Mangin in his elaborate costume selling pencils from his wagon, and Isabelle, the impudent flower girl from the Jockey Club, offering violets on the terrace of Tortoni's. On every corner you would find another charlatan, another purveyor of patent medicine. The search for eternal youth was characteristic of the age, and arsenic pills for rejuvenation were sold everywhere. Indeed, they were said

* "From the shell!"; "From the fishing boat!"; "May your love life flourish!"

to have killed the Duc de Morny, a devoted citizen of the new Paris.

It was a city of noise, and it was a city of crowds. The center of its life lay along the Grands Boulevards, which stretched from the Madeleine to the place de la République and included the boulevard des Capucines, the boulevard des Italiens and the boulevard Saint Martin. Along these wide and busy boulevards strolled the dandies of the day in their richly embroidered vests and square monocles: the *cocodès,* the *gandin,* the *petit crevé.* These were the elegant idlers like M. de Camors in Octave Feuillet's novel of 1867 who described the hardships of his life in the following terms: *"Je me lève généralement le matin."* * There were other, less languid, eccentrics: the "Persian" who attended every theater opening in a bizarre Oriental costume, and M. de Saint-Cricq, who often filled his pockets with ice cream at Tortoni's. As eccentric, and more vocal, were the writers and artists and journalists and Bohemians who gathered daily in the Brasserie des Martyrs in the rue Bréda.

It was a city which sought amusement in public: in restaurants like Voisin, Brébant, La Rue, the Café Riche, the Café Hardy, the Café de Paris. Two of the most famous and expensive were the Maison Dorée at 20 boulevard des Italiens and the Café Anglais at Number 13 at the corner of the rue Marivaux. The latter was renowned for its private dining rooms and its superb chef, Adolphe Dugléré. The most sought-after private dining room was the Grand Seize (Number 16) on the first floor. Here leading courtesans of the day were entertained by the capital's richest financiers and noblemen. At restaurants like the Maison Dorée, waiters were in the habit of adding to the bill the number of the private room in which the meal was served,

* "I generally get up in the morning."

since money seemed so unimportant to their clientèle. In general, a good dinner cost four or five francs and something more elaborate ten francs. Naturally there were restaurants for every taste and every pocketbook. On the rue de Richelieu there was an English Tavern where you could find—if you were foolish enough—boiled vegetables and Stilton cheese and fruit tarts. Galliani in the passage des Panoramas was famous for Italian cuisine.

Before long Paris became the most marvelous and modern city in the world, grander than London and gayer than Vienna. On the continent it was the center of business and art and finance and the hub of all the railroads. As Europe's capital of gaiety and luxury and entertainment, it played host to all the world. There were magnificent hotels for foreign visitors: the Meurice on the rue de Rivoli, for example, and the Bristol on the place Vendôme. These were older hotels, but the Second Empire built its own in the exuberant manner of the day: the Hôtel du Louvre, where Mark Twain stayed during the Paris Exposition of 1867, and the enormous Grand Hôtel facing the boulevard des Capucines with its eight hundred rooms and unsurpassed luxury. In the 1860s you could have a room at the Grand for anything from four to thirty francs a night. An American lady who came to Paris in 1855 stayed at the more modest Hôtel de Tours and left for all time a description of the typical Parisian hotel room: the tented hangings of the bed, the uncarpeted floors polished like glass, the carved ceiling and the marble mantelpiece with its "mass of gilt and burnished brass candelabras" and its "eternal little French clock." For breakfast she was served "three diminutive war-clubs" which she recognized as French bread.

It was a city devoted to entertainment. There were theaters everywhere: the Opéra on the rue Le Peletier, the

Théâtre Italien, the Opéra Comique, the Bouffes Parisiens, the Gymnase—among others in the vicinity of the Grands Boulevards. And there were the famous dance-halls which attracted all the demimonde of Europe. On the allée des Veuves off the Champs Elysées was the city's most popular: the Bal Mabille, founded in 1840. It was lavishly decorated with red damask and gilded mirrors and lighted by five thousands gas jets. In 1862 the price of admission was three and a half francs, and inside there were girls of every description and every price. The orchestra was directed by Olivier Métra, the great Chicard was leader of the cancan and the dancers performed with abandon: Finette, Pomaré, Céleste Mogador, Rigolboche. Next to Mabille was the Château des Fleurs (later joined to it), and here at night you would find some of the more spectacular men-about-town like the Marquis de Galliffet and the Duc de Gramont-Caderousse and Arsène Houssaye and various members of the *jeunesse dorée*. In 1862, while Marshal Bazaine's soldiers were dying of fever in Mexico, a guide to the dancehalls was published: *Cythères parisiennes*. Paris, so careless and unconcerned with tomorrow, had become a modern island of Cythera, abandoned to love and gaiety and pleasure.

It was a sparkling and profligate city, the domain of a debonair tyrant with waxed mustaches. It was a city best seen in springtime when the roses and the lilacs came and the swallows and the nightingales, when you could enjoy the *fraises des bois* and the chilled white wine and hear the polkas and the schottishes and the noisy steam organ in the garden of Mabille. Against the background of a lovely new imperial city, life was a glorious party that never seemed to end. At four o'clock one morning, as they were leaving the Maison Dorée, the Goncourts saw a group of sweepers looking up at the brightly lighted window of one of the restaurant's private rooms. This ragged band could not know that behind the window and under the dancing candlelight a harlot named Sabine lay sprawled on a red velvet couch near a Coromandel screen. She was drunk and her breasts were bare and her slip was pulled up over her knees.

Standing for a moment in the center of the imperial capital, the sweepers looked up with envy at the gaudy window behind which they imagined some scene of surpassing elegance. They too, were citizens of the new and splendid city.

CHAPTER SIX

The Other Paris

Edmond and Jules de Goncourt, innovators in the field of the naturalistic novel as well as accomplished boulevardiers, did not spend all their time in restaurants like the Maison Dorée. They looked into every corner of Paris in search of material for their novels and often came across curiosities unknown to the dandies who lounged on the terrace of Tortoni's. One spring evening in 1855, for example, they attended an entertainment organized by some of their friends: a rat hunt in the slums of Paris. The tracker, silent as a Mohican, led the way dressed in a jockey's vest without a shirt, and there was a piece of cord around his neck instead of a tie. Behind him walked a bearded giant carrying a cage at the end of a pole, and before the evening was out the little safari had managed to capture some twenty rats. All around them Louis Napoleon's new city was rising into the night sky.

As familiar as they were with the salons and cafés and the busy life of the Boulevard, the Goncourts intimately knew another Paris—a city which had nothing to do with the Bouffes Parisiens or the Bal Mabille or the lovely careless evenings of the Tuileries. It was a city which woke in the morning, not to a day of glamour and pleasure, but to a day of work and pain. It was Baudelaire's Paris:

> L'aurore, grelottante en robe rose et verte
> S'avançait lentement sur la Seine déserte,
> Et le sombre Paris, en se frottant les yeux,
> Empoignait ses outils, vieillard laborieux.*

Like London, it was a city illustrating with grim perfection the paradox of European civilization at the threshold of the twentieth century. In every part of Paris you came face to face with the unacceptable enigmas of an age of splendor and wealth and progress. Surely rats had always roamed the streets of Paris and no doubt still do. But hope lay over France in the middle of the nineteenth century, and the birth pangs of the modern age carried with them the promise of a glorious future for all. The more gold that came in from California and Australia, however, and the more wealth that poured into Paris from the mines and factories of the north and the ships and the railroads and the beginnings of colonial expansion, the more obvious was the great chasm in nineteenth-century society— the impossible distance between the rich and the poor. That distance was the greater in proportion to the speed with which Paris was becoming a modern city of luxury and high fashion and lovely vistas. For it was becoming at the same time, and increasingly so, a city of rats and misery and refuse. The march of the *chiffonniers,* it must be said, was one of the characteristic sights of Second Empire Paris: in the first light of day small silent groups of rag-pickers moving from one pile of garbage to the next,

---

* Morning, shivering in her robe of rose and green,
  Made her hesitant way along the deserted Seine,
  While Paris, rubbing tired eyes in its dark,
  Woke like an ancient drudge to another day's work.
              (*Translated by* DAVID PAUL)

hooks and lanterns in their hands, great bundles on their backs, some dragging feet long accustomed to convict chains. Even more apparent after Baron Haussmann's renovations was the image of Paris as a city of contrast where opulence flourished unaccountably in the midst of poverty. Through its mean streets, very near the Grands Boulevards, wandered the débris of the *fête impériale:* beggars, cripples, twelve-year-old prostitutes, thieving bands of Sicilian children, the sick, the mutilated, those without hope. For all of this, the cruel and gaudy city where many a wretched life ended in the common grave at Montmartre Cemetery attracted Frenchmen from every part of the country.

At night in the villages over cheap wine they spoke of that splendid city where a man could earn as much as five francs a day, where there were beautiful women and palaces and gleaming carriages, and where the cafés stayed open all night. When the Second Empire began, migration to the capital in search of money and adventure was no longer an idle dream for the countryman. A growing network of railroads made the journey easy, and the emperor was calling for help in building the imperial city— for masons and carpenters and unskilled laborers of every kind. Yet Paris was not El Dorado, and in 1868 over thirty-five thousand beggars and vagrants were arrested during the course of the year, some taken into custody on their first day in the city.

By mid-nineteenth century an important shift in the alignment of social classes was taking place. Attracted to urban centers, the village laborer had severed traditional ties with the land and given up the relative security of village life. Having exchanged one sort of feudal servitude for another, he could be found in northern France and the English Midlands, in Saxony and along the Bohemian frontier. He manned the textile mills of Yorkshire and Alsace as well as the coal mines of the Ruhr. He became the common soldier of the industrial revolution, without roots or property and dependent for survival on the middle-class capitalist who controlled the means of production. He had nothing to offer but the strength of his back and the labor of his hands. Nevertheless, as time passed, he achieved a position of great political importance. And the pattern of European history through the first half of the twentieth century, as well as the direction of avant-garde art and literature, evolved directly from the presence of the worker created by the industrial revolution.

Two social classes—the one new and other newly important—were gaining strength and definition and preparing for some inevitable conflict. The landed aristocracy had moved from the centers of power, and the industrial age came to be dominated at first by the middle-class capitalist and later by the urban worker. Much of the future of western civilization, in fact, is conditioned by the brutal treatment and just grievances of the worker in the early stages of the industrial revolution. As that revolution spread to various European countries—to England, then to France and the German states, later to Russia and the Austro-Hungarian Empire—exploitation of the poor was the immediate result. The exploitation continued, but by the last half of the nineteenth century the mass of the poor was rising to the surface of European society. It was an inevitable movement dating from the French Revolution of 1789, although, with the exception of certain writers and painters and some unacknowledged visionaries like Louis Napoleon, few people in France were sensitive to its implications. The abuses suffered by the urban proletariat in the early days of industrialism surely contributed to the Paris Commune of 1871 as well as to the Russian Revolutions of 1905 and 1917. European society was broken in two by the co-existence of misery and splendor, and in the end the nineteenth century's glowing faith in science and technology and material progress came to very little.

During the first years of the Second Empire the country worker journeyed to Paris in his thousands, attracted by the city's many small industries. For the most part he settled in the area between the old *octroi* wall and the fortifications built by Louis Philippe—in what were villages and suburban communes like Bercy, Belleville, Vaugirard, La Chapelle, La Villette, Charonne and Les Batignolles. Between 1851 and 1857 the population of these districts rose by two thirds, more than five times the growth rate for the rest of the city. Before long they were heavily industrialized: the railroad companies, for example, filled such districts with repair shops and freight yards and fuel depots. And in 1860 the area was divided into seven new wards, so making the twenty *arrondissements* of modern Paris.

The addition of these seven *arrondissements* served to separate and isolate the poor in a new way. Before the rebuilding of Paris, different social classes had lived in the same neighborhood and often shared the same building. In fact, with the exception of certain well-defined slums, the poor generally had rooms at the top of houses where there were comfortable middle-class apartments on lower floors. This arrangement encouraged some familiarity, a small degree of charity and the absence of direct hostility. Nonetheless, the system was more impersonal than the sometimes benevolent feudalism of village society in the days before the industrial revolution. After the creation of the "red" *arrondissements* in 1860 the inevitable division between the rich and the poor became a literal one, and in the final years of the empire no police agent dared to go alone into sections like Belleville or Ménilmontant. The villager's dream of coming to Paris was no longer impossible, but the realities of city life were something different from the glamorous picture painted in country taverns.

The move to Paris meant the exchange of one kind of desperate poverty for another. Its population ever increasing, the area between the *octroi* wall and the old fortifications turned into an unwholesome complex of shanty towns and tarpaper hovels—in spite of Haussmann's continual building of churches and schools and sewers. That such slums could have developed in the prosperous early days of the Second Empire sets in relief all the defects of Louis Napoleon's urban plan. Paris did not become the model city he wished for, and the construction of the imperial capital was attended by profiteering and brutal evictions and high rents. Most important, his grand design put an end to the vaguely democratic system whereby the rich and the poor lived together. Certainly the emperor was anxious to eliminate the old infected slums of Paris, but he came to concentrate most of his energy on the visual aspects of the city. Little was done to prevent new slums from rising in the place of old, and often, behind prescribed façades and buildings of uniform height, crowded and airless tenements grew up quite as loathsome as the ones which had been torn down.

Even at the center of Paris the poor continued to live in misery, although high rents forced most of them to move to the burgeoning slums of the new *arrondissements*. As the imperial capital increased in splendor, the living conditions of the poor became more and more desperate. All during Louis Napoleon's reign it was possible to find dirty narrow streets in the heart of the city where, against a background of choked gutters and garbage heaps, half-naked children played with mangy dogs and drunken women stumbled through the mud. In a study of Parisian life written at the end of the Second Empire, Maxime Du Camp describes innumerable scenes of the kind. In particular, he singled out the infamous rue Harvey near the place d'Italie: "a cloaca lined with nameless dens." Visiting Paris during the Exposition of 1867, Mark Twain described dismal shops in the faubourg Saint Antoine "where whole suits of second- and third-hand clothing are sold at prices that would ruin any proprietor who did not steal his stock." In the little crooked streets of the faubourg, said Twain, you could hire a murderer for seven dollars.

Gathering material for *Germinie Lacerteux,* a novel of life among the poor, the Goncourts went to the Clignancourt gate near the fortifications and inspected the hovels where the ragpickers lived. Old women, their faces white and moldy as mushrooms, stood in decayed doorways, and ragged children fought with one another in the streets. These, however, were scenes of luxury compared to the flophouses described by Du Camp—those fearful *garnis à la nuit* with their odor of human sweat and spilled wine, their damp walls and their mattresses filled with vermin and wood-shavings. On each mattress was a bundle of rags which turned out to be a man, and Du Camp could only say that he had seen nothing worse on the borders of the Red Sea or among the desert Arabs. Fortunate was the vagrant who could sleep under the Seine bridges or next to the trees in the Champs Elysées or in one of the many buildings under construction. As late as 1862 Baron Haussmann estimated that four-fifths of the population of Paris lived in a state bordering on indigence.

At every hour of every day some heart-breaking scene was to be encountered on the streets of the city. One early morning on the rue du Cherche Midi near the boulevard Raspail a young man came across a woman rooting in a garbage heap for apple cores and lettuce leaves and scraps of cabbage before the arrival of the sweepers and the hungry dogs. On a December evening in 1868 Maxime Du Camp saw another woman trying to pawn some worthless articles of lingerie at the Mont de Piété, the government pawnshop. Refused, she fell down the stairs outside the building and died of malnutrition two hours later in a charity hospital. One winter night the Goncourts reported that a man had been found dead of hunger in a small square, two broom handles crossed under his head as a pillow and his children sleeping next to him in the cold. Fascinated by the darker side of Paris, the Goncourts went to a police tribunal in the summer of 1860. Facing the judge was a little servant girl of thirteen who earned four francs a month and had been accused of stealing jam and syrup from her mistress. The establishment of the Second Empire passed sentence: the judge stern in gold spectacles and white cravat, the clerk of the court very like a Daumier devil, on the wall a picture of Jesus Christ and nearby a plaster bust of Louis Napoleon. The judge took the occasion to lecture the child's father, a mentally defective vagrant, on his failure to imbue her with "a moral sense." Her punishment was four years in the house of correction, and the judge hurried on to the next case—two prostitutes of thirteen and fourteen with eyes like glowing coals.

This dreadful litany continued through all the days of the empire and was based entirely on poverty. Frédéric Le Play, a sociologist of the time, recorded the living conditions of a ragpicker in the faubourg Saint Marceau. The man was an Italian of forty-seven, his wife five years younger and their daughter eight years old. All of them lived in one room, and the furniture was valued at five hundred francs. The family ate two meals a day: coffee with milk and sugar and bread in the morning, and in the evening soup with a plate of rice or lentils or potatoes. Once a week as a treat they bought meat already cooked at the Saint Honoré market, although they were obliged to drink water with vinegar instead of wine. The family's total yearly income from the sale of objects found in the streets—broken crystal and porcelain, bits of clothing, wastepaper, corks, cigar ends, an occasional coin—was 969.69 francs. Not far away Cora Pearl was earning five thousand francs for a single night's work.

The poor of Paris were not all thieves and beggars and ragpickers, however, although living conditions were uniformly impossible. Masons and carpenters had come from all over France for the building of the imperial city, and skilled craftsmen were drawn to the small factories of Paris. For working an eleven-hour day they received between two and four francs, and—in a period of constant inflation—these wages were barely enough to provide food for their families. Living quarters were crowded and unhealthy, and the workers sought forgetfulness outside the home. Factories and shops were generally closed on the Monday following payday, and it was a common sight to see women waiting in front of drinking dens for their men to emerge, in the hope that some money would be left, since the grocer and the butcher no longer extended credit. A few compassionate tavern owners erected shelters in the street for these unhappy women. However, a certain degree of sympathy must be reserved for their husbands. Alcohol was one of the only pleasures available to the worker which could make him forget his misery and deny for a moment the paradox of his life in the splendid city. His solace was pathetic enough: cheap liquor in some tavern with metal cups chained to the wall, coarse bar-maids and shouted obscenities. In a dirty alley between the boulevard Saint Germain and the quai de Montebello you might have found the Bibine du Père Pernette—where laborers and thieves and vagabonds leaned against the walls, slumped over wooden tables or lay drugged with absinthe on the floor.

It was difficult enough to be an honest workman, and the population of criminals grew rapidly. Each day M. Claude, head of the special brigade of the Sûreté, sent his men out carrying *cabriolets*—cords with knots and weights to secure prisoners—and the tribunal of the Police Correctionnelle had never been busier. Crime during the Second Empire was organized with much efficiency: there were, for example, schools for thieves where Sicilian children sold by their parents were given elaborate training. And a flourishing traffic began in the rental of babies by the day, beggars using them to evoke sympathy from strollers on the Boulevard. Certain bars catered exclusively to the criminal element, and of an afternoon you might find successful thieves enjoying their absinthe while glancing through copies of *Le Droit* and the *Gazette des Tribunaux* thoughtfully provided by the management to keep their customers up to date on legal matters. At night you would find the thieves near the rue Mouffetard in dancehalls patterned after the Bal Mabille, where the girls ranged in age from eleven to sixteen. Or you might come across them in a cabaret like Le Guillotine: three dismal rooms where men brought their own bread and sausage and ate in corners like hungry wolves. A guitarist dressed in black with long hair and filthy linen and a drink-ravaged face sang Spanish boleros in the flickering gaslight. When a stranger entered one of these dens, there was a deep and hostile silence. Taverns like La Guillotine

III

were to be found within a few blocks of the Tuileries.

Even closer to the palace were the hordes of street-walkers who clattered through the nights of the Second Empire. "The poor use their daughters," observed the Goncourts, "to avenge themselves upon the rich." In the 1860s it was officially estimated that there were more than thirty thousand prostitutes in Paris, although Maxime Du Camp insisted that the figure should have been four times as high. The police made some attempt to supervise them: they were required to have periodic medical examinations and to carry a card popularly known as *la brème,* since it resembled that flat white fish. Many of the women escaped police supervision, however, and disease was prevalent. Among the prostitutes sentenced to the women's prison of Saint Lazare sixty percent usually could be relied upon to have syphilis or gonorrhea—or both. During a three-month period in 1865 troops of the Garde Impériale lost some twenty thousand duty days in the hospital for treatment of venereal disease. The population of prostitutes included women of every station and every style, although, like Nana, most were the daughters of the poor. At the Dépôt de la Préfecture you would find fourteen-year-old girls awaiting trial who had never been inside a church or a school and who did not even know the first letters of the alphabet. Next to them would be old women who had given themselves to soldiers on the ramparts for half a loaf of bread. And lounging on other benches would be stunningly dressed streetwalkers from the boulevard des Italiens. It was by no means impossible that some of them had been to parties at the Tuileries.

Louis Napoleon was well aware that this underworld of poverty and vice and crime flourished behind the façades of the capital. Only a fool could think of Paris as a city of music and luxury and masked balls. The imperial masquerade could not hide that cruel labyrinth of jails and charity hospitals: Sainte Pélagie, Mazas, the Conciergerie; Saint Louis and Salpêtrière and the Hôtel Dieu. Hunger was everywhere, and wagons still carried condemned men from prisons like Bicêtre to the guillotine in the place de la Roquette. More than most Frenchmen, the emperor knew these things, but he had the vision of something far different.

Among papers found in the Tuileries by the Government of National Defense after the fall of the Second Empire was the sketch of a novel in Louis Napoleon's hand. The plot was simple enough: an honest grocer named Benoît leaves for America in 1847 and does not return to France until twenty years later. His return in 1868 gave the imperial novelist an opportunity to list the wonders of modern Paris—the railroads and the hospitals and the magnificent boulevards and the good life for all. This list, however, does not represent the imaginings of an idle dreamer. The fact is that by 1868 the emperor *had* improved the life of his people in many daring ways.

One of his first acts after the proclamation of empire was to confiscate the property of the House of Orléans and use the money for the poor—for the improvement of slums, for the creation of workmen's mutual-benefit societies, burial associations, public baths and orphanages and for the development of financial aids like the Crédit Froncier.[1] In this, Louis Napoleon was far more modern than most of his contemporaries, and it must be remembered that he was the author of *L'Extinction du paupérisme* and strongly under the influence of the Saint-Simonians. In a number of ways the Second Empire heralds the beginning of state socialism, for the emperor developed many new areas of public welfare and augmented others. A vast welfare organization grew up in Paris with its own commissary, department store, pharmacy, butcher shop, wine cellar and an enormous bakery using six-horsepower steam engines. Assistance was given to the aged and the blind, to the paralyzed and the epileptic and to those with cancer—all of whom received between five and ten francs a month in addition to food and clothing. Whatever the defects of the welfare system, there is no doubt that Louis Napoleon's intentions were good. He was far more concerned with the poor and the disinherited than were the "gilded pimps" whom the Comte de Viel Castel found in such abundance at the Tuileries.

In exchange, the Paris poor developed an ambiguous attitude toward the emperor. At the beginning of the régime he was immensely popular—one has only to think of the early plebiscites—although it is true that his appearance in the streets of the capital often evoked cries of *"Vive la République!"* and *"A bas, Soulouque!"* [2] And Coupeau, the roofer in Zola's *L'Assommoir,* could speak of "that bastard Bonaparte." In 1856, however, after the Peace of Paris which ended the Crimean War, workmen ran through the city shouting *"Vive l'Empereur!"* and over the years there were many reasons for them to have done so. During the course of the Second Empire some important benefits did come to the worker: in 1864, for example, he was given the right to strike, and after 1868 the word of an employer was no longer accepted before his own. The emperor ordered the construction of model homes for the poor in many parts of the city, and Eugénie herself contributed much time and energy to a number of different charities. But all the money and imperial efforts and social legislation were not enough to stem the tide of misery and poverty rising in every part of France.

It must be said that during this period of European history the dreadful working and living conditions of the poor were not peculiar to France, nor can they be blamed entirely on the government of the Second Empire. In the 1860s Daniel Kirwan, a special correspondent for the New York *World,* wrote a series of articles on life in London for his American readers. He described a night he stood on London Bridge, looking out over the great Catharine Docks to the multitude of ships at anchor in the Thames. The sight confirmed the fact that London was the richest city in the world. There was, however, under the very bridge on which he stood, an encampment of ragged and homeless Englishmen who had no share at all in the prosperity which flowed into London daily along the sea lanes of every ocean. Poverty was not new, but it did take on a more desperate cast when seen against the background of the richest city in the world.

As in London, so in Paris: material wealth and bitter want side by side. Maxime Du Camp set down the theme with precision, finding in the French capital "the permanent spectacle of abject misery adjacent to the most grandiose opulence." In the fifty years which preceded the beginning of the twentieth century this inequality came to color all European society. With their gutter wisdom the street urchins of Paris understood it well enough. In the spring, as carriages drove through the faubourg Saint Antoine to the opening of the races at Vincennes, they would shout to the elegant whores riding by: "Make way for the ragpickers of tomorrow!"

It was not immorality which destroyed the Second Empire nor unsound financial practices nor misplaced concepts of glory—nor even the Prussians. The empire fell through its denial of reality—a denial nourished by middle-class hypocrisy and an insolent display of luxury. The immorality of the time is hardly shocking; it is the luxury which offends. In the coarse lexicon of the streets the thief who stole a wallet with fifty francs in it and spent the money on cognac and a low woman did not seem to be much different from the aristocratic clubman who won a thousand times that amount at cards and took some demimondaine (whose father was a coachman and brother a convict) to the Maison Dorée for a midnight supper. No one seriously questioned the morality of either act. It was a matter of degree, and the distance between them was simply too great. Poverty and appalling luxury could not continue to exist side by side, and one day some explosion must occur. "We must prepare for the coming hour," said Disraeli in his novel *Sybil*. "The claims of the future are represented by suffering millions."

In Zola's novel *Germinal* the wife of the mine manager watches striking workers march by, and in the setting sun she sees "the red vision of revolution that on some somber evening at the end of the century would carry everything away. . . . the same terrible troop, with their dirty skins and tainted breath, would sweep away the old world. . . . Fires would flame, there would be nothing left, not a sou of the great fortunes, not a title deed of acquired properties." As early as 1856 the Goncourts understood the new social structure of France: at the top the industrialists, then the "timid grocers" of the middle class and at the bottom the people, "who one bright day would settle accounts with this lovely society." Rich and poor were experiencing the birth pangs of the modern age and sharing the wonder it occasioned. Such rewards as it produced, however, were disproportionately shared.

If his wife and children had jobs, the French workman conceivably might collect 1,800 francs a year, a sum which assured him of poor food and worse living quarters. Did there seem to be any reality in the fact that General Magnan—in his various rôles as marshal of France, commandant of the Army of Paris, senator, *Grand Veneur* and holder of the great cross of the Légion d'Honneur— should receive a total of 196,000 francs a year from the government?

Was there any reality in the fact that almost a million francs had been spent in 1856 on the birth and baptism of little Loulou, the Prince Impérial, while other children died of neglect in the streets? His layette alone cost over a hundred thousand francs, and there were midwives and doctors and ceremonies and musicians to pay for as well. Innumerable contrasts are available: Maxime Du Camp tells the story of a young prostitute and her child in the winter of 1866. They had been without food and shelter for three days, though the mother had managed to earn a few francs singing in cheap cafés. On the third night she fell asleep with her baby in her arms on the doorstep of a house on the rue de Rocher—waking to find that the child had frozen to death during the night.

When poverty was the one consistent fact of Parisian life, was there any reality in a party such as the one given at the Hôtel d'Albe in the spring of 1860, when even Prosper Mérimée thought the luxury too ostentatious and the bared breasts too outrageous? The ladies of the court performed a ballet of the Four Elements, wearing emeralds and rubies and pearls and not a great deal else. And the costumes of the guests themselves were stunning: there were naiads with silver powder in their hair, Mlle. Errazu was marvelously pretty and Princess Mathilde came as a Nubian. The house and garden were lighted by electricity, the servants were dressed as sixteenth-century pages and the empress herself was wearing a white burnoose and a black velvet mask. One popular nobleman came as a tree.

What was the reality when thieves and ragpickers and unemployed workers crowded into the great hangar of a restaurant like La Californie between the barrière du Maine and the barrière de Montparnasse to get a meal for eighty centimes? The place was often so crowded that customers stood up to eat. And there were even cheaper restaurants, like the one in the open air near the Fontaine des Innocents where Mother Bidoche spooned out unidentifiable meat from a huge vat. Not far away the Club des Grands Estomacs met each Saturday at the Restaurant Philippe for a gourmet meal which lasted eighteen hours.

It is true enough that such contrasts could be made today in all the civilized and uncivilized countries of the world. But in most modern nations the inequalities have been lessened to one degree or another. In the time of the Second Empire, when the contemporary world was new, the difference between the rich and the poor was simply too great. There was too much of everything: too much luxury and too much poverty. There were those who had everything and those who had—nothing. The denial of this reality at last led to demoralization and inevitable social conflict. The Second Empire finally must appear to us, as it did to Maxime Du Camp, an age of unreality very like the theater to which it gave such prominence. In the end, it was all false. The silk velvet was cotton, the diamonds were paste and the actors' speeches came from the prompt box.

An extravagant court and an opulent middle class closed their eyes to the existence of the miserable urban proletariat of Paris. It was a form of blindness found in contemporary London, and before long it would be found in Berlin and Vienna and St. Petersburg as well. The blindness was all the more tragic, since the middle of the nineteenth century saw a great surge of progress and prosperity. Industry was developing rapidly, commerce spreading and the wealth of nations increasing enormously. But technology and science and the conquest of the material world did little in France and elsewhere to prevent shutdowns and the decline of craftsmanship, the rising cost of living, the growth of monstrous slums and the prevalence of diseases like syphilis, alcoholism, tuberculosis and cholera. Against a painted backdrop of new splendor, Paris remained a medieval village of disease and poverty. The imperial masquerade could not long sustain that bitter truth.

At the end of their novel *Germinie Lacerteux* (1864) the Goncourts describe how the unhappy servant girl is at last thrown into the common grave at Montmartre Cemetery. Like the street urchins and the sociologists and the scorned painters, they understood the weakness of the Second Empire, leaving for us the portrait of a society broken in two:

Oh, Paris! you are the center of the world, the great humanitarian city, the citadel of charity and brotherhood. . . . Your churches speak of Jesus Christ, your laws speak of equality, your newspapers speak of progress and your government expresses concern for all the people. But here is where you discard those who die in your service, those who destroy themselves to create your luxuries, those who perish in your ugly factories, those who sweat out their lives working for you. They have given you your well being and your pleasure and your splendor. They have created your gaiety and animation. They are the multitude of your streets and the people of your grandeur.

PART THREE

THE MARVELOUS YEAR

"Have some wine," the March Hare said in an encouraging tone.

Alice looked all round the table, but there was nothing on it but tea. "I don't see any wine," she remarked.

"There isn't any," said the March Hare.

LEWIS CARROLL

CHAPTER SEVEN

The Great Fair

IN THE SPRING of 1867 few Frenchmen would have guessed that the Second Empire had come to the beginning of the end. All things conspired to deny the truth: the country had never been more prosperous or Paris more enchanting. The new imperial capital was virtually completed and, as Captain Gronow observed, "decorated with a thousand ornaments, which attract the eyes of the whole world." Even Jules Ferry, bitter opponent of modernization, had to admit that the city was a lovely magnet and the center of the continent. France had reasserted herself, and Louis Napoleon had been a leader among European rulers ever since his rôle in the Peace of Paris. Nevertheless, there were certain melancholy signs abroad for those who cared to read them. In the previous year the Austrians had suffered an unexpected defeat at the battle of Sadowa, and the event marked Prussia's emergence as a military power. But the dark cloud was a small one and the sun bright enough in that optimistic spring of 1867.

On the first day of April, Louis Napoleon's son the Prince Impérial, a boy of eleven, presided at the inauguration of a great new Paris Exposition. There had not been an international fair in the city since 1855, and that had taken place under the shadow of the Crimean War. In the following years enormous material progress had been made in France and in the other industrialized countries of Europe. A summation was called for, and it was appropriate that an exhibition in honor of progress should take place in Paris. Admittedly, London had the greater cachet as a commercial and financial center, but Paris was far more prepared to act as the world's host. It was the entertainment capital of Europe, its gayest and loveliest city, a wonderland of sweeping boulevards and masked balls and operettas, of department stores and haute couture, of cafés and restaurants and hotels. The magnificent new city did attract, as Jules Ferry was afraid it would, undesirables from everywhere, but it attracted as well monarchs and businessmen and tourists from all over the world.

After weeks of rain, the opening day was crisp and clear. The international exhibits were arranged in an enormous glass-and-iron building in the Champ de Mars on the Left Bank of the Seine where the Eiffel Tower stands today. As cannon sounded from the Invalides, Louis Napoleon and Eugénie rode across the pont d'Iéna preceded by a detachment of Cent Gardes. With the exception of this élite troop, all military show was absent: the emperor wore a business suit and the empress a simple dress and shawl in order to emphasize the civilian and bourgeois nature of the exposition. They spent several hours in the fair grounds, passing much of their time in the Imperial Pavilion, an oriental conceit carried out with striped awnings and a multitude of golden eagles. It was difficult to believe that on the very night before the opening the Champ de Mars had been choked with wagons and piles of packing cases. A great deal of energy had gone into the transformation of the bare parade ground into a fairyland of kiosks and domes and minarets. Some two thousand workmen had labored for months on the construction of pavilions and gardens and grottos under the supervision of Adolphe Alphand, builder of the Bois de Boulogne. And since 1863 an Imperial Commission had devoted much effort to arranging the various international exhibits. The commission included two Englishmen: Richard Cobden, Member of Parliament and an early exponent of Free Trade, and Lord Cowley, the British ambassador to France. Other members formed a roll call of the Second Empire establishment: Michel Chevalier, one of Louis Napoleon's Saint-Simonian advisers; General Fleury, the emperor's aide-de-camp; Ingres, painter and member of the Institute; Georges Haussmann, Prefect of the Seine; the Comte de Nieuwerkerke, Director General of Museums; Baron James de Rothschild, the well-known financier; and the Duc de Morny, architect of the coup d'état and president of the Corps Législatif. Unhappily for the stability of the Second Empire, Morny had died in 1865, but he surely would have approved the exhibition in its final form—with its emphasis on money and material progress and "Social Harmony" as the motto on its gold medals. The great fair lasted for seven months and was an extravagant success, attracting over six million visitors from every part of the world. Among them were four amazed natives of Cochin China, twenty-three rabbis, a number of provincial postmasters and 4,750 noblemen of varying degrees of magnificence.

The majority of exhibits could be found in the Palais de l'Industrie and the different national pavilions. There was also an annex on the island of Billancourt in the Seine, and the new tourist boats, the *bateaux mouches,* carried visitors back and forth along the river. The Palais itself was a huge oval building of glass and iron composed of seven concentric galleries. Low and heavy and vulgar, it was something of an architectural monstrosity. An American reporter could only describe it as "a Dutchess county cheese frightfully magnified and decorated with ribbons and little flags." More susceptible to criticism was the materialistic nature of the exhibits themselves. There was little to be admired in the way of fine art, and every attention had been lavished on machinery and manufactured products. It was symbolic enough that a Pavilion of Money stood at the center of the garden around which the oval Palais de l'Industrie had been built. A certain Epicurus Rotundus described this phenomenon to the editor of *Punch:* "And, my dear Sir, the heart of this garden, the centre of all these monster rings, which made you feel as if you had got into Saturn, was a little money-changing office. I liked this cynicism."

As might have been expected, the Goncourt brothers fell enthusiastically upon the theme of materialism. They regarded the exhibition simply as another example of the "Americanization of France" and little more than a collection of steam engines and unnecessarily efficient chamber pots. For them it was a disturbing look ahead into the twentieth century: "a middle class Colosseum" or, rather, "Hadrian's villa reconstructed by a student from the Ecole Polytechnique." This spiteful view of the world of machinery was the characteristic reaction of artists and writers, and the last half of the nineteenth century saw the alienation of the intellectual from middle-class society and all its points of view. On an evening in May, after having attended the unwrapping of an Egyptian mummy, the Goncourts strolled through the fair grounds with Théophile Gautier—all of them sickened by the materialism crowding in from every direction. Many a contemporary would have agreed: the very form of the exhibition building was a symbol of the grossest kind. The inner ring did contain painting and sculpture to nourish the spirit, but each succeeding ring included more and more objects to nourish the flesh—clothing, home furnishings, industrial products—and the outer ring was completely devoted to food and drink.

Predictably, art at the exhibition conformed to middle-class taste, and prizes went to accepted academic painters like Cabanel and Meissonier. These and others like them dominated French art for years to come, and by the end of the century they came to be known as *les pompiers* (fire-men) because of their elaborate canvases on a variety of classical subjects. (Firefighters, then as now, wore elabo-rate brass helmets, calling to mind the classical headgear worn by Greek and Roman heroes in the paintings of Cabanel and Meissonier, for example.) It will surprise no one that avant-garde painters like Gustave Courbet and Edouard Manet found little welcome at the exposition and were obliged to set up their own pavilions outside the Champ de Mars. Manet's private show took place in a shack near the avenue Montaigne, and he charged an ad-mission fee of fifty centimes. On view were some of his finest works: *La Musique aux Tuileries, Le Bain* and *Olympia*. Not a single painting was sold, and the display only provided material for the humorous journals of the day.

The public *was* interested in art, however—had not the emperor himself sent along a voluptuous marble nude from his private collection?—although it is true that visi-tors were far more fascinated with the exhibits in the Gal-erie des Machines. Understandably, the French were the largest exhibitors, with over sixty thousand square meters of floor space, three times the amount allotted to Great Britain. Represented were all the important industrial nations of the world, and even the Grand Duchy of Luxembourg had a few square meters of space. The noise in the gallery devoted to machinery was deafening as wheels and gears turned and pistons rose and fell and steam billowed toward the glass roof of the Palais de l'Industrie. In the French section there were textile machines, electric dynamos, hydraulic lifts and other wonders from the factories of the north. In a special exhibit devoted to trains the French proudly showed the Titan, archetype for the railroad engines of the Compagnie de Nord.

One of the star attractions of the entire exposition, however, was a fifty-eight-ton steel cannon manufactured by Krupp of Essen and displayed in the Prussian section. It was capable of firing a thousand-pound shell, and the French regarded it with a good deal of ironic amusement. A writer for the official bulletin wondered what earthly use it could have beyond frightening everyone to death. More offensive to Parisian sensibility was the fact that it was remarkably ugly, though in the end they did give the cannon a prize. The French themselves were content to exhibit a graceful new rifle advocated by Louis Napoleon: the *chassepot*.[1] In general, however, there was not much emphasis on military matters, although visiting Prussian officers did study with interest a relief map of the French forts thoughtfully provided by the Imperial Commission.

Actually, Louis Napoleon's government was most proud of those exhibits illustrating social progress made under the empire. An entire gallery was devoted to the History of Labor, and all through the exhibition grounds, as well as at Billancourt, there were examples of model homes built for the poor. The displays were impressive enough, although some worker in a blue blouse down from the slums of Ménilmontant might have wondered who really lived in those cozy houses. With a Parisian shrug he might well have turned toward the aquarium and the gardens or wandered through the Temple of Xochicalo or listened to the band of the Guides playing popular music. Instead of looking at mythical model homes, he might have gone into a pavilion built in the form of an Egyptian temple and seen photographs and relief maps of the work so far accomplished by Ferdinand de Lesseps in the construction of a canal through the Isthmus of Suez. This, rather than any social legislation, would be one of the triumphs of the Second Empire.

When the visitor had had his fill of mechanical wonders, he could stop for refreshment at one of the many cafés which lined the outside of the great glass-and-iron building. Particularly at night the fair and the entertainments it provided could be enjoyed at best advantage. Illumination came from the beam of the great lighthouse and from the thousand gas lamps reflected in the glass walls of the Palais de l'Industrie. A workers' restaurant served eight thousand meals a day at the average price of 1.25 francs, wine included. There were innumerable other places to eat and drink in the international pavilions: you could have dark beer from Munich, faro from Belgium, pale ale from England or light Bohemian beer. You could listen to czardas played by gypsies in scarlet blouses. One English reporter described a night he spent in the cafés and kiosks of the outer gallery. He spoke of the Spanish waitresses with their "rich olive complexions, delicate little retroussé noses, low straight eyebrows, and round eyes." He admired their purple satin skirts and white lace shawls and the high combs and damask roses in their raven-black hair. In the Russian café the girls were blonde and wore elaborate diadems with ribbons floating behind. French flower girls wandered through the ground selling Parma violets, and scissors hung from their waists on silver chains. The Swedish waitresses wore red jackets with bright buttons, and in the Tunisian café there were girls with sleepy almond eyes framed in kohl. The Englishman was enchanted with every thing he saw—except for the English tavern, where the girls wore unbecoming clothes in a "Mugby Junction" style and the food was dreadful. Little, however, in these foreign cafés was exactly what it seemed. One evening the Prince of Orange went to the Netherlands Pavilion for a drink. Quite naturally, he spoke Dutch to the waitress, who answered irritably: *"J'comprends pas l'anglais, m'sieur. J'suis d'Belleville."* [2]

During the spring and summer of 1867 a holiday mood came over Europe, and the great fair attracted visitors from everywhere—Frenchmen from the provinces and foreigners alike. Excursions organized by Thomas Cook poured in from London, and travelers arrived from as far away as America. Among the most enthusiastic was Mark Twain, who had sailed from New York on June 8, 1867 on the *Quaker City* in what was one of the first luxury tours of Europe organized in the United States. In Paris he stayed at the new Hôtel du Louvre with his friend Dan Slote, "a splendid, immoral, tobacco-smoking, wine-drinking, godless roommate." They both loved Paris with its music and its life and the bustle of its boulevards. Of course they went to the Bal Mabille and then out to another dancehall in the suburb of Asnières to see the famed aerialist Blondin. In the finale of his act he fastened Roman candles and Catherine wheels to his body, lit them and waltzed across the tightrope in a blaze of light. The two Americans also watched the wicked cancan, and Mark Twain explained to his readers that the idea was to dance as wildly as possible and, if you were a woman, "to expose as much of yourself as possible." The day they chose to go to the fair was the day Abdul Aziz, the Sultan of Turkey, arrived as the emperor's guest. Mark Twain heard distant music and saw a pillar of dust and then the cavalrymen rode in with colors flying and the footsoldiers came in their gorgeous uniforms, and at last one could see the sultan and his imperial host. The American took the occasion to set down a remarkably accurate description of Louis Napoleon: "A long-bodied, short-legged man, fiercely mustached, old, wrinkled, with eyes half closed, and *such* a deep, crafty, scheming expression about them!"

It was possible at this point, however, that the emperor was more tired than Machiavellian. During the seven months which contained the life of the Paris Exposition of 1867 one reception for visiting monarchs followed another, and there were innumerable galas throughout the city. It seemed that some member of European royalty arrived in Paris each day, and Louis Napoleon was generally at the railroad station to greet him and escort him along the boulevards lined with troopers of the Cent Gardes. Even reigning monarchs were delighted to come to Paris for its incomparable luxury and the magnificence of its entertainments. And the busiest center of entertainment was the palace of the Tuileries. 1867 saw its most frenzied array of parties and receptions and balls and dinners. On May 14, for example, the King and Queen of Belgium dined at the palace with the Prince of Wales, the Duke of Edinburgh and Prince Oscar of Sweden. Ten days later the Crown Prince of Prussia came with his little boy, the future Wilhelm II, and the next week Tsar Alexander II of Russia with his two sons, the Tsarevitch and Grand Duke Vladimir. On June 5, Friedrich Wilhelm was entertained at the palace along with his chief minister, Otto von Bismarck. The list of royal guests is endless: old King Ludwig of Bavaria, Don Francisco of Spain, the Khedive of Egypt and at last, in October, Franz Josef, Emperor of Austria and King of Hungary.

Perhaps the most enthusiastic of all the royal visitors was the Prince of Wales. The future Edward VII of England was a handsome young man of twenty-six with a trim figure and a blond beard. As Queen Victoria's representative, he did spend a certain amount of time attending ceremonies at the court and in the Champ de Mars. But he devoted his leisure hours to Hortense Schneider, the glamorous musical-comedy star. She was appearing in one of the Second Empire's great entertainments. *La Grande Duchesse de Gérolstein,* an operetta summing up all the magnificent unreality of the régime's most marvelous year. Offenbach's work was the extravagant crown of the Paris Exposition of 1867.

La Grande Duchesse de Gérolstein opened on April 12 at the Théâtre des Variétés while *La Vie parisienne,* also by Offenbach, was enjoying a revival at the Palais Royal. The première audience included the most elegant figures of the Second Empire: famous authors, bankers, courtiers, ambassadors, demimondaines, celebrities of all kinds. The Prince and Princess Metternich were on hand, as were the dandies of the Jockey Club with their shocks of curly hair and side whiskers *à l'autrichienne,* their shirtfronts bursting forth like great white flowers and square monocles in one insolent eye. Ladies were dressed in the latest fashion —the crinoline was no longer popular—with cloaks and narrow skirts and little military hats perched in front of enormous chignons. That year they favored a shade of havana brown named in honor of Bismarck (although, in retrospect, the complement does seem somewhat tasteless), and coral was much in vogue for necklaces and pins and bracelets.

The sophisticated audience was delighted with the drolleries of *La Grande Duchesse de Gérolstein,* and it was the last great joke of the empire. The amusing Prussian cannon at the Palais de l'Industrie seemed to set the mood, and the operetta took place in the mythical German principality of Gérolstein. There was an amorous Grand Duchess and a chancellor named Baron Puck, who led the country to war simply because he needed some diversion. The army was commanded by General Boum, a courageous and incompetent *miles gloriosus,* who during the course of the play periodically fired a pistol into the air to refresh himself with the smell of gunpowder. On the night Bismarck appeared at the theater in his White Cuirassier uniform the audience was particularly delighted. He seemed to find the evening more entertaining than anyone else, and before long it would be apparent that he had had every reason to have done so. The Frenchmen of the Second Empire entirely misunderstood the realities of the world in which they lived and were unintelligent enough to think of the Prussians as no more than tasteless beer-drinking boors. In the end, Offenbach's joke was on the French themselves—although even Louis Napoleon was highly amused, attending a performance the week after the opening and returning several days later with Eugénie.

1867 was Hortense Schneider's year, and her dressing room at the Théâtre des Variétés became one of the great gathering places for visiting royalty. It was a rose-colored room with Turkey carpets and capitonné armchairs and an enormous mirror the whole length of one wall. Here of an evening you would be almost certain to find the Prince of Wales watching her make up between the acts, and in *Nana* Zola has written a description of this occasion, portraying Edward as the Prince of Scots. Along with the future King of England you might have found the Grand

Duke Constantine of Russia, old Ludwig of Bavaria, the King of Greece and Leopold of Belgium, whom Hortense often kept waiting for hours in front of her hotel. She could afford to do so, since she was the most successful actress—and courtesan—of the year.[3]

Her popularity was enormous: one day Offenbach rushed into her dressing room waving a telegram he had just received. It was from the Tsar of Russia (he had stopped his train in Strasbourg to send the message) saying that he was arriving in Paris that night and would like tickets for the evening performance. Surely an aura of regality did surround Mlle. Schneider. One day, for example, she drove in her carriage over to the exposition in the Champ de Mars and attempted to enter through the porte d'Iéna, which was reserved for royalty. When the guards insisted on knowing her name, she cried out imperiously: "Make way! I am the Grand Duchess of Gérolstein!" In typically Second Empire style, the guards took off their hats, bowed low and let her pass. It is immensely confusing: what was real and what was not in that incredible year?

Perhaps the most awesomely unreal event of the year was the review of the French Army on Sunday, June 6. Some sixty thousand soldiers were to be assembled at Longchamp in honor of the emperor's guests, Tsar Alexander and King Wilhelm of Prussia. Actually, half that number was brought together, but the occasion was unforgettable. The Garde Impériale was under the command of Marshal Canrobert, hero of Africa and the Crimea. Footsoldiers of the Garde lined up in their gorgeous uniforms near the reviewing stand: grenadiers in great bearskin shakos, riflemen in yellow tunics, chasseurs with green plumes and Zouaves in turbans and baggy pants. Cannon sounded from the fortress at Mont Valérien above them, and Louis Napoleon rode into the racecourse on a magnificent black horse. He was escorted by a detachment of Spahis on Arab ponies, and riding with him was a richly uniformed entourage of generals and foreign princes. On his right was the Tsar and on his left King Wilhelm of Prussia.

The most glorious and unbelievable moment in a glorious and unbelievable year had arrived. The infantry regiments passed before the three sovereigns in the reviewing stand, and at a signal ten thousand horsemen wheeled to face Louis Napoleon. There were lancers, hussars, cuirassiers and the dashing Chasseurs d'Afrique. Riding at full gallop across the field, they came to a halt five paces in front of the reviewing stand. They raised their sabers in salute, crying out: *"Vive l'Empereur!"* There had been nothing like it during the Second Empire, and there would be nothing like it again. It was a sight to fill Frenchmen with pride, recalling the victories at the Malakoff and Magenta and Solferino and pointing to the fact that France was the leading military power on the continent.[4] Only an insensitive Prussian could have suggested that this impressive military machine was quite as ineffectual as the comic opera army of Gérolstein. As General Bosquet said, observing the disastrous English cavalry charge at Balaclava: "It's magnificent, but it has nothing to do with war."

However, it is easy to understand the French nation's air of confidence in the spring and summer of 1867. Armed might alone by no means completed the picture: go across the Seine to the Champ de Mars and see the wonders of French science and technology. The great canal at Suez was under way, and the Mont Cenis tunnel through the Alps was being completed. On July 1 prizes were given at the exposition, and the nation paid tribute to the accomplishments of French science and industry and noted progress in every field. One first prize went to a professor of chemistry at the Sorbonne who had improved methods of preserving wine. He was Louis Pasteur, and in his laboratory on the rue d'Ulm he was to devote much time to practical projects associated with the improvement of French industry: he studied the fermentation of wine and vinegar and conquered some of the crippling diseases which had overtaken the sheep and cattle and silkworms of France. In every way Pasteur's career illustrated the usefulness of science. One day, in fact, as he was demonstrating the way in which wine could be heated without destroying its bouquet, the mayor of a small town complimented him upon his discoveries. "I am overwhelmed," said the mayor. "It is as though I were seeing you pouring gold into our country."

To the middle-class mind in the nineteenth century, science and progress came to form the two parts of a miraculous equation. The bourgeois establishment looked through the golden door which science had begun to open. No one foresaw the dark clouds of the future.

"Everywhere trade and the arts flourish," said the prefect's deputy in *Madame Bovary* at the agricultural fair at Yonville. "Everywhere new paths of communication, new arteries within the body politic, are opening up new contacts. Our great manufacturing centers thrive once more. Our ports are full. Confidence returns. At last France breathes again!"

The scene in Flaubert's novel concerns a somewhat earlier generation of Frenchmen, for it is true that the industrialization of France actually began in earnest under Louis Philippe. But the emphasis is the same. All the materialism and optimism of Europe at the middle of the nineteenth century are summed up by the gaudy and vulgar Paris Exposition of 1867. In the tradition of London's Great Exhibition of 1851 it honored the new world of science and industry and technology which was leading Europe into the twentieth century. Its optimism was compelling. "After what we have accomplished here," said an official writer for the Paris Exposition, "nothing seems impossible."

General Fleury, the emperor's aide-de-camp, pointed out that 1867 was the apotheosis of a city and of a régime. The whole country was intoxicated with pleasure and pride—pride in its machinery and magnificent army, pleasure in its money and its beautiful capital.

The future seemed to spread out richly before the nation, although the marvelous year was not without those extremes which form the fabric of the Second Empire. Paradox was there even on that summer day when prizes were awarded at the exposition. Prize after prize was announced, and the cheers of the crowd grew more enthusiastic. On the platform, however, at the center of the festivities, Louis Napoleon and Eugénie sat terrified and alone. That very morning they had received a delayed telegram announcing the death of the Emperor Maximilian. He had been executed by a firing squad in the Mexican village of Querétaro on June 19, and the news was to cast a pall over the entire exposition, a month of mourning subsequently being declared. The death of Maximilian, occurring thousands of miles from France, marked a beginning to the end of the Second Empire—in spite of all the prosperity and splendor and aggressive materialism of the exposition year. Something was desperately wrong, and the news from Mexico contained a part of the answer.

By the middle of October they had begun to dismantle the great exhibition, although the curious still went out to the Champ de Mars to look at the popular Edoux elevator or ride in the captive balloon set up by the photographer Nadar or listen to gypsy music and drink imported beer in one of the many cafés which lined the outer ring of the Palais de l'Industrie. But the magic was fading and with it the memory of the tawdry splendor and the fireworks and the great good times.

CHAPTER EIGHT

The Bombs of Orsini

Y EARS before, at the gorgeous début of the Second
Empire, the poet Alfred de Musset had come down
the grand staircase of the Tuileries after a party. He
turned and looked back over his shoulder. "It's all beautiful today," he said. "Yes, for the moment very beautiful.
But I wouldn't give you two sous for the last act."

Now the last act was beginning, and omens of disaster
could be met with more and more often. They were ex-
traordinarily difficult to accept, however, since one could
see the prosperity and military might of the Second Empire on every side. It was hopelessly confusing and, as
Prosper Mérimée suggested, very like the story of Ro-
land's horse: a splendid animal in every way—except that
he was dead.

By the closing month of the Paris Exposition of 1867,
one friend of Louis Napoleon sensed disaster in the air.
"Fall on the Bourse. The Emperor is unwell. . . . The
situation is growing tense. Can the Empire be coming to
the dusk of its day?" In November the situation was even
grimmer, with rumors along the Boulevard that the government was falling, that secret societies were being

formed and revolutionary proclamations being printed, that there was unrest and savage ill-feeling among the workers. Nothing of this seemed to affect the careless life of opulence and extravagance reserved for the few. In fact, a number of luxurious refinements were being made: there was a new journal called *La Naïade* made entirely of rubber for the comfort of bathtub readers, and the editors of *Punch* had heard of a recently invented playbill made of chocolate which allowed the theatergoers of Paris to be at once well informed and well fed. True or not, this delicious convenience was a further symptom of the temper of the times. The parties went on at the Tuileries and Saint Cloud and Compiègne, and lights blazed all night in the private dining rooms of the Maison Dorée.

In that self-indulgent year of 1867 many of the paradoxes characteristic of the Second Empire came more and more into the open. The paradox of misery and splendor was to be found everywhere. Less obvious, perhaps, though quite as damaging, was another paradox that ran through Louis Napoleon's régime like a hidden river: the continuing conflict between liberty and authority. Under the genial surface of contentment and pleasure and prosperity there was unrest at many different levels of society. One did not have to eat horsemeat or wear a faded blue smock in order to dream of liberty, and threats of freedom assailed the government of the Second Empire from all directions.

A number of political and moral lessons could have been learned from the French failure in Mexico. On the simplest level, however, the execution of Maximilian was no more than a gesture of self-liberation on the part of the abused and nameless followers of Benito Juárez. If the last half of the nineteenth century saw the birth of industrialism, it saw as well the birth of liberalism. And that liberal-

ism expressed itself in nationalistic feelings and in the desire of the common people to do away with tyranny both
at home and abroad. Again and again, in the course of the
century, romantic and desperate gestures were made in
the name of liberty. They took place regularly in Paris:
there was, for example, that early summer day in 1867
when Louis Napoleon was riding back to the Tuileries
with the Tsar of Russia after the military review at Longchamp. Crowds lined the road as their carriage passed
through the Bois de Boulogne. Suddenly a young Polish
patriot rushed forward and fired a pistol at the Tsar. No
one was hurt, but blood from a wounded horse spattered
the imperial party. Berezowski had made his futile gesture
in the name of Polish nationalism and freedom from Russian rule. It was a gesture as futile, and as full of meaning
for the future, as the remark hurled at the Tsar a few days
before by a French lawyer from the steps of the Palais de
Justice: *"Vive la Pologne, monsieur!"* These outbursts
affected the delicate balance of Franco-Russian relations
and prompted the police to undertake more repressive
measures than usual. Known radicals were called in for
questioning, and socialist painters like Courbet were ordered to close the exhibitions they had set up outside the
Champ de Mars. Censorship of the press was already rigid
enough to prevent further insults to the Tsar. In any case,
that angry autocrat left Paris a few days later.

To the liberal mind there was a definite connection between the cause of foreign nationalism and internal opposition to the government of the Second Empire. The irony
is apparent, since Louis Napoleon himself devoted much
time and effort to maintaining the integrity of European
nationalities. Without him Italy would not have been consolidated under Victor Emmanuel in 1861, and Prussia
might not have emerged as the head of a coalition of

German states. As in so many other matters, the contradictions of the empire are contained in the person of the emperor. Sensing this, partisans of many different causes associated with liberty made attempts to kill him over the years. They shot at him as he rode in the Bois, as he arrived for evening performances at the Hippodrome or the Opéra Comique. The threat of assassination is one of the realities with which political leaders have to live, and the attempts on Louis Napoleon's life were no more remarkable than those made on the lives of other European leaders of the time—attempts more frequent and more successful as the turn of the century approached. But the entire structure of a nation and of a régime did not often rest so completely in the figure of one man. He had created the empire from nothing more substantial than his uncle's ashes and, like General de Gaulle in our own day, could have said with conviction: *"Je suis la France."* Across the Channel, Queen Victoria was surely a symbol of England; she was not, however, England itself. As the Second Empire hurried toward dissolution, Louis Napoleon each day became sicker, both physically and mentally.

The politically disaffected had grasped the nature of his rôle as the literal and figurative embodiment of France. If the government exercised tyranny, he was the tyrant. If France was—or was not—interested in the unification of Italy, he was the means by which it could be accomplished. One of the earliest attempts on his life came in the spring of 1855 as he was riding in the Champs Elysées with General Ney and an equerry. Pianori, an Italian nationalist and one of Garibaldi's former followers, leaped from behind a tree waving a pistol. He had time to fire two ineffectual shots before he was dragged to the ground by a detective named Alessandri, known on the force as "the bulldog." As was his habit, the emperor displayed considerable coolness, only calling out to the policeman: "Don't kill him."

The most dramatic assassination attempt took place on January 14, 1858, when Felice Orsini and his fellow conspirators hurled three bombs at the emperor in front of the Opéra on the rue Le Peletier. That evening there was to be given a special performance of *William Tell* as a benefit for the singer Massol. At eight o'clock Louis Napoleon drove up in his carriage, escorted by lancers of the Garde and accompanied by General Roguet and the empress. There was a violent explosion, and then two more. One bomb hit the imperial carriage, which was thrown to the sidewalk in a shower of broken glass from the doors of the Opéra. Smoke filled the street, and one could hear the cries of the wounded and the neighing of dying horses. Alessandri was the first to reach the carriage and, although injured himself, managed to force the door open and help the empress to the street. Her dress was spattered with blood—General Roguet had been wounded—but she spoke calmly enough. "Don't bother with us," she said. "This is our profession. Take care of the injured."

The emperor himself was not harmed, although he did seem shaken and there was a ragged hole in his hat. Nevertheless, he went into the Opéra at once and showed himself in the imperial box. The audience cheered, and the orchestra struck up *Partant pour la Syrie,* the unofficial national anthem. Some time later he slipped out to the pharmacy next door, where some of the wounded were being treated. He bent over one lancer and without a word took a diamond decoration from his lapel and attached it to the dying man's uniform. When the performance was over, he returned to the Tuileries in what amounted to a triumphal march. Crowds with torches lined the streets, and he rode at the center of a squadron of cuirassiers led by the Governor General of Paris. Only when he and Eugénie reached the privacy of their own apartments and stood in their son's nursery did they fall into each other's arms with tears in their eyes.

The bombs of Orsini had accomplished nothing beyond a dreadful carnage in which a hundred and fifty people were wounded and eight killed. In an attempt to dramatize the cause of Italian nationalism Orsini had planned to kill the emperor for not having supported it actively enough. In this sense he was striking a blow against Austrian tyranny, and he went to the guillotine crying out: *"Vive l'Italie! Vive la France! Vive la République!"* But the results of his action were ambiguous: though Louis Napoleon did further the cause of Italian unification and did oppose Austrian occupation of the peninsula with military force, the bombs formed no part of his motive. Ironically, the immediate result of an assassination attempt in the name of liberty was a further loss of freedom in France. The emperor called for a return to the harsh and authoritarian measures which had characterized the new Second Empire in 1852. Although the Orsini affair had little effect on the problem of Italian nationalism, it may stand as a convenient symbol of the struggle between liberty and authority which brought such tumult to the last days of the régime and contributed to the bloody Commune of 1871.

Soon after the assassination attempt a drastic new law was enacted. Among other unpopular provisions, this Law of Public Safety established a quota of arrests for each of the various departments of France. The prefects were obliged, in most cases willingly enough, to fill out the quota with names of known opponents of the Bonaparte régime. The contradiction here is a serious one, for

Louis Napoleon was a declared socialist and honestly wished to create a democratic nation with freedom for all. The Orsini affair, however, only served to strengthen his belief that freedom could not be granted in haste. Liberty must be based upon order, and the people of France had given him a mandate to create that order. "Liberty has never contributed to the foundation of a durable political edifice," he said in a speech to the Assemblée Nationale in 1853. "When the edifice has been consolidated by time, liberty crowns it."

This idea shaped all of his thinking, and at last in the winter of 1867, after many preliminary concessions, he called for the creation of a Liberal Empire with himself as constitutional monarch. It was what the socialist Proudhon described as a "half-turn to the left." Nevertheless, it was even then too late, and the policy of liberalization took almost three years to put into effect. The Liberal Empire provides what is perhaps the most irrational aspect of the whole régime. In the end it was impossible to reconcile any form of authoritarian rule with the liberal spirit of the late nineteenth century—a spirit nourished by industrialism and nationalism. This contradiction has made it easy to dismiss the Second Empire as a brutal dictatorship and to compare Louis Napoleon with the fascist leaders of the twentieth century. The analogy is too convenient, however, since—unlike them—he was sincerely trying to lead his country in the direction of freedom and democracy. To accomplish that end, he felt that he first had to create order, and the creation of order surely meant the elimination of political opposition. He permitted, although he may not have welcomed, the repressive measures of 1852 and 1858.

Nonetheless, in spite of an aura of tyranny the government of the Second Empire closed its eyes to a great many antagonistic opinions. Every shade of political and moral dissatisfaction was to be found in the cafés and salons and coffee houses of Paris. The secret police were everywhere —although not more numerous than under previous French régimes—and careless remarks could lead to unpleasant questioning and even to imprisonment. However, unless you insisted upon wiping your nose on a handkerchief decorated with the emperor's portrait (as did one actor of the day), a great deal of latitude was possible. Moving freely along the Grands Boulevards were Legitimists who favored a Bourbon restoration and Orléanists who longed for the vanished days of Louis Philippe, as well as republicans and radicals of every persuasion: Proudhonists, Blanquists, Anarchists and Internationalists. Even censorship of the press was more severe on paper than in actual practice. It happened that the jail of Sainte Pélagie became a rather comfortable club for journalists briefly removed from the scene for having offended the imperial government in one way or another.

Always more liberal than his own administrators, Louis Napoleon was not upset by contrary opinions. "The empress is a Legitimist," he said one day. "Morny is an Orléanist; my cousin Napoleon is a Republican; I am a Socialist; only Persigny is a Bonapartist, and he is crazy."

Actions, of course, were something else again. All political meetings were banned and agitators dealt with severely. Provocateurs like Blanqui and Delescluze led a dangerous existence one step ahead of the police.[1] When the Second Empire came to an end, these two had spent between them almost fifty years in various prisons and penal colonies. Certainly the Second Empire was a police state in many ways, but it managed to keep a large number of dissenters under some form of control without excessive brutality. Only the régime's most outspoken critics were forced into exile or sent to prison colonies like Cayenne and Lambessa.[2] Victor Hugo's flight to the Channel Islands, it must be remembered, was largely self-imposed.[3] And Louis Napoleon, always sensitive to the misfortune of others, declared a general amnesty in 1859 for all the victims of the coup d'état. Surely he spent his life living under the shadow of those December days.

Anti-Bonapartists breathed the air of Paris freely enough—from the wits at Tortoni's who spent their idle hours commenting on the emperor's sex life to the students of the Left Bank who ran through the streets shouting: "That Eugénie, what a slut!" For all the repressive measures of a police state, there was a constant atmosphere of rebellion in Paris. The city voted against the government in every general election, and there were republicans in all walks of life. "In the attics of students," said Hippolyte Taine, "in the garrets of Bohemia, and the deserted offices of doctors without patients and of lawyers without clients there are Brissots, Dantons, Marats, Robespierres and Saint Justs in bud."

No doubt in an efficient police state these apprentice radicals would have been eliminated. But, as in so many other areas, Louis Napoleon was far too soft for the harsh task he had undertaken. If he had wanted to be a dictator—which he did not—he simply had no stomach for it. His career demonstrates the constant vacillation between caesarism on the one hand and liberalism on the other. At Sedan, when the moment for self-preservation came, he sacrificed himself for his soldiers.

As a result of the emperor's ambiguous attitude, the authoritarian state was often permissive. This was especially true in the case of students who demonstrated violently against the régime and the middle-class writers and professors who supported it. On a number of occasions they broke up performances in theaters, and they were particularly unrestrained in their own schools. In 1864, for example, the architect Viollet-le-Duc was appointed a professor in the Ecole des Beaux Arts. During the induction ceremonies he was jeered at along with the Comte de Nieuwerkerke, director of the school and otherwise remarkable as Princess Mathilde's lover. The demonstration grew out of control, and Viollet-le-Duc and the count fled across the pont du Carrousel to the Louvre pursued by a mob of shouting students. The police were summoned, and in the mêlée Théophile Gautier—uninterested in politics and by no means opposed to the emperor—was arrested. The sergeant who took him in apologized later: "I thought he was one of the demonstrators because of his long hair."

On any afternoon, in some intellectual café like the Brasserie des Martyrs, you would have been hard pressed to find a single advocate of the government. Admittedly, the artists and writers who gathered there would have been nonconformists in any society, but their opposition to the middle-class establishment was often translated into political activity. The caricaturist Honoré Daumier attacked the régime without mercy in *Charivari* and *Le Figaro*. Painters like Manet and poets like Baudelaire, themselves from bourgeois backgrounds, were clearly on the side on the opposition. Gustave Courbet, of course, flaunted himself as a socialist: he took pleasure in refusing the Légion d'Honneur in 1870, and he was at the head of the mob which pulled down Napoleon Bonaparte's column in the place Vendôme after the fall of the empire.

1867 found the tensions and ambiguities of a contradictory régime coming together. There was more to the year than the Paris Exposition and the great military review at Longchamp. It was also a year of strikes: the *hommes-sandwichs* went through the streets wearing placards which read: "The journalists strike! We want ten sous a line!" and the brassworkers walked out of the Barbedienne factories, openly supported by the First International. Hostility was growing among the small craftsmen of Paris: the cabinetmakers of the faubourg Saint Antoine, the goldworkers of the rue du Caire, the ironmongers of Grenelle, the mechanics of Popincourt, the shoemakers of Montrouge. And hostility was growing among the laborers who came down in the morning from the heights of Montmartre and La Chapelle in their faded smocks, tools slung over their shoulders and loaves of bread under their arms. These were the locksmiths and roofers and masons and house painters crowding into Père Colombe's wineshop for the first drink of the day, and Zola has described them in *L'Assommoir*. Their share in the new prosperity was meager indeed, and economic conditions were forcing them to eat horsemeat for the first time. The pastor of the church of Sainte Clotilde could say nervously that the future of the nation was in their hands.

1867 was the year when the Emperor Faustin of Haiti died in exile, and the journalist Henri Rochefort could take the occasion to write what amounted to an obituary of the Second Empire. His article in *Le Figaro* did no more than describe the vicious career of Faustin Soulouque, but the analogy with Louis Napoleon was too obvious to miss. The parallels were astonishing: Soulouque was elected president of Haiti in 1847 and soon proclaimed himself emperor, creating an imperial court and bestowing on his half-savage entourage improbable titles like the Duc de Limonade. Disenchantment with the Second Empire had reached some new level of intensity when Louis Napoleon could be insulted so openly, and Rochefort was by no means through. In the following year he founded the satirical journal *La Lanterne,* which contained attacks on the government and personal abuse of the imperial family. Among Rochefort's many victims was Nero, the emperor's favorite dog. Parisians could hardly wait from one week to the next for another issue of the magazine to appear.

In the last month of the Exposition of 1867 Lord Lyons arrived in Paris as the new British ambassador and was immediately struck by the uncertainties of the French régime. He duly reported his impressions to the Foreign Office in London. "I hear from all quarters," he wrote, "that the Emperor's own position in France becomes more and more critical."

And it was true that Louis Napoleon was slowing down in every way. His eyes had lost their luster, and he was being tortured by gallstones and prostate trouble. His illness was as symbolic as it was painful, since his hold over France was weakening and his prestige as a European leader diminishing. The world had wondered at the fiasco of his intervention in Mexico and had seen his inability to deal with new men of iron like Otto von Bismarck.

The threads of empire were beginning to unravel, and the paradoxes of an age of transition were growing too difficult to resolve. The industrialization of Europe had brought with it enormous social changes, and the old and the new were coming into inevitable conflict. Poverty was struggling against luxury and liberty against authority, and under the gaudy surface of empire there had been too many defeats. In the beautiful new city of Paris the poet Baudelaire had found only the flowers of evil, and now the laughter of the humorists was bitter. Dissatisfactions were hardening, and Louis Napoleon seemed to drift helplessly with the tide of events. By 1868 they were playing *The Last Days of Pompeii* at the Théâtre Lyrique, and Rochefort was writing his ironic tribute to the long-dead son of the first Napoleon:

As a Bonapartist, I prefer Napoleon II; it is my right. I shall even add that he represents, to my mind, the ideal sovereign. No one will deny that he occupied the throne, since his successor calls himself Napoleon III. What a reign, my friends, what a reign! Not one tax, no useless wars . . . no consuming civil list, no pluralistic ministers at one hundred thousand francs for five or six functions. Ah! yes, Napoleon II, I like you and I admire you without reservation. Who, therefore, will dare to say that I am not a Bonapartist?

Rochefort's cleverness at last forced him into exile in Brussels, but for a while he managed to smuggle his flame-colored scandal sheet into France—on one occasion hidden in some plaster busts of Louis Napoleon.

There was an uneasy atmosphere throughout the country, and the emperor's sickness and spiritual depression were infectious. France was beginning to lose confidence in his régime, and periodic general elections pointed up the trend. The government won by a substantial margin in 1863, but it was defeated in every one of the large cities: in Paris, Lyon, Marseille, Toulon, Brest, Le Havre and Bordeaux. Over the years the margins of victory began to narrow until by 1869 only a little over half a million Frenchmen would voice their approval of the empire.[4] In itself the narrowing margin was no cause for alarm, but it did indicate a new and dangerous mood. More disturbing was the fact that the revolutionaries were now coming out into the open.

In the fall of 1868 a journalist named Eugène Ténot wrote an inflammatory description of Paris during the coup d'état of 1851. In his vivid account of those famous December days he devoted a good deal of attention to the story of a leftist deputy named Victor Baudin who had died on the barricades fighting the Bonapartist seizure of power. Surprisingly, in this obscure and long-forgotten figure, republicans and radicals of every kind found a rallying point and a hero. On All Souls Day a group of students and revolutionaries went out to Montmartre Cemetery to look for Baudin's grave. They were led by Charles Delescluze, the editor of *Le Réveil,* a journal antagonistic to the government. When they finally found the grave—it was almost covered with grass—they threw flowers on it and turned the occasion into a near-riot. In his paper Delescluze demanded that a monument be erected to commemorate the fallen hero who had fought against the empire nearly twenty years before. Under the Law of Public Safety, which had gone into effect after Orsini's attempted assassination of the emperor, Delescluze was arrested and brought to trial for having incited a riot. He was represented by Léon Gambetta, a fiery lawyer from the Midi, who soon saw that there was little point in trying to defend his client. Instead he turned the trial into an indictment of Louis Napoleon's government and of the coup d'état upon which its power rested. Where were the generals Lamoricière and Cavaignac? he asked. Where was Thiers and where were the Orléanists and republicans of 1851? In an impassioned oration to the court, Gambetta answered his own questions by saying that these victims of Louis Napoleon's insane ambition were now in prison at Mazas and Vincennes or rotting in the jungles of Cayenne and Lambessa. His provocatory speech did not prevent Delescluze from being found guilty, but it gained wide currency in Paris and put Gambetta himself into sudden prominence. It was easy enough to understand, for he had succeeded in expressing the mood of many a liberal Frenchman.

The heroes of the moment were two radicals, Baudin

Left *Louis Napoleon Bonaparte, emperor of the French from 1852 to 1870. Below His Spanish empress, Eugénie.*

Above *1848: the triumphal proclamation of the republic. Louis Napoleon was its president.*
Right *1869: the parliamentary régime commenting on Louis Napoleon's granting of parliamentary government after seventeen years of personal rule. Cartoon from* Vanity Fair.

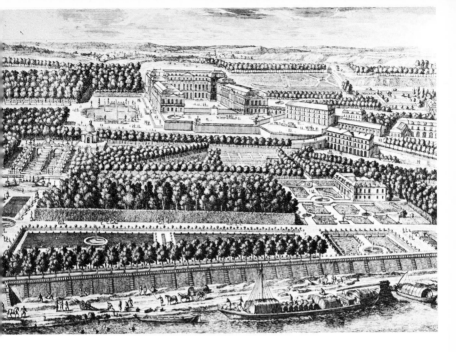

Above *Saint Cloud, a sumptuous château on the Seine, often used for entertaining foreign royalty.* Below *Demonstrations among the women workers at Le Creusot, an industrial town near Dijon.*

Napoleon III at the battle of Solferino, 1859.

Above Orisini and his fellow conspirators hurl bombs at the Emperor's carriage. Below Baudin at the barricades. A leftist deputy killed in the fighting of 1851, he was later idealized by liberals opposed to Napoleon III.

Princess Pauline Metternich: "two parts whore and one part great lady". Wife of the Austrian ambassador, she was Eugénie's friend and the Second Empire's unofficial mistress of ceremonies.

Above left *Hortense Schneider, the musical-comedy star who counted the future Edward VII of England among her admirers.* Above right *Auguste, Duc de Morny, the statesman who helped his half-brother, Louis Napoleon, seize the Imperial throne.* Below *Jacques Offenbach, satirized by André Gill.*

Manet's La Musique aux Tuileries.

Paris gloriously re-built. Above Part of the original official design.
Much of the old city was torn down and surrounding villages were
engulfed to form suburbs. Below The peasants in Daumier's
drawing exlaim: "We are Parisians now." Above right The
demolition of part of the Quartier Latin.

Below left *An excursion in the sewers. Paris was as new beneath as above.* Below right *Baron Haussman—caricatured with money falling through his sieve—was the chief architect of the lovely city.*

G. Larosso

The Second Empire was a time of industrial, technological and scientific progress. Above The central garden during the opening of the Paris Exhibition of 1867. Below Louis Pasteur, the chemist famous for his work on bacteria.

Above *The building of the Suez Canal, which was opened in 1869.*
Below *Fragment of Manet's painting of the execution of Maximilian, the puppet emperor of Mexico.*

Above *The poet Baudelelr*. Below left *Viollet-le-Duc, the architect famous for his restorations of old buildings*. Below right *Cézanne: self portrait*.

Above *Zola, the realist novelist, painted by Manet.* Below left
The poet Verlaine towards the end of his life. Below right
*Alexander Dumas, novelist and playwright and son of an equally
popular father.*

Above *Edmond and Jules de Goncourt, brother writers and chroniclers of French society.* Below *"Le revers de la médaille de Sainte-Hélène." The Second Empire ended with the battle of Sedan and the humiliations of French defeats at the hands of the Prussians.*

and Gambetta, and—thanks to Rochefort—the ghost of Napoleon II. At the same time, however, the liberalization of the empire was under way, and this fact effectively neutralized the complaints of the radicals. True enough, in the large cities of France intellectuals and workers and many aristocrats were opposed to Louis Napoleon, but retrospect alone has made his régime appear so close to the brink of disaster. The country as a whole supported him, particularly the great majority of the middle class and the villagers in the provinces. Of course, they were tired of relinquishing their money and their sons for wars and colonial adventures like those in Mexico and Syria and China. But they were not displeased with the prosperity and new conveniences enjoyed under the Second Empire. The middle class in particular was willing to follow the emperor. The industrialist and the small shopkeeper had little sympathy for the poverty of the urban proletariat or for the emotional outbursts of the Baudin trial or for the disorder caused by fanatics like Orsini.

In spite of many debilitating encounters between liberty and authority, the nation was behind Louis Napoleon— more so than ever in the final days of empire when even the workers welcomed the Franco-Prussian War with enthusiasm. It is not difficult to understand why this should have been so: the prosperity of the empire was real enough and so were the wonders of its scientific discoveries and technological triumphs. Those who had seen the Paris Exposition of 1867 were convinced that a glorious future lay ahead. The middle-class businessman looked to his profits, and the worker hoped for a better life.

CHAPTER NINE

The Pragmatists

T HE triumphs were there, and no amount of political dissatisfaction could deny them. France was in the early stages of the modern industrial era, and on every side the material world was being brought under domination. The products of a new age had been displayed at the Paris Exposition of 1867, and the country's prosperity rested more and more on the scientific and technological achievements of a number of talented Frenchmen. Scientists like Pasteur were giving Paris back its reputation as an intellectual center, French engineers and laborers were helping to cut the Mont Cenis tunnel through the Alps to Italy, and at the eastern end of the Mediterranean, Ferdinand de Lesseps was bringing Europe and the Orient closer together by constructing a canal through the Isthmus of Suez. One of his favorite mottoes could well describe the mood of industrial and scientific Europe in the 1860s: *Aperire terram gentibus* (To open the world to all people).[1]

The world was being opened in every conceivable direction. Disease was being conquered, and speed and transportation and communication were becoming the hallmarks of a new age of discovery. More and more reliance was being placed on machines and steam engines and the useful applications of science. All over France clouds of smoke were rising from new factories, and the whistle of the locomotive was heard throughout the countryside. Activity on the stock market was intense, and prosperity was spilling over into many different levels of society—even, during the first years of empire, to the workers themselves. In the manner of the American New Deal of the 1930s, Louis Napoleon's government was subsidizing railroad companies and steamship lines, supporting vast public works and pouring money into the economy through easily available credit. Initially, the results were impressive: a network of railroads was growing in all directions, ships were being built for the Atlantic run at Brest and Toulon, telegraph lines were going up everywhere and Paris was becoming an efficient and modern city.

Economic and industrial growth during the Second Empire was remarkable, and in almost every way the period marks the birth of modern France. Life in the large cities was moving rapidly toward the twentieth century, although the greater part of provincial France continued to follow pre-Revolutionary patterns. The statistics are dramatic enough: by 1870 there were more than twenty-five thousand steam engines at work, four times the number one could have found when Louis Napoleon became president of the Second Republic. By the end of the empire there were over ten thousand miles of railroad track where there had been two thousand in 1850. In addition, French engineers were building railroads in Spain and the Americas, and French capital was helping to finance them. These new projects were followed with enthusiasm by the emperor. Under the influence of his Saint-Simonian advisers, who were businessmen as well as mystics, he developed financial institutions to encourage investment at home and abroad: the Crédit Foncier for agricultural development and the Crédit Mobilier for the development of commerce and industry. They were the economic tools appropriate to a modern age.

It has often been suggested that Louis Napoleon forced the growth of material prosperity in order to make his countrymen forget the liberties denied them under an authoritarian state. The argument does not make a great deal of sense, for industrialism and new wealth would have come to France with or without the Second Empire. A growing population with more money to spend demanded the articles being mass-produced in the textile mills and factories of northern France and distributed in the great department stores of Paris. More clearly than most of his contemporaries, Louis Napoleon came to understand that the world soon would belong to the Many and not to the Few—and he greeted each new development of the modern age with pleasure.

He was especially proud of the private railroad train which often took him from Saint Cloud to the military camp at Châlons or from Paris to Compiègne. It was of the latest design, although the interior décor was eclectic and rather out of date in the Second Empire manner: a dining car paneled in oak and leather with golden crowns on the chairs of the emperor and empress, a salon car in Louis XV style with Aubusson tapestry covering the furniture, and a sleeping car with four bedrooms and four private bathrooms. In attempting to combine the old with the new, the imperial train was symbolic of an age of transition. It was something of a contradiction, but so was Louis Napoleon. In spite of the aura of First Empire he carried with him, he was a man of his own time and no worshipper of the past for its own sake. At the Paris Exposition of 1867 he had ordered a dinner service made out of the new wonder metal aluminum, and it is said that when he died in exile at Chislehurst he was working on an improved stove for the poor.

Generally uncomfortable with art and literature and music, he preferred the intricacies of machinery and science and technology. In this he was a man of the twentieth century, and his interest did not come from curiosity alone. No one could fail to see that the nation's industrial growth and future prosperity would be in the hands of the pragmatists: the technicians and the engineers and the men of science. They were discovering new sources of wealth, and scientific knowledge was beginning to be equated with money—an equation appealing strongly to the middle-class industrialist and businessman. To keep abreast of new developments, the emperor often arranged for lectures on modern subjects to be given at Compiègne and elsewhere. One of his favorite speakers was the chemist Louis Pasteur, whom he first met in 1863.

Of all the practical scientists at work during the reign of Louis Napoleon, Pasteur must rank as the first. In the course of a long career he made innumerable contributions to both applied and theoretical science. He made discoveries about the structure of the chemical molecule, the mechanism of fermentation, the rôle played by microorganisms and the theory and practice of immunology. Although his personal inclinations lay in the direction of pure research, he came to devote almost his entire career to the useful applications of science to French industry and agriculture. In terms of wealth his contributions to the economy were enormous. After the fall of Paris the government of the Third Republic was able to pay the indemnity imposed by the Prussians with remarkable speed—largely out of profits from the wine industry which had been so improved by Pasteur's researches into fermentation and the nature of micro-organisms. In 1863 he had undertaken a study of the wine industry at the urging of the emperor himself. It was a business that generated five hundred million francs a year, and French wine was in great demand abroad. However, it traveled badly and was subject to a number of ruinous diseases. The well-known process of pasteurization was the result of his investigations, and later it was used to improve the production of beer and milk as well. For this he received a prize at the Paris Exposition of 1867, and he continued to devote his career to improving the economic health of France by solving many another industrial and agricultural problem. As much as Louis Napoleon—whom he greatly admired—he was a man of the modern age. "Science, in our century," he pointed out shortly after the Franco-Prussian War, "is the soul of a nation's prosperity and the well-spring of progress of all kinds."

This view reflects the nineteenth-century middle-class faith in science and material progress, and Pasteur was to believe in it all his life. Born in 1822 in a small town in the eastern part of France, he was brought up to honor the bourgeois virtues of sobriety and decency and conformity. Unlike some other scientists of the day, he was troubled by no religious doubts or political eccentricities. He even managed to die, as good taste dictated, with one hand in his wife's and the other holding a crucifix. As a young man he had studied at the famous Ecole Normale Supérieure in Paris and, while a graduate student in 1848, gained a small reputation for a paper presented to the Academy of Sciences outlining his work on the optical activity of the tartaric acids. However, in terms of his contribution to French industry, the most significant date in his life was 1864: in that year he was appointed dean and professor of chemistry in the new Faculty of Science at the University of Lille.

Lying on a rich agricultural plain a hundred and fifty miles northeast of Paris, Lille is the capital of the Département du Nord. The city is located near the coal deposits of the Valenciennes basin and convenient to the ports of Boulogne and Calais and Dunkerque. In the early days of the Second Empire it was one of the important centers of the French industrial revolution. The town was filled with textile mills, breweries, dye works and plants for the manufacture of heavy machinery and steam engines and railroad cars. Pasteur accepted the post at the university with the clear understanding that he would devote his time to teaching industrial chemistry and serving as a consultant to Lille manufacturers. He put aside his own studies and concentrated on the practical needs of his country. The official appointment had been quite specific: "M. Pasteur must be continually on his guard not to be carried away by his passion for pure science."

On an autumn day in 1856 an industrialist named Bigo came to the young professor with a problem. He was a manufacturer of beet alcohol, and for the past few months his product had been ruined by what he called "bad" fermentations. What could the professor do to put his business back on a profitable basis? In the course of solving M. Bigo's difficulty, Pasteur came to the revolutionary conclusion that fermentation was not a chemical process but a "phenomenon correlative of life" and caused by the action of living micro-organisms. Certain of these micro-organisms aided the course of fermentation, while others damaged it. He found that partial heating would destroy or inhibit unwanted organisms and so took the first steps in the direction of pasteurization. From these studies the germ theory of disease began to evolve, and in 1857 Pasteur published an important paper on the subject. His work prompted the Scots surgeon Joseph Lister to use carbolic acid for the destruction of the microbes causing infection and so lay the foundations of antiseptic surgery.

Convinced by nature and upbringing that it was an obligation to use his knowledge for the benefit of the French government and his fellow citizens, Pasteur devoted himself to the solution of practical problems. In 1865, at the request of one of his former teachers, Jean Baptiste Dumas, he headed a commission organized by the Ministry of Agriculture to study a disease then on the point of destroying the French silk industry. He led a team of scientists into the Cévennes, where silkworms were dying by the thousands. With only a primitive laboratory at his disposal, he managed to isolate and make provisions for combatting two separate diseases. The silk industry was saved from disaster, and the economic consequences of his work were far-reaching. For the rest of his life French industry and agriculture continued to benefit from his genius. One of his most dramatic triumphs came in 1881 when he conducted the famous experiment in immunology at Pouilly-le-Fort in the Brie district near Paris and saved the sheep and cattle of France from an epidemic of anthrax. Four years later he achieved world-wide fame by giving a young Alsatian boy named Joseph Meister the first anti-rabies inoculations tried on a human being.

At the end of his life Louis Pasteur regretted that he had not spent more time in theoretical studies of crystallography and molecular asymmetry.[2] Nevertheless, he stands as the perfect symbol of his time: the practical man lecturing the Whitbread brewers in London, astonishing the farmers at Pouilly-le-Fort and putting his faith in science and material progress. Out of his work came improvements in many different areas—in farming, in the manufacture of cloth and in the production of beer and wine and milk. He had taken his contemporaries on a voyage of discovery and revealed to them a new world of minute organisms. Most important of all—in terms of the era in which he lived—he had shown them how to make a profit and increase their wealth.

The Second Empire saw many other improvements and developments which brought new wealth to the country. Among the men of genius who discovered new worlds was Ferdinand de Lesseps. Like Louis Pasteur, he was the symbol of a new era, a modern man dedicated to the improvement of the century in which he lived. This desire he shared with men of science and with Louis Napoleon himself. Like them, he put his faith in material progress and spent a lifetime turning a dream into reality.

In 1832, as a young man of twenty-seven, Lesseps came to the Egyptian port of Alexandria to take up his duties as French vice-consul. The ship on which he arrived had been placed under quarantine, and he spent his enforced leisure looking through the volumes of the famous *Description de l'Egypte*—a massive work compiled by scientists and scholars attached to the French army which invaded the country under the command of the first Napoleon in 1798. In particular, the young man was fascinated with a report written by Lepère, Napoleon's chief engineer. It contained a survey of the Isthmus of Suez and discussed the possibilities of building a canal across it. The isthmus was a hundred miles wide, lying between the delta of the Nile and the Sinai Peninsula and separating the Mediterranean from the Red Sea. In ancient times there had been a Canal of the Pharaohs from the Nile at Zagazig through to the Gulf of Suez. Then, as now, Egypt stood at the crossroads of two worlds and was the link between Europe and the Orient. For centuries Greek and Arab traders had carried the riches of Asia across the desert by canal and caravan to Alexandria for shipment to all the ports of the Mediterranean. They brought tigers from the Punjab, leopards from Afghanistan, wool from Kashmir, silk from China, furs from Tibet, sapphires from Ceylon and spices from the islands of Southeast Asia. Long after the Canal of the Pharaohs was abandoned, caravans continued to cross the desert—until a new and more efficient route to the Orient was discovered by the Portuguese explorer Vasco da Gama in 1498. He opened a sea lane to India around the Cape of Good Hope at the southern tip of Africa, and traders gradually gave up the difficult desert journey across the Isthmus of Suez.

When Lesseps arrived in Egypt, the isthmus was a wasteland given over to cranes and flamingos and the few fishermen who lived on the shores of Lake Manzala. There was a great silence. The caravans had gone and there was nothing on the desert but the occasional black tent of a Bedouin. Nevertheless, the young vice-consul became obsessed by the idea of building a canal, and one day in his office he received a strange visitor who increased his interest even more. This was Prosper Enfantin, a Saint-Simonian mystic who dressed in a flowing white robe. He had come to Egypt to interest the viceroy, Mohammed Ali, in building a canal through the Isthmus of Suez, and he was asking Lesseps to exert some influence on his behalf. Though he had sent surveyors out into the desert, nothing ever came of the project.

More and more in those early years the idea of a canal was occupying Lesseps' thoughts, but finally his career in the French diplomatic service called him away from Egypt. He was sent to a variety of posts: to Rotterdam and The Hague, to Barcelona and Málaga and Madrid. By 1849 he had retired and was living the life of a gentleman

farmer at La Chênaie, an estate in central France. Five
years later his quiet life was interrupted by the report that
Prince Said, an old friend, had become the new viceroy of
Egypt. This was a stroke of luck, for Lesseps had never
given up the idea of building a canal at Suez. Moreover, it
was now mid-nineteenth century, and the time for such a
canal was ripe: European factories desperately needed the
copra and ore and jute and cotton of the Orient, and
steam engines and iron ships were being perfected to carry
these bulky raw materials. Soon Mohammed Said had invited his old friend to Egypt, and within a short time Lesseps managed to convince the viceroy that a canal at Suez
would bring glory and profit to Egypt. On November 25,
1854, in the great hall of the Citadel in Cairo, Mohammed
Said announced to the foreign diplomatic corps that he
had granted a concession to Ferdinand de Lesseps to build
the canal.

That day marks the beginning of a long and desperate
struggle to create what is now one of the great waterways
of the world and the finest technological triumph of the
Second Empire. From the start Lesseps faced three almost
insurmountable obstacles: the British government, which
was firmly opposed to any French influence along the
route to India; the absence of money to complete the project; and the hundred miles of sand and swamp that lay
between the Mediterranean and the Red Sea. The story of
his eventual victory is one of the great adventures of modern times. And he won in the end, to a large extent because he instinctively grasped the nature of the era in
which he lived and used all its new techniques of finance
and technology. Under the directions of his indomitable
will, money and machinery conquered the desert.

The project began badly. In 1858 Lesseps arrived in
Paris after having spent many months in Constantinople

in a futile effort to gain the permission of the Sultan of Turkey—Egypt was then a part of the Turkish Empire—to proceed with the canal. He had spent as many months in England in an equally futile effort to charm the antagonistic Lord Palmerston. The circumstances were discouraging, and Lesseps made up his mind to begin the canal on his own. The first thing he needed was money, and it happened that the Paris of the Second Empire was exactly the place to find it. Money was discussed everywhere, and talk of stocks and bonds filled the cafés and restaurants. Everyone was looking for instant profit, and the city had begun to rival London as the financial center of Europe. There were a thousand legitimate businessmen and—it was typical of the Second Empire—a thousand more shady speculators and adventurers and confidence men.

Greed was never his motive, and Lesseps was careful to avoid this financial underworld. Nonetheless, he needed at least two hundred million francs to begin his project.[3] He approached Baron de Rothschild for help in selling public shares in a Suez Canal company. The baron was happy to set up a subscription, only adding that there would be a five-percent commission. "Five percent on two hundred million?" repeated Lesseps. "Why, that makes ten million! I shall hire a place for twelve hundred francs and do my own business equally well."

He was as good as his word and soon rented a small office in the place Vendôme, operating on what amounted to an amateur basis. The wolves of high finance found it all very amusing, but Lesseps obtained a small amount of capital from friends and worked tirelessly through the fall of 1858—establishing contacts, using his considerable charm and keeping in touch with the Tuileries. It was fortunate that the Empress Eugénie was his cousin, since he hoped through her influence to obtain the emperor's favor. Meanwhile, he managed to persuade Prince Plon-Plon to act as unofficial protector of the company, so gaining the prestige of the Napoleonic name and the entrée which the emperor's cousin had in high places. Lesseps planned to issue 400,000 shares of stock with each share selling for five hundred francs. Half of the shares were reserved for the French public, and the subscription began on November 5, 1858.

Fortunately, the idea of the Suez Canal had become a popular subject of conversation around the Boulevard. Some people were convinced that the project was another of the financial swindles so common at the time of the Second Empire. Others, however, believed in Lesseps and were strongly motivated by patriotic and anti-British sentiments. There is a story told that a gentleman came into the office on the place Vendôme one day in a very aggressive mood. He announced loudly that he wished to buy some shares in the new Swedish railroad. His mistake was explained: it was a canal, and it was at Suez. "It's all the same to me," said the aggressive gentleman. "Provided it be against the English, I subscribe."

The sale closed on the last day of November, and all but a few thousand shares had been sold. Twenty thousand Frenchmen had seen fit to invest their money, most of them small stockholders with an average of nine shares apiece. They came from every walk of life, but mostly from the middle class, though it did begin to seem that every waiter and delivery boy and taxi driver in Paris had bought a share or two of the new company. One morning Lesseps rode to his office in a cab and, as he was stepping down, the coachman shook his hand and announced: "Monsieur de Lesseps, I am one of your shareholders." In those prosperous early days of the Second Empire everyone who could manage it joined in the frenzy of speculation and profit-seeking. Thanks to such an attitude, Lesseps was able to incorporate the Compagnie Universelle du Canal Maritime de Suez in 1858 on the day after Christmas.

For a moment his financial problems were solved, and he was ready to attack the Isthmus of Suez itself. On the morning of April 25, 1859, four merchant ships anchored in the Bay of Pelusium at the eastern end of the Mediterranean and began to unload supplies for the first phases of construction.

At the beginning they faced the task with little mechanical equipment of any kind, relying on the shovels and palm-leaf baskets of Egyptian laborers. The first thirty miles were to pass through the swamp of Lake Manzala until the desert began at El Qantara, and this part of the canal was constructed largely by hand. Workmen scooped armfuls of dripping mud from the lake bottom, put them out in the sun to dry and so produced primitive building blocks. In this way, slowly and painfully, they built up the banks of a narrow service canal, the skeleton of the completed waterway. Lesseps rode back and forth in sun helmet and burnoose, constantly demanding more from engineer and workman alike. For several years the work went on in this manner, and suddenly in 1864 everything came to a standstill. Largely through the maneuvers of the English, a horrified world learned that the French company at Suez was using what amounted to slave labor supplied by Said and his successor, Ismail Pasha. The workmen were taken away, and without them Lesseps could do nothing. At last he decided to ask Louis Napoleon for an impartial ruling on the labor dispute. The emperor decided in favor of the Suez Canal Company, and possibly Eugénie had used her influence in the interests of her cousin. The Egyptian government was ordered to pay eighty million francs as a form of indemnity.³ With this money Lesseps was able to begin an entirely new phase of construction. For the first time he could make use of modern technology, and professionals moved in to complete the job.

The principal work was done by the French firm of Borel et Lavalley, and the amateur days of pick and shovel were over. Lesseps and Voisin Bey, his director of engineering, joined with the contractors in designing and building a fleet of steam excavators and mechanical dredgers. These powerful machines were capable of digging out the canal at the rate of six million cubic feet a month. Set up on barges in the canal, they scooped mud from the bottom by means of endless chains of buckets. Each of these machines was specifically designed for the Suez project. They marked an enormous technical advance in the field of heavy construction, since little precedent existed for a work of this magnitude. By 1869 the giant machines had enlarged the service canal to such a degree that it was now capable of accommodating ocean-going vessels. Lesseps' dream of almost forty years had become a reality.

On Wednesday morning, November 17, 1869, the Suez Canal was opened in a ceremony that stands as the last great spectacle of the Second Empire. In the new harbor of Port Said lay a gaudy flotilla, ready to enter the canal and sail through to Suez on the Red Sea. At the head of the flotilla was a black steam yacht which flew the French imperial flag. Shortly before eight o'clock the Empress Eugénie appeared on the bridge with her cousin, Ferdinand de Lesseps. Cannon sounded from the shore, and the harbor was filled with the hissing of steam whistles and the sounds of military music and the cheers of the crowd. With deafening blasts from her siren the French imperial yacht *L'Aigle* started up, her paddlewheels churning the water as she turned to enter the canal. On the shore the band was playing *Partant pour la Syrie,* and in single file the flotilla began to pass through the entrance of the canal.

There were nearly fifty ships in all: the second in line was the *Greif,* which carried Franz Josef of Austria-Hungary, and then a frigate with the Crown Prince of Prussia on board and a Dutch yacht with the Prince and Princess of Holland. A Russian gunboat carried two representatives of the Tsar, and *Psyche* steamed by with the British ambassador to Constantinople at the railing. A British officer watching from the deck of a merchant ship described it as "an enchanted scene": the silent ships floating in the desert and white-robed Bedouin watching from the banks of the canal.

Ismailia, in the natural harbor of Lake Timsah, marks the halfway point between Port Said and Suez, and it was here that the Khedive of Egypt had decided to give a party that would combine Oriental opulence with Second Empire extravagance. His party was said to have cost over thirty million francs. It was not difficult to believe: for the occasion Ismail had built a sumptuous palace in less than six months' time and furnished it with gilt chairs and marble-topped tables and paintings from Paris. The great party began on Thursday night. The palm trees in front of the palace were hung with brightly colored lanterns, inside there were a thousand servants in powdered wigs and scarlet liveries, and five hundred cooks were preparing a feast of wild duck and pheasant and partridge.

It was a fair imitation of the Tuileries itself. Diamonds and rubies and sapphires gleamed in the candlelight along with military decorations and the jeweled handles of scimitars. The dinner began and Eugénie, wearing the imperial coronet, sat with the Khedive and the Emperor Franz Josef. Together they drank toast after toast in champagne: to France and to Egypt, to peace and to international harmony. In such a manner the last ironies of the Second Empire were consummated. Less than a year later it would exist no longer.

The Second Empire vanished, but, like Louis Napoleon's Paris, the great canal at Suez survived. Soon the warehouses at Port Said were filled with merchandise from the Orient, and one could smell the spices of Canton and the curries of Delhi and Benares. Almost from the beginning the canal was a commercial success, although it never became the source of international harmony which Lesseps had anticipated. In spite of his idealism, and quite in keeping with the mood of the Second Empire, the canal stands as an entirely materialistic accomplishment. It was based on money and technology and opened a new era of trade and communication and prosperity. The Suez Canal had been the work of one Frenchman perceptive enough to make use of all the financial and technical tools newly available in those exciting years when modern Europe was born.

CHAPTER TEN

Syllabus of Errors

T HE Goncourts had a cousin who prayed to God daily in somewhat special terms: "Oh, Lord, may my urine be less cloudy and my hemorrhoids less annoying. May I live long enough to make another hundred thousand francs, may the Emperor stay in power so that my income will increase and may Anzin Coal continue to rise on the stock market."

The prayer has much to say about the middle-class mind as it existed in France during Louis Napoleon's reign. The requests of the Goncourts' cousin were nothing if not materialistic and largely concerned with money. They seemed appropriate in an age devoted to industrial growth and stock-market speculation, when even science was being put to more and more practical uses each day.

It is not materialism, however, which stands condemned in mid-nineteenth-century France—but, rather, the abuses of it. They were abuses which existed elsewhere in the industrialized Europe of the time, although materialism must be found to some degree in a modern world concerned exclusively with the visible and the tangible. There was, for example, little inherent evil in the philosophy of Positivism which gained many converts in France as the century advanced. That philosophy had been set forth by Auguste Comte, a graduate of the Ecole Polytechnique and a former teacher of mathematics. It was a system based on the recognition of positive facts and observable phenomena and clearly evolved from the new European interest in science and technology. As a consequence, there was a growing dissatisfaction with received religion, a discipline which did not thrive on fact, and the Catholic Church was losing some of its authority in France. In 1849 Comte himself published a calendar which substituted the names of famous men for the names of saints, and Ernest Renan issued the first volume of his controversial *Vie de Jésus* in 1863. These were works appropriate to an age of scientific realism and in themselves not the products of the devil. But there were dangers in unrestrained materialism and the narrower applications of Comte's philosophy—dangers obvious in the extent to which the middle class in France and England had become obsessed with profit and money. These obsessions led the establishment to turn aside from many an unpleasant fact. In France the *rentiers* collected their dividends greedily enough, perhaps unaware that the workers of Lille lived in caves and that children in the mines of northern France were chained like animals to coal wagons.[1]

The Goncourt brothers were among the first to understand the direction their country was taking in the new age of science and industry and practical men. In 1857—at the height of Second Empire prosperity—they could say that the French character was turning in upon itself and that people were concerned only with "figures and money and arithmetic calculations." "The whole nation," they said, "is like Molière's miser, closing its fingers around dividends and property, ready to submit to any pretorian or Caracalla, ready to endure knowingly any shame—so long as its profits are safe."

If all Frenchmen were like Harpagon, many of them were refreshingly naïve. On one occasion a group of stockbrokers offered to erect a statue of Louis Napoleon in front of the Bourse as a token of their gratitude. The emperor, fortunately, had the good sense to refuse. That gesture simply indicated the prevalence of the profit motive among his subjects, and such a point of view was by no means restricted to the industrialist or businessman or shopkeeper of the middle class. The bourgeois mentality was not the unique product of any one class but rather a universal state of mind. Many an aristocrat at the Tuileries had made a fortune in real-estate speculation during the rebuilding of Paris. And throughout the 1850s it was common enough to see crowds lined up at night outside the city halls of the various *arrondissements* waiting for the doors to open and another National Loan subscription to begin. The crowds were composed of simple people eager to invest their small savings and realize some instant profit: cooks and water carriers and street vendors and the gatherers of broken china and cigar ends. The world around them dealt with tangibles, and even the golden eagles of the Second Empire were not heraldic and imaginary in the manner of Napoleon Bonaparte's but copied with scrupulous care from birds in the Jardin des Plantes. The atmosphere was heavy with money and scientific pretension and misdirected realism.

Looking back, the journalist Arthur Meyer saw that the disaster of 1870 had been mitigated by the Second Empire's financial successes. The extent of its inherited wealth saved the Third Republic from ruin, and in many ways the country emerged less damaged than its conquerors. During Louis Napoleon's reign, and long afterward, the heart of middle-class Paris was to be found in the place de la Bourse. The Stock Exchange was a temple of money not far from the Opéra and the expensive cafés of the Grands Boulevards. Viewed from one of the galleries, in fact, the great hall of the Bourse looked very like the Opéra itself during one of those famous masked balls. Stockbrokers appeared to dance back and forth across the floor like drunken revelers; there was the same noise and confusion and only the dominos were absent. Outside in the arcades of the Bourse one came across the equally animated bustle of the Curb Exchange.[2] Here you might have seen M. Isidore Dreyfus with his deep voice and imperious gestures, and there the gigantic figure of M. Lange, whose tailcoat flapped around a covey of excited clients. The Coulisse swarmed with bankers and brokers and financiers, and at the bottom of the steps uniformed messengers waited with bicycles to rush telegrams to the Central Post Office in the rue de Grenelle. Even at nine or ten o'clock at night the hoarse voices of the Coulisse could be heard as far away as the boulevard des Italiens or the passage de l'Opéra. In those exciting and profitable days one of the more successful of the Parisian stockbrokers was a young man named Paul Gauguin.

For certain people the obsession with profit reached the proportions of an epidemic disease. Eugène de Mirecourt was fond of telling the story of a well-known physician caught between his devotion to medicine and his love of money. One day he was summoned to the bedside of a patient near death, and on the way his carriage happened to pass through the place de la Bourse. The doctor stopped to look at the latest quotations, returning to his carriage some time later, gray and shaken. When he finally reached his patient, he first of all took the man's pulse.

After a few minutes he looked at his watch and whispered: "It's going down!" And later, in a louder voice: "It's still going down!" The patient was overcome with terror and cried out in despair, sensing that the end was upon him. Relatives rushed into the room and asked the doctor for an explanation. "At two o'clock," he muttered wildly, "it was at 76.80!"

There is no information as to whether the patient died or the doctor's shares rose in the next day's market. Both events were likely, and the anecdote simply illustrates the moral confusion so characteristic of the Second Empire. As confusion existed in the worlds of fashion and sex, so it existed in the world of money. It was in the nature of the times to idolize the actual and the tangible. And what could be more tangible than women and clothes and money? Everything came to complement a new point of view which honored monetary profit and the practical accomplishments of science and technology. The emphasis on materialism was extensive and produced a degree of spiritual illness and some distressing lack of human feeling. In Rome, Pope Pius IX—ironically, a liberal at the beginning of his papacy—was horrified at the world he saw growing up around him. He felt obliged to issue an encyclical in 1864 condemning a number of aspects of that world. In particular, he denounced the worship of science and the spread of liberalism and the appearance of all those anti-religious sentiments which excessive materialism had generated. His encyclical was called the *Syllabus of Errors,* and it was thought to have been directed largely against the French Second Empire and the acquisitive society it was producing with such enthusiasm.[3]

Yes, General de Saint Arnaud admitted to the emperor, he *had* been gambling on the stock market and he *was* deeply in debt. "Fould counts on the market going down," he explained.[4] "I have confidence in your star, Sire, and invest on the principle that the market is going up. And I am the one who has been hurt!"

There was little Louis Napoleon could say to that, and he personally settled the general's debts. Almost no one— from the highest to the lowest ranks of society, from the minister of state to the girl of the street—escaped the frenzy of speculation which dominated the early years of the empire. For the most part, money poured into the hands of those who needed it least. Between 1852 and 1870, for example, the Anzin coalminers did receive wage increases of thirty percent, but during the same period the dividends paid to the company's shareholders tripled. In the confusion of new enterprises and new businesses and new opportunities for profit, simple greed and healthy materialism often came close to the borders of the criminal.

The incarnation of the Second Empire may well have been the elegant person of Auguste de Morny, half-brother to the emperor, who was elevated to a dukedom in 1862. In his devotion to the tangible pleasures of clothes and money and sex, the Duc de Morny had few peers, and among his legacies to the future was the creation of Deauville on the Channel coast near Le Havre. For years to come this fashionable resort would perpetuate his consuming interest in women and society and ostentation. When he became a figure of importance in the government of the Second Empire, he indulged his natural tendencies to live *en prince* quite without shame. It was to have been expected, since extravagance had been his way of life in the days when he had no money at all. During his years of power there were few financial enterprises in which he did not have a hand, and at one point he even tried to remove Ferdinand de Lesseps from the Suez Canal Com-

pany. Surely he would have approved the well-known remark in *La Question d'argent,* a play written by Dumas
fils in 1857: "Business? Why, it's very simple; business is
other people's money."

And the Duc de Morny required a great deal of money
to support tastes that ran to race horses and Old Masters
and personal chefs. One of the great legends of the Second
Empire has grown up around the entourage he took to St.
Petersburg in the summer of 1856, when he acted as
French ambassador at the coronation of Tsar Alexander
II. A special ship sailed from Le Havre carrying horses
and carriages, fine china and silverware and a number of
paintings from his private collection. His staff included
Joachim Murat, who was Louis Napoleon's cousin, three
general officers and those dashing spendthrifts, the Duc de
Gramont-Caderousse and the Marquis de Galliffet, then a
sub-lieutenant in the Guides. There were secretaries and
aides-de-camp, a government artist and a head chef, several Russian scholars and a leading lady from the Comédie Française. In St. Petersburg the embassy occupied a
sumptuous residence on the left bank of the Neva not far
from the Hermitage and the Winter Palace, and one opulent party followed another. When he returned to Paris,
Morny brought along with him an eighteen-year-old
bride, the Princess Troubetskoi, as well as a concession for
the Crédit Mobilier to build railroads in Russia. There was
a rumor that the diplomatic pouch contained a large sum
of money in gold.

It was hardly a secret that the Duc de Morny was often
rewarded for his influence in high places, and in the careless atmosphere of the Second Empire little opprobrium
was attached to simple acts of bribery. One of his enterprises, however, did seem to have some uglier implications. In the spring of 1860 Mexico was in a state of civil

war, and among other disasters its most important foreign bank had failed. The head of the bank was a Swiss named Jecker whose clients were largely French and whose chief assets were bonds that had been issued by the Mexican president, General Miramón. In the following year the general was ousted by Benito Juárez, who took the occasion to repudiate all previous debts, including the bonds held by Jecker. Jecker himself traveled to Paris, where he became a naturalized citizen with uncommon speed and soon had a number of important connections in the French capital. At the end of 1861 an expeditionary force of French and British and Spanish soldiers landed at Veracruz to protect European financial interests. The landing marks the beginning of French intervention in Mexican affairs—an intervention resulting in the creation of an imperial régime under Maximilian and supported by Louis Napoleon's government. A persistent rumor went around the Boulevard that the Duc de Morny had encouraged the French expedition in return for a thirty-percent commission from Jecker when the bonds were made good. Many years later, however, the Empress Eugénie—the Mexican adventure was popularly thought of as her war—denied that Morny had had any part in the decision to send French troops to Veracruz. Nevertheless, there were certain unexplained circumstances, and he was surely involved with Jecker in some way or another. No one was too upset, and, if slightly dishonorable, the Duc de Morny was never charged with anything more specific than greed. It did not matter a great deal, since by 1865 he was dead.

Other contemporary adventurers were less successful than Louis Napoleon's charming half-brother. One of the notorious financial scandals of the day came to revolve around the person of Jules Mirés, an intimate of the Duc de Morny and the father-in-law of the Prince de Polignac. Mirés was less a financier than a blackmailer in the grand tradition. His career began in Bordeaux, where he was the editor of a newspaper which was given to printing elaborate obituaries, in each case carefully naming the dead person's physician. The doctors of Bordeaux soon understood what was happening, and before long Mirés moved on to Paris with a comfortable sum of money. Once there, he started a journal devoted to railroad news, often containing articles by the Péreire brothers, and he lost no time in printing details of frauds and accidents and irregularities. Gradually less and less news appeared, as more and more railroad companies exchanged money for silence. Mirés went to other questionable activities and had a number of dealings with the Crédit Mobilier. Finally in 1861 he was arrested for fraud, and it was said that among the various bribes listed in his private books was the following entry: "To Monsieur X, government minister, the sum of 40,000 francs for having taken my arm in the foyer of the Opéra."

Surely the most successful financiers and businessmen of the early Second Empire were the Péreire brothers. Emile and Isaac were Jews as well as Saint-Simonians, a remarkably happy combination in an era devoted to money and industrial growth. The Saint-Simonian philosophy was tailored to industrialism and hoped to establish a new society of talent directed by scientists and engineers and given over to useful public works—and profit. During the reign of Louis Philippe, Saint-Simonians had proposed the rebuilding of Paris, and it was one of their leaders, Prosper Enfantin, who had tried to arouse interest in a Suez Canal in the 1830s. Since then Saint-Simonian businessmen had made a number of contributions to improving the production and distribution of goods in France and to developing modern methods of finance. During the first half of Louis Napoleon's régime the Péreire brothers were involved in many considerable enterprises in metropolitan France as well as in North Africa and other parts of Europe. They were behind railroads in the Midi, public utilities and transportation companies in Paris as well as being in control of department stores like the Louvre and the Grande Maison de Blanc. They were responsible for financing the Grand Hôtel and the Imperial Ottoman Bank and the Austrian State Railroads. Their Compagnie Générale Transatlantique built one of the first ocean liners in France, launching the *Impératrice Eugénie* at Saint Nazaire in the spring of 1864.

The most famous and disastrous enterprise they undertook was the creation of the Crédit Mobilier, a private investment bank which sold shares to the public and made funds available for promising projects in every part of the world. When the Second Empire began in 1852, they inaugurated their company with the blessing of Louis Napoleon and his financial advisers. The traditional banking community under the leadership of the Baron de Rothschild regarded the Péreires as unsound, but the country responded with enthusiasm and quickly bought up all the first shares issued at 500 francs apiece. Within a few hours the shares had risen to 1,100 and were up to 1,600 a week later. At the beginning the savings of the middle class poured into the Crédit Mobilier without apparent end. Conservative bankers, however, soon joined together to crush these arrivistes, and a long financial war began. The Rothschilds started their own Société Générale, set up the Kreditanstalt in Vienna and forced the financing of the Mexican War on the Péreires. By 1860 the price of a Crédit Mobilier share was down to 800, and dividends were being paid out of capital rather than from current earnings. After the Mirés scandal—he had been closely involved with the Péreires and the operations of the Crédit Mobilier—Louis Napoleon withdrew his support. The company suffered severe losses each year, and by the fall of 1867 the price of a share had plunged to 140 francs. The company soon collapsed, and the Rothschilds had won again.

As Arthur Meyer pointed out, money was king in those exhilarating early days of the Second Empire. It dominated many aspects of Parisian life. Loose morals and easily available credit were an irresistible combination, and there was much justification for the Pope's *Syllabus of Errors:* the society of the Second Empire *was* putting materialism and physical gratification above everything else. Money and luxury and the love of possessions were leading the weak into immense difficulties. The Comtesse de Rougé, for example, whose husband was the curator of the Musée Egyptien, awoke one morning in 1858 to find that she owed some four million francs to a band of moneylenders and couturiers and jewelers. Her husband had no choice but to send her off to a convent and begin the task of paying her debts.

In those early days of the modern industrial world there was too much of everything, and materialism and extravagance led into many dark areas. It was a simple step from the pleasure of monetary profit to the pleasure of physical gratification. Strong sexual undercurrents, perverse and otherwise, flowed just beneath the surface of a venal society. At the races at Longchamp a foreign visitor could look around him and ask: "Where are the honest women?"—and be told that there were none. Homosexuality and lesbianism were more prevalent and more easily accepted: the Goncourts could point to the Coin affair of 1864 in which a play was put on where women were insulted and replaced on the stage by naked men. The Goncourts went on to tell the story of a bureau chief in the Ministry of War who was supplying rich homosexuals with so many soldiers from the Garde Impériale that the government began to suspect a military conspiracy. They spoke of the growing practice of blackmail and described the famous register of pederasts and prostitutes kept by M. Félix, a member of the Vice Squad for thirty years.

No one was more interested in gossip of this kind than the Comte de Viel Castel, who filled his diary with the ripest scandals of the day. He spoke of a discreet little house at Saint Germain-en-Laye which several ladies of high society rented in order to entertain army officers and young dandies. One of the ladies was a plump marquise who enjoyed boys and girls with rare impartiality. And Viel Castel lingered over the story of another noblewoman who had given an unmentionable disease to several of her more intimate friends. As a consequence, Lord Henry Seymour spent four months visiting Dr. Andral, the well-known specialist. At dinner one night in Princess Mathilde's house the Comte de Viel Castel heard her describe a journey to Compiègne on the imperial train: a sudden movement swung the door to a private compartment open, and there was Louis Napoleon sitting on Marianne Walewska's lap, kissing her passionately and plunging his hand down the front of her dress. The empress was reading in the next compartment. Other piquant stories of the day dealt with popular actresses who were lesbians, and there was one very important gentleman who had been apprehended by the police at the center of a group of young men, some dressed as society ladies and others as nuns.

These were diversions appropriate to the last days of an empire, and such decadence and over-ripeness evolved entirely from the material preoccupations of the day. There had been too much of everything: too much money and too much time and too much poverty and too much sex. The insolence of those who gratified their every wish was appalling. They said that at one of his parties—it happened often enough—the Duc de Morny disappeared into an upstairs dressing room during the course of the evening with a magnificent Polish girl. Some time later she came down the stairs, on her lips the sphinx-like smile so characteristic of the Second Empire and around her neck the Légion d'Honneur. The Duc de Morny followed at a discreet distance.

Important as sex may have been, money was more important, and success in that area was greatly admired. This was nothing new in French life, and even before the beginning of the imperial régime the poet Heinrich Heine had described the day he saw a uniformed lackey coming out of Baron de Rothschild's office with a chamber pot. As the servant passed along the corridor, at least one speculator up from the floor of the Bourse raised his hat in reverence. With industry expanding and money pouring in from all directions during the major part of the Second Empire, admiration for financial success grew more and more pronounced. The heroes of the day were businessmen and bankers, and pretty ladies were inclined to favor rich escorts over handsome ones. At least this was the attitude which Nana took, and Zola has given us a description of her lover Steiner—the banker Bischoffsheim in real life—"that terrible German Jew who brewed money." Whatever their lack of charm and unlovely greed, Steiner and those like him were the new men, the operators, the realists in harmony with their time.

The boulevards of Paris were full of them, and the provincial capitals of France were crowded with their less successful brothers. All of them were middle-class in their thinking, and to a man they believed in money and science and progress—and their own personal profit. Some, like the Duc de Morny, were aristocrats to the tips of their lemon-colored gloves, while others, like Homais the chemist in *Madame Bovary,* were near the bottom of the social scale. It was during the reign of Louis Philippe that artists and writers had begun to find the middle-class point of view a source of amusement and inspiration. The symbol of the prosperous and banal bourgeois under the July Monarchy was the figure of M. Joseph Prudhomme, Henri Monnier's famous caricature which added a new word to the French language. With his considerable stomach and loud voice and collection of platitudes M. Prudhomme is the quintessence of the French middle class. He was often seen in the days of the Second Empire. "Shakespeare's Polonius," said Nestor Roqueplan in the 1860s, "is one of those solemn idiots whom one finds today described as a 'Prudhomme.'"

Gustave Flaubert's novel *Madame Bovary* was first published in the *Revue de Paris* in 1856. Although the story itself took place some years earlier at the time of the July Monarchy, it was a universal indictment of middle-class morality. As such it outraged bourgeois readers, and Louis Napoleon's government prosecuted Flaubert and the editors of the magazine for having committed an offense against public morals. In the end Flaubert was acquitted, and the trial turned his book into something of a bestseller. But the fact remains that he had, particularly in the case of the apothecary Homais, created a devastating portrait of all that was wrong with the materialistic world of the Second Empire. In the novel, after the death of Emma Bovary, the victory goes to M. Homais, the modern man who believed in progress and was in the habit of contributing to scientific journals.

"His practice grows like wildfire," wrote Flaubert at the end of the novel. "Authority respects and public opinion protects him. He has just been awarded the Legion of Honor." Like the Duc de Morny's Polish friend, the apothecary Homais had received his decoration, the ultimate accolade of a middle-class society. It is perhaps easy to understand why the painter Courbet rejected the honor so violently.

The bourgeois world was devoted to tangibles and could not entertain the romantic or the rebel or the eccentric. In it there was no room for an Emma Bovary or a Courbet or a Baudelaire, no place for a Cézanne or a Rimbaud. The concern of the Second Empire was with profit and progress, and the idols of the day surely were not unfaithful wives and alcoholic poets and failed painters. You wanted a hero? There was M. Schneider, the head of Le Creusot,[5] and there was the epitome of middle-class success: old Baron James de Rothschild himself.

On February 17, 1862, Louis Napoleon paid a visit to the baron's sumptuous new estate at Ferrières. Imperial banners and Rothschild family colors flew from the towers of the château. Liveried servants lined the great hall as the emperor walked along a green velvet carpet embroidered with golden bees. He walked past wall after wall hung with paintings by Rubens and Vandyke and Velásquez. In the dining room he ate from Sèvres china decorated by Boucher and listened to music composed for the occasion by Rossini. Whether he knew it or not, Louis Napoleon was paying homage to an empire far more substantial than his own.

Money was king.

PART FOUR

VOICES OF DISSENT

A creator is not in advance of his generation but he is the first of his contemporaries to be conscious of what is happening to his generation.

GERTRUDE STEIN

CHAPTER ELEVEN

The Establishment

ToDAY in Montparnasse Cemetery you will find a simple tombstone that has much to say about the conflicting currents of Second Empire society. It marks the grave of the poet Charles Baudelaire who is buried there along with his mother and his stepfather, General Aupick. Dying in Paris on August 31, 1867, at the age of forty-six, Baudelaire is described simply as Aupick's stepson. The general's name dominates the tablet:

> JACQUES AUPICK
> *Division General, Senator,*
> *Former Ambassador*
> *at Constantinople and Madrid,*
> *Member of the Conseil Général,*
> *Département du Nord, Grand Officer of*
> *the Imperial Order of the Legion of Honor,*
> *Decorated by Several Foreign Nations,*
> *Died on 27 April 1857,*
> *At the age of 68.*

There is nothing on the tombstone to indicate that his stepson was a poet, not to mention one of the most original writers of his time and largely responsible for creating a new idiom in French art and literature. The omission is understandable, since Baudelaire's genius lay well beyond the confines of the Second Empire.

This was not the case with General Aupick. In terms of the moment in which he lived, he was an effective and important citizen, a gratifying example of middle-class status and success. His stepson, on the other hand, was a disastrous failure: a depraved and alcoholic Bohemian, dying in poverty of a shameful disease. Surely the liquor and the drugs and the hallucinations represented in part Baudelaire's struggle to resolve the paradox of his presence in mid-nineteenth-century Paris. The bourgeois world which surrounded him was content to turn its back on the future, while he and others like him were hurrying to meet it. For this eccentricity he was cast aside by the arbiters of Second Empire taste, although he continued to defy the established order until the end.

The majority of his contemporaries saw little reason to swim against the tide. They had an abiding faith in money and a belief in the virtues of tradition and fixed patterns of morality. Even today, as Sanche de Gramont has pointed out, the French live "in a codified environment where every situation is either legislated or determined by usage." It is an atmosphere affecting many different areas of life. During the Second Empire, for example, and well into the days of the Third Republic, the rules governing art and literature were easy enough to understand. One played the game, and the rewards were enormous. The artist did not have to starve in some garret on the Left Bank, and those who won the Prix de Rome were assured of an enthusiastic reception by the critics of the Salon.[1] Painters like Cabanel and Winterhalter and Meissonier made comfortable fortunes and lived in un-

Bohemian luxury. A novelist like Octave Feuillet, virtually unread today, saw his books go into many editions, found himself welcomed in the highest circles and at last was awarded the prestigious post of Imperial Librarian. To a successful man of letters or portrait painter the fate of the nonconformist under the Second Empire must have seemed like divine judgment: Baudelaire dying penniless and insane, Zola pawning his clothes, Renoir depriving himself of food in order to buy paints. True, the era was obsessed with business and industry and profit, but there was plenty of room for the artist. It was only necessary to cater to the tastes of a newly opulent middle class.

By the last half of the nineteenth century the patrons of art and literature were no longer wealthy aristocrats with inherited advantages of education and leisure and good taste. The new patrons came from every level of an arriviste society: there were bankers and financiers, rich industrialists and successful businessmen, prosperous courtesans and the horde of bourgeois noblemen created by the emperor.[2]

"We are all of us newcomers," said Louis Napoleon with engaging frankness—a remark not only describing his own career but summing up much of the atmosphere of the Second Empire. That régime came to preside over the dissolution of the old order, and it marked an age of transition, an age of insecurity on the threshold of a new century and a new dispensation. For the moment, in spite of the gaudy aristocracy of the imperial court, the age was dominated by the middle class. A bourgeois point of view could be met with everywhere and was not restricted to any one social class. It was as common among the shopkeepers of Paris as among the foreigners and actresses and demimondaines who crowded the parks and forests of Compiègne and Fontainebleau and Saint Cloud. They had similar tastes in art and literature, and they lived by the same specious code of morality. Most important of all, they shared the new prosperity which flourished so luxuriantly at the beginning of the empire.

Few of them, however, had the education or the background or the time to create a cultural milieu for themselves. It really did not matter. In an age of materialism and easy speculation, money was quite enough. They bought their culture ready-made and accepted the agreeable products of competent and not infrequently venal craftsmen. Whether novelists or painters or architects or playwrights, these craftsmen had no ambitions to die insane or go without their meals, and they gave the middle-class public exactly what it wanted.

The tastes of that new public can be established most accurately in a consideration of what it did not want. One of the characteristics of modern art is to bring to the surface a number of things the average person would like to forget. The trend began in the early days of the empire, and against every form of opposition new movements in poetry and painting and fiction developed—movements we often have thought of as the contributions of a far later period in European history. To many it may come as something of a surprise to learn that the foundations of realism and symbolism and impressionism were set down in France in the 1850s and 1860s. This illustrates another of those misunderstandings which have served to diminish the Second Empire and deny its importance as a period of profound cultural change. Paradox plays its accustomed rôle: many of the familiar structures of the modern world were erected against the backdrop of Louis Napoleon's harlequin empire. In a time of intellectual ferment, when traditional molds were being broken with regularity painters and writers of the avant garde found their material and their inspiration in the newly developed urban environment and among the growing mass of the industrial poor—areas of interest which since have become the particular province of our own century.

What fascinated the avant-garde intellectual, however, was bound to repel members of the middle-class establishment. To the extent he had time for them, the rich bourgeois looked upon painting and writing as a means of escape from everyday life. He did not care to dwell on the ugly new world of industry which was supplying him with his money, nor did it please him to make a study of the poor, from whom nothing of taste or good manners could be learned. Least of all did he have any desire to take a closer look at himself. What middle-class factory owner in 1854 would have been comfortable with a book like Charles Dickens' *Hard Times,* in which the misery of a modern industrial city is described? Perhaps it was true, but there was no need to pretend that it was art. And surely there was no art in a volume of poems like *Les Fleurs du mal,* which contained endless descriptions of beggars and decayed old women and other monstrosities best hidden from the general view. What was the profit in reading a novel like *Madame Bovary,* in which the whole code of middle-class conduct was held up to ridicule? It was more than understandable that Baudelaire and Flaubert should have been prosecuted by the imperial government and put on trial for immorality.[3]

Certainly the middle class did not wish to hear about its own weaknesses, nor did it see any reason to wallow in the ugliness of contemporary life. In the struggle to achieve status, many members of that class had become all too familiar with the darker corners of their world. When success came, they were anxious to put such things behind them. The fact that they were paying the bills now gave them a new arrogance. At the very least they expected the artist and writer of the day to provide them with some pleasant form of relaxation. Understandably insecure in the rôle of patron, the nouveau riche felt most comfortable with those traditional forms of art sanctified by the past. He came to regard anything experimental as absurd, if not actually indecent. Sustained by pseudo-science and a love of the practical, he was convinced that art must be useful in one way or another—either as moral instruction or pure entertainment or as tangible evidence of his newly exalted station in life. Naturally he derived the most pleasure from the work of craftsmen who indulged his enthusiasm for luxury and ostentation. Soon enough the awkward millionaires of the industrial revolution began to confuse materialism and vulgarity with good taste. They were simply following in the footsteps of the uncertain noblemen who filled the palace of the Tuileries.

Gold leaf and red velvet blossomed everywhere, and elaboration grew from elaboration. The tendency toward pretentious magnificence could be seen in all areas of cultural life, and it was by no means a French obsession. The Second Empire does correspond in time with the flowering of the Victorian Age in England. "Ornamentation is the principal part of architecture," said the art critic John Ruskin. On both sides of the Channel the industrial revolution had created new wealth and with it a new public— a public eager to display recent acquisitions and encouraged to do so by an atmosphere of abundant materialism. In England as well as on the continent, mid-nineteenth-century painting and architecture and interior design accurately reflected an almost universal and indiscriminate love of ostentation. In France the passion for display could be found even in the trivial aspects of daily life. On Sundays children of the middle class, answering to fashion-

able names like Léon and Emile, went to the garden of
the Tuileries dressed in black velvet suits with lace collars
and wearing little hats with pompoms. Later in the day
their parents would receive guests in some crowded room
very like Sarah Bernhardt's salon, photographed by Nadar
in all its gaudiness—a room choked with paintings and
furs and flowers and crystal chandeliers. On a winter's
afternoon the same bourgeois family might take a ride
through the snow in the Bois, the sleigh fashioned to look
like a swan or a bull and the horses decorated with crimson and yellow plumes. Nothing seemed too bizarre or
elaborate, and display became the certain measure of
worldly success. As befitted his position in society, the Duc
de Morny had a sleigh more luxurious than most: it was
shaped like a dragon and his horses wore silver bells and
red morocco harnesses outlined in gold.

In the rich decade which followed the coup d'état of
1851 Louis Napoleon began the rebuilding of his capital,
and Paris soon became a giant construction site. It was a
chaos of scaffolds and paint pots and unfinished façades.
Public buildings and private houses were rising on all
sides, and architects and decorators swarmed through
them. The refashioning of an entire city offered exciting
possibilities for the development of modern design. But,
with a few exceptions, the builders of the Second Empire
rejected innovation and did not attempt to use new materials or original concepts.[4] They simply turned back and
made a summary of the European past, and imitation became the keynote of the day. Although poised at the edge
of the twentieth century, Haussmann's decorators and architects did no more than re-create a number of antique
styles—all of them ostentatious and all of them reflecting
the royal history of France.

The bewildering eclecticism of the time was accepted

without question by the rich bourgeois, since it corre-
sponded entirely with his own views on art and decoration. Surely there could be no offense to good taste in duplicating the accepted styles of the past. In this he was
hopelessly wrong, and the evidence of his mistake could
be found everywhere. It was only necessary to walk along
some wide boulevard of Louis Napoleon's Paris—near the
Parc Monceau, for example—and go into one of those new
apartment buildings with their creamy white façades and
wrought-iron balconies. Knock on any door, and you
would soon find yourself carried back into the past. The
hallway itself might be Gothic and the salon almost certainly in the style of Louis XIV. A Henri II dining room
and bedrooms done up in the most involved style of Louis
XV would carry you into other periods of French history.

The rooms would be crowded with vaguely classical
paintings, pseudo-Gobelin tapestries and an explosion of
bric-à-brac. The imitation period furniture was wildly
elaborate: boulle cabinets, wardrobes decorated with
ormolu, rosewood bureaus with china plaques painted at
Sèvres or Limoges, baroque consoles and gilded tables
with crimson velvet tops. There would be other tables of
lacquered papier-mâché, decorated with silver and bronze
and mother-of-pearl. And here and there you would see
chairs hung with black satin and passementerie. Marble
and onyx and crystal shone on every side, and gold leaf
adorned the walls and ceilings and mirrors. Rare and exotic wood abounded: gray maple, bois de rose, amboina,
violet wood. However, much of this middle-class furniture seems almost stark when compared with the mar-
queterie pieces ordered by the Empress Eugénie from her
cabinetmaker, Georges Grohé, who quickly grasped the
nature of her Latin temperament. Today, in the reception
rooms of the château of Compiègne, you can still see a

good deal of that imperial furniture—heavily Victorian with additional touches of French and Spanish excess. Originally, much of this furniture was at Saint Cloud, a palace which the decorator Cruchet filled with poufs and causeuses and fringed ottomans of surpassing ugliness.[5]

There were many architects to provide the involved backgrounds necessary for the display of such furniture. Among the most successful were Viollet-le-Duc and Hector Lefuel and Charles Garnier, each of whom contributed enormously to the extravagant scenery of the Second Empire. Viollet-le-Duc, awash in scientific and scholarly pretension, devoted much of his time to the restoration of ancient buildings. He rebuilt the Sainte Chapelle and the cathedral of Notre Dame, reconstructed the ruined château of Pierrefonds near Compiègne and repaired the crumbling ramparts of Carcassonne and Avignon. On August 14, 1857, Hector Lefuel completed the building of the Louvre and at last connected it with the Tuileries. His additions were inspired by Renaissance and seventeenth-century designs, and he was a master of baroque redundancy—crowding the Louvre with dormer windows, huge fireplaces, ornate caryatids and all manner of vermiform embossing. However, few contemporaries were disturbed by his excesses, and the passion for elaboration grew. Nowhere, of course, could this passion be seen more blatantly than in the opera house designed by Charles Garnier and completed after the Franco-Prussian War. It is the supreme example of *le style Napoléon III* and a many-layered symbol of middle-class pretension. Like so much else in an age of broad contrast and materialism, Garnier's work is at once brilliant in its virtuosity and appalling in its vulgarity—though not without considerable charm.

In the wake of public buildings the new rich indulged

themselves to a spectacular degree. The uniformity of Haussmann's façades and boulevards notwithstanding, they created houses and apartments even more stylistically incoherent than the Opéra or the additions to the Louvre. The *"démon du pastiche"* (the frenzy of imitation) was everywhere. As always, the example came from on high: there was Plon-Plon's Pompeian villa on the avenue Montaigne, and at the Tuileries Eugénie was busy re-creating the era of Marie Antoinette. The middle class built somewhat more modestly: Norman chalets in their hundreds, elaborate cottages echoing the Middle Ages and small Renaissance palaces of varying degrees of magnificence. One of the most sumptuous of them, and a building standing today, was a mansion on the Champs Elysées designed by the architect Pierre Manguin for La Païva. That this house should have belonged to a prostitute reflects much of the ambiguity of Louis Napoleon's empire. It was to be expected, of course, at a time when so many other things were false: marble was often only stucco, and plaster regularly took the place of wood. There are still imitation Cordovan leather walls at Fontainebleau ordered by the emperor, and a certain Ruolz, who worked for Christofle et Cie., invented an electroplating process which provided many of the table decorations at the Tuileries. Imitation was a normal feature of Second Empire life: little was real, and little was what it appeared to be on the surface.

Quite naturally, painting conformed to the temper of the times and mirrored all the deficiencies of architecture and interior design. Artists catered to the newly rich consumer and produced work which had as its appeal an escape into the past. They soon learned that it was not profitable to deal with any of the anxieties or realities of modern life. Endlessly repeating the stale conventions of other centuries, these academic painters fashioned easy and agreeable canvases—comfortably narrative and mildly sensual, fitting as harmoniously on the walls of the Tuileries as in the villas of the middle class. Official art caused no controversy, was digested with ease and much appreciated for its ostentation.

Sharing the interest of his contemporaries in machinery and practicality, Louis Napoleon was not at home with art and actively opposed the new and the unusual. Although he did initiate the famous Salon des Refusés, his artistic perceptions were not otherwise remarkable.[6] In 1853 he went so far as to strike at Courbet's painting *The Bathers* with his riding crop. And some years later Eugénie, offended by Manet's *Olympia,* hit the canvas with her fan, although her husband bought one of Cabanel's voluptuous nudes at the same exhibition, rewarding the artist not only with money but with the Légion d'Honneur as well. More than hypocrisy is involved, and we are present at the clash of two irreconcilable points of view. It is not too difficult to understand why the nudes of Courbet and Manet should have shocked the establishment. The emperor's anger was perfectly honest, even though his private record of sensuality and marital infidelity might have made the most rebellious painter blush. It was simple enough: the trouble with Olympia, to take an example, was not that she was naked but that she was too real. You did not buy a picture in order to look at the mistress you had visited between five and seven the previous afternoon.

Since the art world was so rigidly controlled, this kind of offensive painting did not often come to the attention of the general public. Among the most influential figures in that world was the Comte de Nieuwerkerke, Director General of Imperial Museums, a handsome and stultifying man well known as Princess Mathilde's lover—albeit an unfaithful one. In his diary Viel Castel, who was on the staff of the Louvre, took every occasion to set down descriptions of the various young women who were accustomed to slip into the director's office toward the end of the working day. However doubtful his private morals may have been, Nieuwerkerke's professional life conformed to the code of the establishment, and he supported the whole structure of contemporary art: the exhibitions at the Salon, the gold medals, the Prix de Rome, the Ecole des Beaux Arts. By the end of the nineteenth century the Salon had become completely sterile and quite divorced from reality—the natural result of a system which for so many years had rejected any form of original work. Nevertheless, during the Second Empire and well into the beginning of the twentieth century the only path to financial success lay through the labyrinth of the official establishment.

The academic painters who flourished under Louis Napoleon were making enormous sums of money, while artists like Manet and Renoir and Cézanne could hardly sell their work at any price. As a matter of fact, it was rather difficult to be a failure: there was a growing demand for art to hang on the walls of new houses and government buildings, and the painter with a modest talent and a few connections and the money to hire a luscious model or two would not starve for very long. From the ateliers of artists like Cabanel and Baudry poured innumerable classical allegories—a hundred Births and Triumphs of Venus, countless Auroras and Judgments of Paris. These practical men played the game without regret, and their credentials were neatly in order: Léon Bonnat, Second Grand Prix de Rome, 1858; William Bouguereau, Grand Prix de Rome, 1850; Edouard Detaille, student of Meissonier; Carolus-Duran, Grand Officier de la Légion d'Hon-

neur; Jean Jacques Henner, Grand Prix de Rome, 1858—
the list is endless. Perhaps the most successful of them all
was Ernest Meissonier, who came to command almost any
price he wished for his work. In a studio on the Ile Saint
Louis, his long beard wrapped in a scarf, he painted enormous historical canvases like *1814,* which sold for more
than eight hundred thousand francs and was much
admired for its photographic attention to detail. *His* grenadiers never lacked for a gaiter button.

Painting was a lucrative business, and the artist who
sought tangible profit could not afford to waste time expressing himself or making comments about the contemporary world. Pictures were to be sold, and the Second
Empire was crowded with commercially minded technicians who painted an overwhelming number of canvases
about nothing at all. In the scale of values the painter was
perhaps a little beneath the architect and slightly above
the interior decorator. There was no profit in dwelling on
the unusual or the paradoxical: far better to glide along on
the surface of things. The middle-class patron wished it
so, and in the matter of taste there is nothing remarkably
different about the general public in France and England
and America today.

If it required no extraordinary talent to make your way
in the art world of the Second Empire, it did require a
certain degree of self-promotion. Among papers found in
the Tuileries after the fall of the empire was a letter written to one of Louis Napoleon's aides a few months after
the coup d'état:

Paris, 21 April 1852

GENERAL:
The acclamation of December 20th, without parallel
in history, should be celebrated on canvas. I have

sketched out a project for a painting to represent the French nation welcoming Prince Louis Napoleon as president of the republic. I ask you to consider the project. . . . Before beginning the work, I should like to know whether it is agreeable to the Prince.

DUBUFE,
Painter of History
Chevalier of the LÉGION d'HONNEUR
36 rue Saint Lazare

This is one of many letters which arrived at the Tuileries during the course of the empire. It is obvious enough that government approval would enhance an artist's reputation enormously.

What was true of the painter was also true of the writer. Volume upon volume of ponderous and flattering works filled the palace offices—books like *Les Césars et les Napoléons,* sent in by a certain Amédée de Cesena for the emperor's edification. The general public was more comfortable with popular novels of a pseudo-scientific nature, such as Jules Verne's *Voyage to the Center of the Earth.* And by the 1860s Emile Gaboriau's detective stories were being widely read for their entertainment value and semi-intellectial stimulation.[7] But perhaps the most popular novelist of the day was Octave Feuillet, tall and elegant with exquisite manners. A member of the estabishment in good standing, he was elected to the Académie Française in 1862, taking the seat left open by the death of Eugène Scribe, the well-known dramatist. A familiar figure in imperial circles, Feuillet perfected the *roman mondaine:* the novel of life in high society, of which the finest example is *Monsieur de Camors.* This study of a rich and idle dandy was written in 1867 while the author was spending a good deal of time in Fontainebleau as the emperor's guest. Though far less welcome at court, contemporary journalists provided the public with witty comments and easy entertainment. On the Grands Boulevards and in the cafés they coined epigrams and laughed their way toward the unhappy dénouement of the empire: Nestor Roqueplan, Aurélien Scholl and Villemessant's editorial staff at *Le Figaro*—among a multitude of others.

The theater, however, was the most appreciated literary form of the era, and perhaps it has never been more active in Paris than during the Second Empire. The leading playwrights were by no means without talent: Emile Augier and Dumas *fils* and Victorien Sardou. They were skilled craftsmen who wrote well-constructed plays that dealt lightly (and, for the most part, morally) with such subjects of universal interest as sex and money. Augier, in particular, upheld the bourgeois virtues of honesty and common sense and married love. But the most popular performances of the time were rather less stern. Taking the lead from Offenbach's operettas, theatrical producers offered one salacious musical comedy after another, and nowhere can the fundamental hypocrisy of the Second Empire be seen more clearly. The Folies Bergère itself opened in the spring of 1869, although it was not successful until after the Franco-Prussian War.

On New Year's Eve in 1860 the Goncourts went with their friend Gavarni to see the revue at the Variétés: *Ooh! La La! Qu'c'est bête, tout ça* (*How silly it all is*). The title alone should have kept them away, and, predictably, they were disgusted by what they saw. The revue was in three acts and twenty-two scenes, and most of the action took place in a photographer's studio. This device allowed the producers to stage a series of almost naked *tableaux vivants* and so capture the attention of the audience. It could only remind the Goncourts of the reception room in a brothel, although their moral outrage is somewhat diluted by the accuracy of the observation. "The director of this exhibition," they said, "has been awarded a decoration."

This should have surprised no one, and there is little virtue in criticizing the ephemeral theater of the Second Empire for its lack of taste. A certain degree of pornography was flaunted, and even at the Exposition of 1867 nude photographs with the superimposed heads of Eugénie and the Duchesse de Morny were circulated. To be irritated by this kind of thing is as unrewarding as to lament the fact —from the remove of another century—that Cabanel was a successful painter and Manet was not. The point to be made is that hypocrisy was abroad in every field of the arts. Under the patronage of a middle class which could afford to support them, the novelists and painters and playwrights of the day were designing products almost entirely for amusement and escape. When possible they included a degree of mild, and not so mild, sexual stimulation.

It is difficult to believe that many of the foundations of twentieth-century art and literature could have been laid down in such a context. At first glance it would seem that the Second Empire was a period particularly unconducive to the development of anything new or modern or significant. Yet the artificiality of the empire and the doubtful tastes of the middle class forced the serious artist to react in a way which would not have been possible in an atmosphere more favorable to experimentation and innovation.

This ambiguity has been apparent in later years and in other cultures. Speaking of the Habsburg Empire, the painter Oskar Kokoschka remarked that it was something wonderfully concrete to react *against*. And perhaps the only other city in European history as rich as Second Empire Paris in the vulgarity of its popular styles and as significant in the development of new and modern movements was Vienna before the First World War. Attending an exhibition of Kokoschka's work, the Archduke Franz Ferdinand was heard to say: "We should break every bone in that fellow's body." It has a familiar ring. We can only think of Louis Napoleon slashing at Courbet's canvas with his riding crop, and the official establishment in Vienna was quite as antagonistic to innovation. And yet, against the background of Hans Makart's pretentious paintings, the art of Kokoschka and Egon Schiele developed; not far from the florid façades of the Ringstrasse rose the modern buildings designed by Adolf Loos and Oskar Wagner and Josef Hoffmann; out of the masquerade of the Dual Monarchy came the novels of Franz Kafka.

So it had been in Paris a half-century earlier: for all its financial stability and authoritarian government and echoes of the Napoleonic past, the Second Empire was a period of continuous revolution. Social and political and intellectual upheavals of every kind were taking place, and far from silently—upheavals which mark the beginning of the modern world we live in. The reflection of these upheavals is to be found in the work of rebellious writers and painters and poets who spurned the glossy temptations of the age and chose instead to record their impressions of a new era dawning in Europe. Out of their sensitivity, and against every objection, they created a language and an idiom and a life style appropriate to the modern industrial age. They were either ignored or ridiculed for their pains, and a contented middle-class nation did not even care to glance at their vision of what was happening to Europe in the middle of the nineteenth century.

The scorned artists reacted normally enough, and in their turn rejected all the values of the bourgeois society which had rejected them. Some showed their defiance by wearing long hair and eccentric clothes, others through drugs and alcohol and peculiar sexual arrangements. And all of them defied the establishment by producing work which to the average person seemed uglier and uglier and more and more incomprehensible. Even a blue-stocking intellectual like Juliette Adam could say: "Now we've seen everything—Germinie Lacerteux in literature and the black cat with dirty paws in painting." [8]

In order to make a new beginning the serious artist felt that he had to break all the traditional patterns of the past. As the years went by, he retreated more and more into the sanctuary of his art until the estrangement from bourgeois life became complete. This was a far more significant rebellion than the cheerful attempts of Henri Murger's Bohemians to defy tradition and authority. Anxious to concentrate on a diagnosis of modern life, the anti-establishment artists of the Second Empire realized that the whole outmoded structure of the past had to be pulled down in order to make way for the future.

As the level of popular culture sank and as the contemporary love of imitation grew, so did their defiance increase. And perhaps only the anti-intellectualism and vulgarity of the day could have provided such a strong impulse toward innovation and discovery. In every area of life—social and political and artistic—the old and the new were coming into violent conflict. Oddly enough, the glittering and insecure and tasteless Second Empire gave an unexpected depth to that conflict, the very artificiality of the empire serving to set it in bolder relief.

With his accustomed clarity of mind Louis Napoleon saw what was happening, if he did not fully understand why it was happening. It is ironical that no other contemporary ruler had accepted the necessity of the social and political revolution to the extent which he had. As much as any impressionist painter or symbolist poet or realistic novelist he was aware that Europe was at the beginning of a new dispensation. He had no understanding, however, of the artist's rôle in that beginning. "There is nothing less than a conspiracy of men of letters against my government," he said, recognizing the conspiracy but failing to see the reasons for it.

Like those rejected artists, he knew that France stood at the threshold of a new age. Unlike them, he did not understand the themes which gave unity to their rebellion— hatred of materialism and the realization that the greatest weakness of his empire and of the middle-class establishment which supported it was an awesome denial of the real world.

CHAPTER TWELVE

Against the Grain

As a young man Théophile Gautier had been a rebel, attending the famous opening night of *Hernani* in 1830 wearing a flame-colored doublet and leading the claque in praise of Victor Hugo's romantic manifesto. The years went by, and his passions grew more restrained. Under the Second Empire his career was devoted largely to writing literary and art criticism for papers like *La Presse* and *Le Moniteur* (almost the official voice of the government) and magazines like *La Revue de Paris*. He did not lose his spirit of rebellion entirely, however, and he was sensitive enough to recognize some of the changes that were taking place in the intellectual world by the middle of the nineteenth century. The romanticism in which he had believed so ardently was becoming as outmoded as classicism before it, and there were new and imperfectly defined trends in the air. In 1850 he considered some of them as they applied to architecture:

Mankind must create a totally new architecture, born of today, now that use is being made of new systems created by the industry that is just coming into exist-

206

ence. The application of cast iron allows and demands the use of many new forms, such as can be seen in railway stations, in suspension bridges, in the arches of greenhouses.

His comments were set down before the completion of several of those few original contributions made to architecture during the nineteenth century in Europe: the Crystal Palace in London (designed by Joseph Paxton, a builder of greenhouses) and the pavilions of Les Halles in Paris, which had been proposed by Louis Napoleon himself. Well in advance of many of his contemporaries Gautier began to understand the implications and necessities of the modern age, and his pleas for a new approach in architecture can be applied equally well to the other arts. It is ironic that he was unable to make the application himself, seeing in Manet's *Olympia,* for example, "only the desire to attract attention at any price." The old rebel had little sympathy for the young one.

However, Manet was doing nothing more unusual than attempting to create an art "born of today"—to use Gautier's own phrase. And it is the work of those Second Empire painters who moved against the grain of their era that we find the genesis of the modern sensibility. In contrast, French architecture of the day—with the exception of Les Halles and the additions to the Bibliothèque Impériale—had turned its back to the present. A movement forward was more obvious in the field of painting. Reacting against the imitation classicism and faded romanticism of Gérôme and Cabanel and the other *pompiers,* young artists were fitting their work to the measure of man and trying to express the reality of the times in which they lived. In retrospect their point of view does not seem so very daring: surely the Greek and Roman heroes, the woodland nymphs and chubby angels who filled the walls of Salon exhibitions at the Palais de l'Industrie had little relation to the pressing problems of the nineteenth century. They were remarkably silent on the subjects of social injustice and materialism and grimy industrial cities.

In order to focus on the image of modern man in the setting of everyday life the rebellious painters were obliged to find new means of expression, new coins of exchange not worn thin by the pressure of many hands. In every field of art the search for a new style and a new language and a new way of seeing took different forms and different directions as it appeared in the work of individual painters and poets and novelists. They all shared certain similarities of approach, however, and they may be grouped together as realists. In some ways it is an unsatisfactory definition, for who could have been a more "realistic" painter than Meissonier? But the realism of the anti-establishment artist took a rather less literal direction. It became an attack on traditional habits of seeing and thinking, and it made use of the compelling new facts of an industrial age: the emergence of the common man and the urban environment which was nineteenth-century Europe's most ambiguous gift to the future. As befitted members of a minority, the rebellious artists were outspoken. "Show me an angel," said Gustave Courbet, "and I will paint one."

His words were designed to shock a respectable middle class sufficiently horrified by his coarse ego and socialistic tendencies. The very word *réalisme,* in fact, first gained currency in France in the 1850s to describe Courbet's paintings of peasant scenes and ordinary people—subjects then considered beneath the dignity of art. His earthy canvases offended a generation brought up on helmeted classical heroes and misty romantic landscapes. It was easy enough for an establishment spokesman like the Comte de Nieuwerkerke to dismiss such painting as the work of "democrats," noting that its exponents were not difficult to recognize since they never changed their linen. Before long Courbet and other realist painters found themselves at the center of a number of controversies. The battle between the innovators and the traditionalists took on many social and political overtones: Courbet against the imperial government, the middle class against the workers, the old versus the new and, above all, youth versus age. The broad lines of conflict could be seen in a novel like *Les Misérables,* published by Victor Hugo in 1862 and expressing, in Javert's pursuit of Jean Valjean, something of the eternal conflict between liberty and authority.

Looking back, we find the young innovators of the Second Empire inspired more by the logic of art than by political revolution, but their enthusiasm for reality was bound to unsettle some of the foundations of Louis Napoleon's government. It was a régime which did not thrive on fact and was sustained by show and decoration and sleight of hand—by all those devices familiar to the academic painters it supported so strenuously. Under an authoritarian government, art and politics were inextricably bound together, and the realists formed an unacknowledged party of the opposition. Nevertheless, their radical point of view came from other directions than from the desire for social reform and an end to tyranny. Courbet outlined with rare simplicity the reasons for his rebellion:

> I wish to put myself in the position of being able to translate onto canvas the customs and ideas and aspects of my own era as I see them. In a word, it is my ambition to create art which is alive.

The positive thrust of these remarks is not open to criticism: they are, or should be, the statement of any artist's credo. The negative thrust, however, generated violent antagonism among members of the Second Empire establishment. And surely there are a number of revolutionary ideas behind Courbet's remarks: not only the denial of the official Salon, but the desire to break away from the traditions of the past, to put an end to rhetoric and sentimentality, to eliminate from painting all of the heroic and the monumental. For these irrelevancies Courbet wished to substitute a scientific study of contemporary life.

To this end, he concentrated on portraying the peasants of the district in which he was born, as well as the Parisian workers. He took every occasion to record the ordinary and even sordid aspects of everyday existence, and very often these interests served only to amuse art critics of the day. His *Wrestlers,* exhibited at the Salon of 1853, caused a good deal of merriment. "These two men are fighting to see which is the dirtiest," wrote one critic. "The victor will receive a four-cent bath ticket." And he added that "none of the muscles of these wrestlers will be found in its usual place."

Courbet, whose opinion of the bourgeois mentality was low, did not concern himself with criticism of this kind. However, his ego surely suffered under the emperor's censure. Years later Courbet took pleasure in refusing the Légion d'Honneur when it was offered to him at last. After the fall of the empire he became a member of the Commune, a group remarkable for the diversity of its radical opinions and its common hatred of Louis Napoleon. During the Paris Exposition of 1855 Courbet found that a number of his paintings, including *The Burial at Ornans,* had been rejected by the hanging committee of the Salon. Gathering up this canvas, so criticized for its delineation of peasant life, and others like *The Bathers* and *The Studio,* both of which contained offensively realistic nudes, he opened his own exhibition in a wooden gallery on the avenue Montaigne not far from the Palais de l'Industrie. The title of the exhibition was simply: *Le Réalisme—G. Courbet.*

The same concern for reality and the same interest in the life of the ordinary man is to be found in the work of Honoré Daumier, who reached a far wider public than did Courbet. At the time Daumier's more serious work in painting and sculpture was largely unknown, but he was popular for the brilliant caricatures and cartoons he had begun to contribute to Paris newspapers during the July Monarchy. He carried these bitter satires into the richer field of the Second Empire, and his drawings appeared regularly in *Charivari* and *Le Figaro* and elsewhere. Among his most memorable creations was the angular and sinister figure of Ratapoil, the Bonapartist agent, who gave Daumier the means to articulate his own opposition to the imperial government. Perhaps that opposition was inevitable for anyone who studied, as he did, the incontestible realities of the day: political oppression and social injustice and urban poverty. "We have to be men of our own time," said Daumier, and he revealed his consternation at the social implications of an industrialized urban age. In such an atmosphere only the most commercial and insensitive artist could continue to elaborate the narratives of Greek mythology and draw sentimental pictures of little girls with their dogs. In his paintings and cartoons Daumier set down the essence of the city hidden behind Haussmann's façades: the Paris of hunger and despair and unheroic struggles for survival.

It was to be expected that the author of *Les Fleurs du mal,* so at home in that dark city and so familiar with its misery, should have been attracted to Daumier. "Dip into his work," said Baudelaire, "and before your eyes will pass, in all its fantastic and arresting reality, all that a great city contains in the way of living monstrosities."

Curiously enough, it was not Daumier—or Courbet or Manet—whom Baudelaire singled out as "the painter of modern life." It was Constantin Guys, basically an illustrator, and an artist with little reputation today. Nevertheless, Baudelaire was a perceptive art critic, and his reasons for having chosen this painter above all others are unexpectedly valid. He was attracted by the modern quality of Guys, by his success in recording the varied images of Second Empire life. The artist's early career had prepared him thoroughly for such a rôle: he had been a correspondent for the *Illustrated London News* during the Crimean War, and his battle sketches were sent regularly to England to be turned into engravings for the magazine. In the Crimea he developed an accurate eye, not only for the uniforms and military display of which he was so fond, but for the movement and tempo of the immediate present. Returning to Paris, he devoted himself to the narrative of city life. His friends were artists who shared his point of view: Honoré Daumier, the photographer Nadar and the Goncourt brothers, who were among the originators of the naturalistic novel.

In 1863, in a series of feuilletons published by *Le Figaro,* Baudelaire discussed the work of Constantin Guys. In the articles Baudelaire set forth one of the principles unifying the work of realists as different as Courbet and Manet, as Daumier and Guys himself: "The pleasure which we derive from the representation of the present does not depend solely on the beauty with which it may be invested, but also on its essential quality as the present."

This theme can be found in all of Baudelaire's art criticism and particularly in his remarks about Manet. In their emphasis on painting contemporary life both Manet and Guys were innovators, although it is difficult to appreciate the extent of their innovation today. Far more than Manet, Constantin Guys succeeded in creating a panorama of Second Empire life from its highest to its lowest social levels. The quality of his painting remains dubious, but through his eyes you still can see and feel the movement and vitality of a vanished era: its love of war and sex and gambling, its theaters and military reviews, its horses and carriages and uniforms, its elegant demimondaines and its five-franc whores. With far greater impact and depth Baudelaire had done the same thing in his *Tableaux parisiens,* and perhaps this is the reason he had such sympathy for Constantin Guys. The painter, after all, had "searched everywhere for the transient, fleeting beauty of actual life, and for the character of what, with the reader's permission, I have called *modernity."*

Through his study of Constantin Guys, Baudelaire had grasped the essentials of that avant-garde art which was developing in the face of every obstacle. The far superior painters who came to be known after 1874 as the Impressionists began their careers under Louis Napoleon and shared Guys' consuming interest in the present. It is true that they turned their attention to matters of technique primarily, but more often than not they did paint what Baudelaire has called "landscapes in stone": studies of ordinary Parisian life in the middle of the nineteenth century. It is strange that the work of these young artists should so have offended the middle class. For the most part their pictures dealt with the pleasanter aspects of bourgeois life: pretty women, children, circuses, theaters, regattas, restaurants, cafés, gardens and flowers—all the colorful backgrounds of the contemporary scene. But the public was not conditioned to think of such things as suitable subjects and looked to the Salon for guidance. It imagined art to be something removed from daily life, fashioned with a traditional palette under studio lights. There could be no art in painting the streets and cafés and gardens of the real city. The public saw them every day and could learn nothing from them.

The artist whom Baudelaire might well have described as the "painter of modern life" was Edouard Manet, a rebel in spite of himself. Ironically, he was anxious to find a place for himself in the art establishment, and no one longed for the honors and gold medals more than he did. On the surface Manet was a conventional product of the upper middle class: a wit, a dandy, a man-about-town, elegantly dressed, well known in the cafés along the boulevard des Italiens and the friend of beautiful demimondaines. Nevertheless, he was the most revolutionary of contemporary painters, the most "modern," the first to receive the full force of middle-class condemnation.

Manet's father had wanted him to become a lawyer, but he gave in at last and allowed the young man to study painting with Thomas Couture, one of the most successful and least imaginative academic painters of the day. Manet began his apprenticeship in the winter of 1850 and was soon dissatisfied with the stilted and imitative work produced in the master's studio. He constantly annoyed the models posing as naked Greek and Roman heroes until he managed to make one of them pose *in* his clothes. Couture was horrified, and Manet, finding the studio as interesting as a tomb, went his own way—rejecting traditional art and choosing instead to use the rich new materials of the present which lay around him in such abundance.

In 1858 he met Charles Baudelaire, and an inevitable friendship developed. At their first meeting Baudelaire's eyes were dancing with the effects of ether, and he was wearing what the Goncourts described as his "guillotine dress": a tight blue frock coat with gold buttons, a white collar and a huge black cravat. He had already endured the scandal following the publication of *Les Fleurs du mal,* he was suffering from syphilis and he had begun his long affair with the mulatto Jeanne Duval. Perhaps as only the most proper bourgeois could have been, Manet was attracted by this strange person's eccentricity and rebellious nature. For all the overlay of affectation and satanism, he saw in him a fellow spirit. Baudelaire reacted in the same way and was one of the first to recognize Manet's genius. "He will be a *painter,*" said Baudelaire, "a real painter, who will know how to seize on the epic quality of modern life, and make us see and understand how important and poetic we are in our cravats and patent-leather boots."

This is almost exactly what Baudelaire came to say about Constantin Guys. Although his coverage of Second Empire Paris was more limited than the extensive panorama created by Guys, Manet shared the same impulse to discover "the epic quality of modern life." His technique was unquestionably superior and the depth of his vision far greater. Like other realists, Manet found his subject matter in the immediate present and wasted no time on a distant and inappropriate past. For his obstinacy in abandoning traditional techniques of perspective and chiaroscuro he was condemned to a lifetime of scorn and rejection. Denied all honors until his last years, he was insulted by the critics of the Salon and laughed at by the general public. It was all the more painful for Manet to find himself classified as a rebel and nonconformist since his fastidious nature prevented him from feeling entirely at home in the smoky cafés of the anti-establishment. In centers of intellectual revolt like the Brasserie des Martyrs and the Café Guerbois he felt uncomfortable and disliked the posturing of his fellow artists. They formed a group eccentric by any standard: Cézanne looking as if he had slept in his clothes (which he had), Courbet drinking beer and exercising his considerable ego, the novelist Champfleury in a rumpled chocolate-colored suit, and all the less talented rebels—loudly advertising their rebellion and laughing with those cherished whores, Mimi la Bretonne and the girl known as "Fried Eggs." Manet would sit observing the scene dispassionately; Manet with his top hat and eyeglass, his walking stick and lemon-yellow gloves; Manet, the most revolutionary of them all.

Baudelaire, so disturbed by the middle-class world symbolized in the person of his stepfather, General Aupick, might well have been offended by Manet's conventional exterior. But he sensed the revolutionary within, particularly when he came to observe Manet's method of composition and to understand what the artist was trying to do. The preliminary sketches for *La Musique aux Tuileries* were taken from life as Manet walked through the garden with Baudelaire himself. Completed in 1862, the painting is a fine example of Manet's eye for the contemporary scene. This was a talent he shared with Baudelaire, and in their work both of them were concerned with capturing the reality of the present. Like many of the poems in *Les Fleurs du mal,* Manet's painting of the garden of the Tuileries is a vivid record of the urban scene, a "landscape in stone." Although unsympathetic critics found it only a meaningless jumble of aggressive colors, Manet was guilty of no other error than producing a work given over to "modernity," in the sense in which Baudelaire used the term. Even today the canvas is alive with the immediacy of the present, and it is a penetrating comment on the nature of Second Empire life. However, through this painting, and through others of the same period, Manet first came to experience the agony of total rejection by the majority of his contemporaries.

The famous Salon des Refusés, on the surface a magnificent gesture in the name of innovation and artistic freedom, served only to turn the public against Manet as well as against most of the other young painters of the day. In preparing for the exhibition of 1863 the hanging committee of the Salon outdid itself and succeeded in rejecting almost three thousand canvases submitted for consideration. The rejected artists reacted loudly and violently. It was understandable enough: there were few art dealers in Paris, hardly any with independent ideas, and the only road to commercial success lay through the official channels of the Salon. The anger of the young artists was heard at the Tuileries, and on April 22, 1863, Louis Napoleon himself appeared unexpectedly at the Palais de l'Industrie and asked to see the paintings in question. After having looked at some forty of them, he sent for the Comte de Nieuwerkerke. The Director of Imperial Museums had vanished discreetly, and Louis Napoleon ordered one of his assistants to see that all of the rejected work was accepted without delay.

The emperor's command was obeyed. When the exhibition opened in May, all the rejected paintings had been hung in auxiliary rooms. For weeks the wits along the Boulevard had been referring to the coming exhibition as the Salon des Refusés; the name caught on and it proved to be the intellectual event of the year. For the first time a large audience had the opportunity of seeing the work of young and unknown painters, and within a few hours over seven thousand tickets had been sold. This unprecedented attention was disastrous for the young painters, since the public soon discovered the rich irony of the occasion: although the rejected artists did include Cézanne and Renoir and Manet, the majority of the work displayed was poor. In fact, as one critic said with some restraint, it was more than poor; it was "deplorable, impossible, insane and ridiculous." Most of the work was far from being experimental and nothing more than inferior academic painting of the worst kind. The public was delighted, however, discovering that it was great fun to look in on the "Clowns' Exhibition" and jeer at all the pathetic failures and bearded revolutionaries who never would be able to paint like Cabanel and Meissonier and Gérôme. Much of the work exhibited at the Salon des Refusés was worthless, but public antagonism was directed largely against one of the least imperfect paintings on display. It was on the end wall, in the last room, and it was called *Le Bain*.

Parisian wits soon changed the title to something more amusing: *Le Déjeuner sur l'herbe*. In this famous painting Manet succeeded in offending every canon of taste and every artistic tradition of the day. The presence of two naked women at what appeared to be a bourgeois picnic shocked his contemporaries. Popular reaction should not have surprised Manet, since he had shown the painting two months previously at Martinet's gallery on the boulevard des Italiens. There the few visitors who came had booed it openly and in some cases threatened to puncture the canvas with their walking sticks. They thought the picture disgusting, at best a brash echo of Raphael and Giorgione and otherwise incomprehensible. No one knew what it meant, and people searched helplessly for a story. They had been brought up on narrative art: in a painting they expected to find Jupiter in disguise or the history of a betrayed wife or the record of one of Napoleon Bonaparte's famous battles. When *Le Déjeuner sur l'herbe* appeared at the Salon des Refusés and reached a larger public, it only managed to offend more people. With every good intention Louis Napoleon had managed to produce a negative result. After 1863 the general public was the acknowledged enemy not only of Manet, but of all the young painters not approved by the Salon.

No matter how he longed for acceptance, Manet was unable to change the way he painted and could only continue to set down the vision of modern life as it came to him. In 1865, unhappily for Manet, that vision took the form of *Olympia:* the portrait of a naked demimondaine with her maid and black cat. The painting was simple and elegant and in some ways as realistic as a photograph. But its daring technique—among other things, the painting scorned perspective—and controversial subject matter condemned it to disapproval. In fact, that it had been selected by the Salon committee at all was surprising, and the painting was subjected to unprecedented abuse. In a city given over to sensuality and all the refinements of vice Manet was held up to ridicule as an offender of public morals simply because he had seen fit to paint a naked prostitute. *Olympia* was the great scandal of 1865. "Who is this odalisque with a yellow belly?" asked the prominent critic Jules Claretie. "A degraded model picked up I don't know where and who has the pretension to represent Olympia. Olympia! What Olympia?"

Another journalist cautioned young girls and pregnant women against looking at the painting, and Saint Victor, critic and friend of the Goncourts, noticed with anger that "the public pressed around the putrefying *Olympia* as if at the Morgue." Naturally, Baudelaire was disgusted by the hypocrisy of such comments and could only think of the occasion when he had taken a harlot of his acquaintance to the Louvre, where *she* had been shocked by the nude statues and pictures. Public taste ran true to form, and the most popular painting at the Salon of 1865 was a rustic trifle by Jules Breton called *The Haymakers' Repose*. It was bought for a large sum by Prince Plon-Plon himself.

Manet's failure to find acceptance in the art world of the Second Empire haunted him for the rest of his life, and it is said that on his deathbed he asked after the health of Cabanel, a painter whose success had always irritated him. Perhaps the most depressing comment of all was made by the English novelist George Moore, who studied art in Paris in the 1870s. "We were taught at the Beaux Arts," he said, "to consider Manet an absurd person, or else an *épateur* who, not being able to paint like M. Gérôme, determined to astonish."

However, Manet was simply following in the footsteps of Courbet and Daumier and Constantin Guys, searching for an "art born of today." Sensing some of the new directions of modern life, these artists were more sensitive to the beginnings of change than most of their contemporaries. And that sensitivity made it inevitable for Manet and the others to be regarded as revolutionaries, since any interest in realism cut deeply into the artificial structure of Louis Napoleon's government and offended middle-class sensibilities. In many ways it appeared that the Second Empire's most consistent pleasure lay in the avoidance of reality in all its forms. To his discomfort and final glory, Manet saw that reality with a clear eye and recorded it with a more elegant hand than most.

Unlike Manet, there were young artists who consciously courted the disapproval of the middle class. Perhaps the most flamboyant was Paul Cézanne, a painter even more significant in the future development of modern art than Manet but whose most important work did not appear until after the fall of the empire. Cézanne arrived in Paris in the second decade of the régime, coming up from the south and immediately assuming the role of bearded avant-garde painter. For the time being he was content to

defy the establishment, not with his painting—for he was
slowly learning the fundamentals of his art—but with his
appearance and general conduct. Although his father was
a wealthy banker in Aix-en-Provence, few people would
have suspected his middle-class background. Emile Zola,
an old friend from the Midi, described his habitual costume: a "black, shapeless, rusty" felt hat, a stained and
faded overcoat covered with green patches and dirty trousers which were too short. To complete this vision of Bohemia, he wore his hair and beard long and delighted in
being boorish and obscene. His life was disorganized and
his studio a pig-sty. For all the accoutrements of genius,
however, he was still an awkward painter.

He had come to Paris in 1861 during the most prosperous and elegant period of the empire. With little enthusiasm his father had given him an allowance, and the
young man began painting in the Académie Suisse on the
Ile de la Cité. It offered no instruction and simply provided models for the boisterous students who gathered
there to insult Louis Napoleon and laugh at the successful
painters of the day. Cézanne soon became discouraged and
went back home to work in his father's bank. Inevitably,
the moment of conformity was a disaster, and he returned
to Paris more determined than ever to shock the great
bourgeois majority that was unaware of his existence and
had no interest in him at all. Although he still received
an allowance from home, he took to sleeping on park
benches as a measure of his defiance. By 1865, after many
visits back and forth to Aix, he was painting in a studio in
the Marais, continuing a lonely apprenticeship in the face
of every discouragement.

His slovenly exterior hid a great sensitivity and a keen
awareness of new intellectual trends. He even recognized
some of the absurdity of his own rebellious pose: having

failed the entrance examination at the Ecole des Beaux Arts, he wrote to a friend that his hair and beard were "more abundant than my talent." Among his friends were Pissarro and Sisley and Auguste Renoir, the son of a poor tailor, who was studying at the Beaux Arts in a state of continual frustration. Renoir could not understand why the academic traditions of the day demanded that "the big toe of Germanicus must have greater majesty than the big toe of the coal-merchant on the corner." This was a point of view with which Cézanne had sympathy, and he was drawn more and more into the realist avant garde. His earlier enthusiasm for Victor Hugo and Alfred de Musset was waning: he had learned *Les Fleurs du mal* by heart, and he admired Manet's work at the Salon des Refusés. But he had not outgrown youth's obsession with the externals of revolt. As a friend observed, he spent a good deal of time saying "the most terrible things about the Tyrant," perhaps because it was fashionable to criticize Louis Napoleon in intellectual circles. He refused to shake hands with Manet at the Café Guerbois "because I haven't washed for a week." And he was given to uttering all manner of paradoxical statements. "The day will come," he once said, "when a single original carrot will be pregnant with revolution."

It was fortunate that Cézanne had at least one friend as determined as he and rather more stable. Emile Zola had been his boyhood companion in the Midi, and they both found themselves in Paris at the beginning of their careers in the freezing winter of 1861. Zola had made up his mind to be a success at any cost, and he spent that winter practicing to be a poet, writing one alexandrine after another until there was no more fuel and money and food left. Nothing stopped him: he pawned his clothes and wrapped himself in a blanket—and continued writing.

Fortunately, he was soon offered a small job in the advertising department of Louis Hachette's publishing firm, and he supplemented his salary with free-lance journalism. By 1866 he was associated with Villemessant's evening newspaper, *L'Evénement.* It gave him the opportunity of reaching a large public, and there might even be a chance to help some of his friends.

The art world was still in a turmoil after the disaster of the Salon des Refusés and the scandal of *Olympia* in the previous year. It was assumed that the hanging committee for the exhibition of 1866 would show some signs of acknowledging new movements in painting. However, the committee maintained its fossilized point of view and monotonously rejected new work by Cézanne and Renoir and Manet, among others. Probably with Zola's help, Cézanne wrote a letter to the Comte de Nieuwerkerke demanding a reconsideration of his own rejected work and suggesting another Salon des Refusés. No answer came from the recesses of the Louvre, and Cézanne wrote into the great silence a second time. At this point Zola felt, since so many of his friends were painters of the neglected avant garde, that he had found an opportunity to help them and in addition provide a series of entertaining articles for *L'Evénement.* Villemessant, a great believer in scandal and indiscretion of every kind, was quick to agree, and Zola began work on a number of articles designed to provoke the Parisian art world. The first two of them appeared at the end of April and created something of a sensation. Zola's general theme was the myopia of the Salon in the face of recent developments in art, and his writing took the form of a diatribe. By May 4, 1866, he had warmed to his subject, pointing out that in the arts it was now a time of struggle and excitement and that the Salon was meeting the challenge with "an accumulation of mediocrity." He praised the new painters extravagantly, took time to defend the infamous *Olympia* and suggested that space be reserved on the walls of the Louvre for Manet himself and Courbet as well.

Public reaction was violent, and letters of protest poured into the editorial offices of *L'Evénement*. Cézanne was overjoyed at the hornets' nest which Zola had stirred up: "God knows, he puts those bastards in their place all right!" But Villemessant, threatened with a flood of canceled subscriptions, was less enthusiastic. He compromised by assigning an art critic with more traditional views to alternate with Zola for the rest of the series, which was curtailed in any case, and the controversy gradually died away. In the same year Zola salvaged something from his defeat by publishing the articles in book form. He went so far as to dedicate *Mon Salon* to Cézanne himself, who was then entirely unknown to the general public.

"Do you realize," said Zola in the dedication he wrote to his old friend, "that we were revolutionaries without knowing it? I have had the opportunity of saying out loud what we have been whispering these ten years past."

CHAPTER THIRTEEN

The Scientific Eye

IN SPITE of his enthusiasm, Emile Zola was far from being an art critic. He approached painting from a literary point of view and found in the young rebels what he wished to find. It was their subject matter which interested him, and, having rejected romanticism in his own work, he was pleased to find them dealing with the realities of contemporary life. He did not understand that their most significant rebellion lay in matters of technique: in the use of light and color, in the approach to form and line. It was enough for Zola that they had abandoned the dead end of traditional painting and were recording the moods and movements of a new era. Over the years his appreciation of modern art diminished, and in the end he repudiated even Cézanne, whose mature work, subtly concerned with the re-creation of nature, he found to be incomprehensible. Perhaps it was impossible that he should have grasped the meaning of Cézanne's reduction of nature to its basic components of cone and sphere and cylinder, for by the end of the nineteenth century Cézanne had advanced well beyond the Impressionists. His influence on the future of modern art was to be profound, and echoes of his originality exist today. It is no criticism of Zola to suggest that he did not have the genius to follow in Cézanne's footsteps. He did accompany his old friend on the first stages of the revolutionary journey, although he was content to stop along the way and devote his talents to an imitation of nature—and not to a re-interpretation of it.

The definition of nature itself was being expanded rapidly in those years when modern France began. Nature had always meant more than trees and rivers, country landscapes and farmers tilling the soil, and it included all aspects of the material world. By mid-nineteenth century, however, under the impetus of the industrial revolution the material world was taking on a number of new and startling aspects. More and more often there were factories and railroads, great urban centers and complicated machines where there had been none before. The old order of agricultural Europe was gradually coming to an end, and many a peasant left the land to find work in increasingly crowded cities, forming what amounted to a new social class. The movement had begun in England during the last years of the eighteenth century, and by 1850 it was well under way in France. A new civilization was waiting, and on every side there were new facts to be absorbed and acted upon: the presence of industry, the speed of urban development, the increase in population and the varied accomplishments of science and technology. Louis Pasteur's research in microbiology and Ferdinand de Lesseps' efforts to build the Suez Canal received extensive publicity, and knowledge of other advances was brought to the attention of a wide public through newspapers and magazines and books of scientific popularization. Alexander von Humboldt's *Kosmos,* for example, appeared in five volumes between 1842 and 1865 and was translated into many languages. It was the work of a Prussian naturalist who attempted to summarize all scientific knowledge to date.

The emphasis on science gave a new direction to European thought. Disillusioned by the failure of the revolutions of 1848, a number of people were rejecting the idealism which had given birth to those revolutions and were searching for a more realistic approach to the human condition. They were receptive to any point of view which relied, not on romantic imprecision or the mythology of religion, but on fact alone: on the data of perception and on the realities of the material world. In 1859 Charles Darwin's controversial book *The Origin of Species* seemed to elevate science above accepted religion, and many Europeans were to find in science—and most particularly in a misapplication of Darwin's theories—the basis for a new philosophy. They put their faith in the scientific method and, whenever possible, applied it to business and social life. Inevitably, the concept of matter took its place as the supreme reality and informing principle of nineteenth-century thought. That concept did encourage a number of extreme views. "Man," announced a teacher at the University of Tübingen, "is not a work of God but a product of nature." It is perhaps unnecessary to add that the professor soon found himself without a job. Whether in the German states or France or England, the scientific point of view by no means gained immediate acceptance, not even among the middle-class who were to profit from it the most.

Nevertheless, the simpler aspects of the scientific method were greeted with enthusiasm by bourgeois capitalists interested in money and material progress and concerned with industry and technological improvement. However, their acceptance of it occurred at a somewhat superficial level. The changes taking place in Europe were so rapid that the average person could not grasp the wider applications of the scientific method. He could not see, for example, how it might be applied in painting or in literature. Unscientifically, he came to deny the data of his own senses, preferring to think of Europe as the abode of sunshine and happy peasants and yielding nymphs which popular art suggested it to be. The realities of the century were quite otherwise, and many shadows were falling over contemporary life. But in France the nonconformist writer and painter of the Second Empire began to apply the scientific method to his art and, by the very nature of that art, to life itself. A new school of realism was the result, and young artists devoted themselves to the truth, presenting a vision of modern life in all its ugliness and complexity. In the manner of the scientist, they dispassionately gathered facts and reproduced them with candor.

Realism was nothing new: it was evident in Chaucer's *Canterbury Tales,* the plays of Shakespeare and the picaresque novels of eighteenth-century England. To some extent it could be found in Renaissance painting and in the work of writers as different as Cervantes and Rabelais. Until the middle of the nineteenth century, however, realism did not give rise to a school and had never influenced an entire generation of painters and poets and writers. But after the abortive revolutions of 1848 a number of European intellectuals began to search for new ways of seeing and thinking consistent with the facts of a civilization which was coming to be dominated more and more by science and materialism. They soon made use of the tools which science itself was providing. In France painters like Courbet and Manet, anticipating the shift in sensibility, turned in the direction of scientific realism. It remained, however, for the prose writers of the nineteenth century to elaborate the philosophy of realism most fully and to demonstrate all the virtues and defects of the scientific method.

The novel was the most popular and successful art form of the century. This could be seen, not only in France, but in most of the other European countries as well. Newspapers and magazines had created a large reading public, and many famous novels of the day first appeared in serial form. It is only necessary to think of the work of Charles Dickens, and in France *Madame Bovary* was published originally in *La Revue de Paris*. During Louis Napoleon's régime there was an avid audience for novels, and the output was enormous. It ranged from Flaubert's social criticism to the science fiction of Jules Verne and the detective stories of Gaboriau, from the sociological novels of the later Victor Hugo to the worst kind of romantic and historical trash patterned after Alexandre Dumas. The variety was impressive and the food of novels never ending. Later in the century Emile Zola described something of the literary atmosphere of the Second Empire. "During the winter," he said, "from September to May, hardly a day passed without two or three novels pushing their way up like mushrooms from under the ground."

Of the abundant fiction published in Europe during the middle of the nineteenth century not a great deal has survived into our own day. However, the survivors are extraordinary. Among others, you will find Dickens, Thackeray and George Eliot in English; Tolstoy, Turgenev and Dostoevsky in Russian; Balzac, Zola and Flaubert in French. Many of these novelists are widely read today, and the reason for their popularity is not difficult to understand. In one form or another, much of their work reveals a particularly modern theme: man's alienation in a world dominated by things.

In France perhaps the first movement in the direction of the realistic novel came with Stendhal's *Le Rouge et le Noir,* written during the Restoration which followed Napoleon Bonaparte's final defeat. But a more consistently realistic panorama of French life is to be found in Honoré de Balzac's series of novels, *La Comédie humaine,* published between 1842 and 1848. In them he presents hundreds of characters taken from different levels of society, concentrating on a study of vice and passion and illustrating the difficulty of human relationships in a period dominated by money and power. Balzac's influence on the following generation of writers was enormous. In 1866 Emile Zola, well on his way to extending the realistic novel into the further reaches of naturalism, was invited to speak at a scientific congress in the south of France.[1] He was unable to attend, but he sent in a speech to be read at the meeting on the subject of Balzac as novelist. Balzac, he said, was "the anatomist of the soul and the flesh" and could be considered a Doctor of Moral Sciences:

> He dissects man, studies the interplay of passions, examines each fibre, analyzes the entire organism. Like a surgeon, he feels neither shame nor disgust when he plunges his hands into the wounds of humanity. His only concern is with truth, and he exhibits our heart to us on the operating-table. Modern science has presented him with the instrument of analysis and the experimental method. He proceeds like our chemists and our mathematicians.

Although these remarks apply generally to Balzac, it is apparent that Zola was indulging in a rather humorless display of self-analysis. In many ways the quotation from the speech read at Aix is a perfect definition of the naturalistic writer Zola himself came to be. The basic ideas he touches upon, however, do form a composite portrait of the nineteenth-century realistic novelist: a writer who respected science and the scientific method, although not unaware of the dangers of excessive materialism, and one who had a consuming interest in the facts of contemporary life—no matter how brutal and unpleasant they might be.

The battle for realism began in Courbet's studio on the rue Hautefeuille between the boulevard Saint Michel and the boulevard Saint Germain in the heart of intellectual and radical Paris. The café next door was called the Brasserie des Réalistes, and in his large studio Courbet surrounded himself with friends and models as interested as he was in enjoying the pleasures of the real world and in setting down on canvas and on paper all of its life and vitality. That vitality contained in equal measure the ugly and the beautiful, and Courbet and his fellow artists did not hesitate to record the shadows and blemishes of contemporary life. In describing *The Stonebreakers,* one of his early paintings, Courbet stated the case for realism clearly enough. "I have invented nothing," he said. "I saw the wretched people in this picture every day as I went on my walks."

Something of the atmosphere of Courbet's circle can be felt in his enormous painting *The Studio,* one of the works rejected by the Salon at the time of the Paris Exposition of 1855. It is a rather contrived image of the contemporary scene, the realism that had been denied in every square inch of canvas hanging in exhibitions at the Palais de l'Industrie. In the middle of the painting Courbet is seated at his easel, watched by a nude model and an admiring child. A dog and a cat are playing on the floor, and on one side of the room there is a group of Latin Quarter students dressed in the costumes of mid-nineteenth-century France: as beggars, priests, cloth merchants, professional mourners, unemployed workers. On the other side of the room we find a number of Courbet's friends and fellow artists—among them, the novelist Champfleury and the poet Baudelaire, who is absorbed in reading a book. Though not in the painting, the well-known photographer Nadar, Flaubert and the brothers Goncourt were also frequent visitors to his studio.

Jules Husson, who chose Champfleury as his nom de plume, has been described as the father of realism in the French novel. Perhaps it would be more accurate to think of him as one of its earliest and most enthusiastic exponents. In 1856 he published—before running out of money—two issues of *La Gazette de Champfleury,* a manifesto of realism. And there is little doubt that he wrote the program notes for Courbet's personal Salon des Refusés in 1855, in them sketching out a basic definition of realism in the arts. Like many of his intellectual circle, Champfleury was excited by the recently developed art of the daguerreotype, sensing that some of the methods of photography could be applied to writing and to painting. Surely it is no coincidence that the first exhibition of the Impressionists took place in 1874 in Nadar's studio on the boulevard des Capucines.[2] Champfleury himself wrote a number of now forgotten novels which use elements of photographic realism: novels like *Les Aventures de Mademoiselle Mariette,* published in 1853 and containing a much less sentimentalized version of the *vie de Bohème* than could have been found in Henri Murger's stories of Rodolphe and Mimi. For all his activity at the center of the battle of realism, Champfleury remained a minor novelist, ending his career on an unexpected note of conformity as the director of the State Porcelain Factory at Sèvres.

Far more significant in the history of French realism are

the brothers Goncourt, figures central to the social and intellectual life of the Second Empire. In a characteristic moment of self-congratulation they announced that there were only four honest writers in the whole of France: Gustave Flaubert, Charles Baudelaire and themselves. They pointed out that all four had been brought before a police tribunal, and they had been attacked by readers and critics alike. Their offense? Only to have displeased the middle class by setting down some of the realities of the world in which they lived. Although they were charged with having offended public morality, the charges served to obscure the fact that they were being punished for entertaining radical points of view which moved against the grain of the establishment. Like so many of their friends, they belonged to the new school of realism.

Writing in collaboration, Jules and Edmond de Goncourt had begun their careers with historical studies of life in the eighteenth century. They soon turned their attention to the contemporary world, bringing to the modern novel their methods of historical research. Between them they developed the technique of the *roman documentaire,* the naturalistic novel based on the facts of real life and brought to its ultimate perfection by Zola in the last quarter of the nineteenth century. More and more often in the course of their career, research carried the Goncourts into the poorer sections of Paris, and they filled their journal with descriptions of the ugliness which lay hidden behind Louis Napoleon's façades. Perhaps their best novel, and a good example of the *roman documentaire,* is *Germinie Lacerteux,* the story of a servant girl whose secret life of vice and debauchery led at last to her death in the workhouse. The novel, published in 1864 and much admired by Zola himself, aroused the wrath of the critics and was considered offensive by most readers. The middle-class public had no particular quarrel with the techniques of the realistic novel; but it objected violently to the subject matter chosen by authors who were focusing their attention increasingly on poverty and other sordid aspects of life. It is true that many writers were motivated by the desire to shock a complacent middle class and add some provocative note of drama to their work. But the fact remains that despair and poverty and vice were the disturbing realities of modern life, and no honest writer could afford to ignore them. Flaubert and Baudelaire and the Goncourts were criticized not for their immorality—even Princess Mathilde could find little immoral about *Madame Bovary* —but for their insistence on presenting the real world to an audience which did not care to acknowledge it. It was apparent that the revelation of vice and poverty and hypocrisy constituted an attack on the structure of middle-class society itself. However, in all honesty there was no other course for the realistic novelist to follow.

Although he never considered himself a realist, Gustave Flaubert emerged as the finest of the new writers, demonstrating qualities of style and depths of psychological insight not reached by Zola or the Goncourts. In spite of a desire to dissociate himself from the exponents of realism and naturalism, he occupied a position at the heart of nineteenth-century avant-garde literature—a position which assured him of automatic rejection by the middle-class public. Although acquitted, he and the editors of *La Revue de Paris* were brought to trial in 1856 after the magazine had published *Madame Bovary* in serial form. The scandal attached to the trial turned his novel into something of a best-seller, and Flaubert soon came to be classified as one of the new realists. Commenting on *Madame Bovary* in *Le Moniteur,* the influential literary critic Sainte Beuve sketched a portrait of the author: "M. Gus-

tave Flaubert holds the pen as others hold the scalpel."
And there is a famous drawing by the caricaturist Lemot
in which Flaubert is shown standing over Emma Bovary's
body laid out on the operating table. He is brandishing
her heart at the end of an autopsy knife, and here we have
the same scientific imagery used by Zola to describe Balzac. It is not surprising to learn that both Flaubert's father
and brother were physicians and—again to use Zola's terminology—Flaubert himself might well be described as a
Doctor of Moral Sciences. No matter what he said to the
contrary, *Madame Bovary* is a realistic novel—realistic in
its portrayal of middle-class society under the July Monarchy and realistic in its psychological analysis of Emma
Bovary, whose heart's corruption came from the un-
breachable distance between dream and reality. In any
event, Flaubert did not deny the merits of realism. "The
greatest art," he said, "is scientific and impersonal."

This statement does little to explain the brilliances of
Madame Bovary, but it does point up the technique employed by more and more writers as the nineteenth century progressed. On every side there were new justifica-
tions for the use of the scientific method, and it became a
commonplace to equate the writer and the medical man.
In 1865 one of the most influential books written during
the course of the Second Empire was published by the
physiologist Claude Bernard. His *Introduction to Experimental Medicine* was taken as gospel and often misap-
plied by followers of the naturalistic school—particularly
by Emile Zola. A professor of medicine at the Sorbonne,
Bernard had carried out important research on liver function and the vasomotor system, and in the last years of the
empire Louis Napoleon built a laboratory for him in the
Natural History Museum at the Jardin des Plantes. In the
Introduction to Experimental Medicine Bernard described

the nature of research and outlined the rôle of the scientist. Medicine, he felt, was entirely a matter of experiment and observation, and he pointed out as well that many diseases could be explained in terms of heredity and environment.

When writing *Les Rougon-Macquart,* his cycle of novels describing various aspects of French life during the reign of Louis Napoleon, Zola fell with enthusiasm upon Bernard's concept of heredity as well as upon the techniques set forth in the book for gathering and classifying material.[3] The application of science to literature was not Zola's alone, and in the course of the nineteenth century more and more forms of writing came to be influenced by elements of the scientific method. In 1863, for example, Hippolyte Taine made the famous remark in the preface to his history of English literature that virtue and vice were simply products of nature "like vitriol or sugar." Even Sainte Beuve developed a quasi-scientific approach to criticism by studying the life and cultural background of the authors he reviewed. His weekly column of literary criticism appeared on Mondays during almost the whole of the Second Empire in important newspapers like *Le Temps* and *Le Moniteur* and *Le Constitutionnel.*[4] Ernest Renan, historian and philologist, was professor of Hebrew at the Collège de France and in 1863 published the first volume of his controversial *Vie de Jésus,* a biographical and psychological work of realism which set Christ in historical context and in many ways denied the validity of the Bible story. The historian Jules Michelet, whose *History of France* is often romantic and subjective, nevertheless approached original documents with scientific precision. His training had made such an approach inevitable: for many years he had been Keeper of the National Archives, and toward the end of his career he wrote several perceptive books on natural science.[5] During the last half of the nineteenth century a growing number of talented Frenchmen was drawn in the direction of scientific research—learning to apply that modern discipline to history and criticism, to poetry and religious thought, to painting and fiction. "Anatomists and physiologists," said Sainte Beuve, "I see you everywhere!"

The thrust toward realism had predictable political results: like the rebellious artists and writers, Renan and Michelet soon incurred the displeasure of the establishment, and both of them lost their chairs at the Collège de France through opposition to the imperial government. The impartiality of the scientific method did not encourage acceptance of the empire and only served to turn a cold light on its many inconsistencies.

Combining the roles of social critic and journalist, historian and novelist, Emile Zola himself turned the coldest light of all on the weaknesses of the Second Empire. Almost his entire literary career was devoted to a study of French life during the reign of Louis Napoleon. And perhaps in the work of no other contemporary writer can one find the scientific interests of the age put forward so clearly and the results of the intellectual battle for realism illustrated so completely. There is little doubt that Zola came to think of himself as a scientist in the manner of Dr. Claude Bernard, for example, although fortunately he very often managed to transcend the limitations of pseudoscience which he imposed on his work. Whatever prejudices and misconceptions may be found in the twenty novels comprising *Les Rougon-Macquart,* they do form a portrait of Second Empire society which cannot be equaled in richness and depth. It is true enough that all the novels were published between 1871 and 1893 after the empire had fallen, but they have an air of immediacy which surely can be traced to the scientific methods used

237

by Zola in gathering material. His naturalistic approach was a logical extension of realism, and in many instances the novels are literally case histories. This was a technique the Goncourt brothers and Champfleury and even Flaubert had used before him. Novel by novel, Zola built up a dossier of Second-Empire social history, recording all aspects of business life and urban poverty and considering art as well as the development of industry. The completed work—reaching its thematic culmination in *La Débâcle*—is a summary of the political and social and military factors which led to the collapse of an entire civilization.

From the beginning Zola aroused the antagonism of most critics and took his place as one of the exponents of that new *"littérature putride"* which was concentrating on the unpleasant aspects of contemporary life. In 1864 his first novel, *La Confession de Claude,* was dismissed as an example of "hideous" realism, and the suspected immorality of the author came to the attention of the establishment. Zola's rooms on the boulevard Montparnasse were searched, and the police asked questions at Hachette, the book shop where he worked. In the end no charges were brought against him, but Zola felt under a moral obligation to resign from his job. From that moment on he devoted his time to free-lance journalism and to his own writing, and two years later his second novel appeared. The reception given *Thérèse Raquin* was predictably hostile, since, among other disturbing elements of realism, it dealt with a particularly gruesome murder. Critics soon understood the extent to which he had been influenced by the rebellious new painters who scorned traditional rules. "M. Zola," said a writer for *Le Figaro,* "sees women as M. Manet paints them, mud-colored with pink make-up."

There is little doubt that Zola's friendship with the avant-garde painters led him to look at the contemporary

scene under a new light. In that second decade of the empire he saw the magnificent materials of modern life
which lay all around him, waiting only for a scientific
synthesis. While still under thirty and in every popular
sense an unsuccessful writer, Zola had the courage to con-
ceive the entire ambitious plan of *Les Rougon-Macquart.*
As early as 1868 he began to read all the medical and scientific books he could find, seeking some logical explanation for the movements of the modern world. At the same
time he took elaborate notes on the various crafts and businesses and professions characteristic of the Second Empire. He described slums and tenements and urban poverty and set down the argot of the poor; he took notes on
hotels and theaters and department stores; he documented
the shadow world of the demimonde and gathered material on politics and the army and the Stock Exchange.
There was no detail too small or too sordid to escape his
scientific eye, and through the massive accumulation of
fact he provided himself with the background necessary to
write an epic of contemporary French life. He wished to
achieve nothing less than a comprehensive portrait of
every phase of Second Empire society, explaining the
weaknesses and triumphs of its people in terms of heredity
and environment. As he pointed out in the preface of
Thérèse Raquin, his goal had always been "a scientific
one." In the spring of 1869 he set about writing the first
novel of the series, *La Fortune des Rougon,* a study of
provincial life after the coup d'état which brought Louis
Napoleon to power.

It was no part of Zola's plan that the Second Empire
should so soon become recorded history instead of contemporary life. The end of the empire, while more than
agreeable to Zola the citizen, had some unhappy effects on
Zola the novelist. Since most of his novels were written in

the 1870s and 1880s, he was guilty of a number of inconsistencies and often mixed the facts of the Third Republic with those of the Second Empire. Much of his antagonism to the evils of government under Louis Napoleon seemed outdated when applied to social abuses which had been corrected to a degree by the final years of the century. It is ironic that some of these abuses were being rectified even as the empire came to an end. For example, the brutal working conditions seen in the coal mines of *Germinal* are not really factual either in terms of history or within the context of the Third Republic. Although unscientific, Zola's description is nonetheless compelling as a literary symbol of exploitation and oppression. His criticism of Louis Napoleon's government was often overstated, but *Les Rougon-Macquart* is almost exactly what the subtitle suggests it to be: "The Natural and Social History of a Family under the Second Empire"—a thoroughly documented study of five generations of Rougons and Macquarts who lived their lives at every level of society in the transitional years when modern France was born.

   L'Assommoir (*The Tavern* or *The Drinking Den*), published in 1877, was the first novel in the cycle to bring Zola fortune and success. Its subject matter and method of composition clearly reveal his scientific eye and naturalistic bent. In the Bibliothèque Nationale there are two octavo volumes containing the manuscript of the novel as well as some of the notes the author made in preparation for writing it. Since the book deals with drink and poverty and the life of the poor, there are detailed notes on alcoholism and descriptions of streets and cabarets and dance-halls, small shops and public laundries in the slums of Paris. There are contemporary newspaper clippings and some forty pages of working-class slang. Most of this material found its way into the completed novel—particularly the language of the poor, which Zola used not only in dialogue but in many narrative passages as well, something of a stylistic innovation for his day. The central characters are Gervaise and Coupeau, a laundress and a roofer, whose lives are joined at first by love and then by despair. Destroyed through the effects of alcohol and poverty, they play out their unhappy rôles in the ruined quarter of Paris lying between the porte de la Chapelle and the gare du Nord, their horizons limited by a slaughterhouse on one side and a charity hospital on the other.

Zola's realism is stark, and he has painted a vast canvas of vice and poverty and hopelessness against the background of decayed buildings and filthy streets. The author's scientific eye is frank and brutal: Coupeau's dance of delirium tremens in the Lariboisière Hospital is one of the heartbreaking images of the book, as is the final disintegration of Gervaise herself. Having lost everything, she is reduced to selling the wool from her mattress to the second-hand dealers on the rue Belhomme for a few sous. Her death is almost unbearable, as Zola points to its real cause: not malnutrition or alcohol, but an accumulation of filth and weariness and poverty. Her last days are spent in a sort of closet under the stairs of the tenement on the rue de la Goutte d'Or:

> According to the Lorilleuxs, she died like a pig in its sty. One morning, noticing a bad smell in the corridor, folks remembered that she had not been seen for two days. They found her in her cubbyhole already turning green.

A pervasive theme dominates *L'Assommoir,* and it is the same pervasive theme which dominates the whole of the Second Empire: the paradox of poverty in the midst of overwhelming luxury. Woven into the fabric of the novel are descriptions of the great new capital being built by Louis Napoleon—a city, in Zola's words, "so brilliant with gilt and glitter." But all the façades of empire could not hide those accusing streets where vice and poverty denied every success of business and finance and industry. Zola's factual material led him to an inevitable conclusion, and hatred of the Second Empire was the result. His twenty novels form the portrait of a rotting society, a society sick with greed and materialism and indifference.

Surely someone was responsible for the wasted lives of *L'Assommoir,* and Zola put the blame firmly on the ruling caste presided over by Louis Napoleon. Descending on Paris in search of pillage and money, its members had left little in their wake but despair and poverty. Greed became more obvious the higher one went in society, and for Zola the symbol of that decadence was *la curée:* a word describing the part of an animal thrown to the hounds after a hunt and freely translated as "the spoils." In fact, it is the title of one of the novels in *Les Rougon-Macquart.* And in another novel, *Son Excellence Eugène Rougon,* largely devoted to court life, Zola set down a description of *la curée* as it regularly took place at Compiègne during the hunting season. After dinner the hounds would be brought into the courtyard of the château and the spoils of the hunt were distributed by grooms. Under the torchlight the hungry animals swarmed over the remains of a stag, for example, in a frenzy to devour everything. Above them Louis Napoleon's guests watched in silence, and the only sound came from the crunching of bones below:

> On the balcony and at the window, satisfaction showed itself in the tight smiles of the ladies, clenching their white teeth, and in the heavy breathing of the gentlemen, bright-eyed, twisting toothpicks they had brought away with them from the banqueting hall.

242

In miniature this was Zola's vision of the Second Empire. And although he approached his subject with the scientific tools of realism and naturalism, he was unable to maintain any degree of impartiality. His cycle of novels is a savage indictment of the régime and all its works. In *Les Rougon-Macquart,* as in the paintings of Daumier and Courbet, there is a hatred of oppression as well as the artist's sympathy for the poor and the outcast. That sympathy presupposed a denial of authoritarian government and middle-class supremacy, the twin foundations upon which Louis Napoleon's empire rested. Zola's antagonism often led him into extremes of invective: in *L'Assommoir,* for example, he describes a scandalous book printed in Belgium on the subject of the emperor's sex life. One of the illustrations showed Louis Napoleon, wearing hardly more than the ribbon of the Légion d'Honneur, in lustful pursuit of a little girl.

There is a grim appropriateness to the fact that Zola should have used the techniques of science to condemn a society given over to materialism and the worship of progress. Indeed, the ambiguity of progress is one of the striking features of the last half of the nineteenth century, a period when spiritual development fell far short of the advances of science and technology. The phenomenon was not uniquely French, although Zola's distaste for Louis Napoleon and the masquerades of his régime obscured much of the larger significance of *Les Rougon-Macquart.* The novels comprising it illustrate a theme by no means restricted to the twenty years of the Second Empire. Like Baudelaire and Flaubert and certain of the avant-garde painters, Zola can have a special appeal to the twentieth century, not for the analysis of an era long gone and forgotten, but for a realistic appraisal of modern life. The civilization created by the industrial revolution is with us still, and from the beginning it put a dangerous emphasis on science and materialism. Often that emphasis was sustained at the expense of human values, and the failures of a machine age have provided endless material for poets and painters and novelists in the hundred years which followed the coup d'état of 1851. During that period the triumphs of science and technology created more serious problems than they solved, and the French school of realism flourished under the impact of this paradox. By the middle of the nineteenth century many areas of European society were beginning to be dominated by mechanical objects and man-made things, and the stencil of the future had been cut.

Throughout *Les Rougon-Macquart* Zola gives life to a number of inanimate objects: the department store in *Au Bonheur des dames,* the food markets in *Le Ventre de Paris,* the locomotive in *La Bête humaine,* the coal mine in *Germinal,* the still in *L'Assommoir* and Paris itself in *Une Page d'amour.* Little by little these things of steel and iron and glass were destroying the men who made them, and the materialistic environment of the modern world was crushing their humanity. Zola to the contrary, the cruelties and indifferences of an urban civilization cannot be blamed on Louis Napoleon alone. The impersonality of money and machinery was creating new faces of terror in the industrialized countries of Europe, and realists who studied the meaning of contemporary life were united in their vision of despair.

In France it remained for Charles Baudelaire, a greater artist than Zola, to diagnose the nature of the human condition at the threshold of the twentieth century.

CHAPTER FOURTEEN

Flowers of Evil

C HARLES BAUDELAIRE addressed the first harsh lines of
Les Fleurs du mal to his reader:

> La sottise, l'erreur, le péché, la lésine,
> Occupent nos esprits et travaillent nos corps,
> Et nous alimentons nos aimables remords,
> Comme les mendiants nourrissent leur vermine.*

This point of view could scarcely have recommended his
poems to a public which delighted in the paintings of
Bouguereau and the novels of Octave Feuillet, in the operettas of Offenbach and the waltzes of Métra. Baudelaire's
volume of poetry was published in 1857, the year following the Congress of Paris which had ended the Crimean
War: Louis Napoleon's prestige was at its height, the régime's most prosperous and glamorous years were beginning and almost every area of French life was dominated

* Infatuation, sadism, lust, avarice
  possess our souls and drain the body's force;
  we spoonfeed our adorable remorse,
  like whores or beggars nourishing their lice.
  Translated by ROBERT LOWELL

245

by the middle class. However appropriate Baudelaire's words may seem to the twentieth century, it is not surprising that *Les Fleurs du mal,* the work of a relatively unknown and entirely dissipated writer, should have offended the arbiters of the Second Empire. If nothing else, the style was "unpoetic" to the highest degree: it was a mixture of archaic and colloquial language, and much of its imagery was taken from the most sordid aspects of everyday life. *Les Fleurs du mal* confused the contemporary reader, but it is strange that Baudelaire should have been depressed by the adverse criticism his work received. There have been few authors in any era more intoxicated with the desire to displease or more sustained by an aristocratic belief that poetry was for the initiated alone.

Like other anti-establishment artists and writers of the day, he devoted his life to a rebellion against the canons of middle-class taste—at first, like Cézanne, through his conduct and then, like Manet, through his work. That defiance took many forms and ranged from painting his head green to wearing exotic clothes and experimenting with drugs. Such gestures, however, have no more significance than Barbey d'Aurevilly's habit of walking a lobster on a leash along the Grands Boulevards. If Baudelaire's defiance of society had taken no other direction, he would be remembered today, if at all, as a minor curiosity in a city crowded with polished eccentrics. The fact remains that Baudelaire was one of the first and most subtle analysts of the modern sensibility, and his poetry represents a turning point in the history of literature. As Victor Hugo said, he was responsible for creating *"un frisson nouveau,"* a new wave in contemporary writing. His influence on the succeeding generation of symbolist poets cannot be overstated, and modern writers from Apollinaire to T. S. Eliot have learned from him. He is one of the few creative artists of any period whose work may be called germinal. That he should have appeared in Paris during the high noon of the Second Empire is not as strange as it may seem on the surface. The cultural awakening which accompanied the decline of the Second Empire cannot be denied. The age of Louis Napoleon saw the beginning, not only of modern French industry and finance and social reform, but of modern poetry and painting and fiction as well. Baudelaire was among the first of his contemporaries to have understood the implications of the future and to have set an intellectual course for the twentieth century. He freely admitted that he had been inspired by the Muse of Modern Times, and that rebellious daughter of Zeus provided him with an unusual clarity of vision.

In every sense his personal life was tragic and wasted, and he fought a losing battle against the bourgeois establishment which controlled so much of the world into which he had been born. The symbol of everything he despised in the middle class is to be found in the person of his mother's second husband and his own hated stepfather: the reactionary Colonel (later General) Aupick, Chevalier de Saint Louis, officer of the Légion d'Honneur and aide-de-camp to Prince von Hohenlohe. At the time of his mother's remarriage in 1828 Baudelaire was only seven years old, but a long and hopeless rebellion began almost immediately. His early history is one of loneliness and melancholy, of problems at home and difficulties at school. However, by the 1840s he had achieved some measure of freedom and was leading the undisciplined life of a Latin Quarter student.

These were the years when the *vie de Bohème* was at its most appealing. The boulevard Saint Germain and the boulevard Saint Michel had not been built as yet, and the Left Bank of the Seine was a maze of dirty narrow streets where students with long hair and beards wandered around in velvet hats and bedroom slippers. Perhaps for the first time in his life Baudelaire was happy. The atmosphere was immensely congenial: all the young men were in revolt against society, and they proclaimed their new freedom by going to bed with careless *grisettes* and now and then enjoying the oblivion of opium or hashish.[1] They admired eccentricity for its own sake and in their innocence equated disorder with genius. It was not long before General Aupick came to the conclusion that the *vie de Bohème* was having an unfortunate effect on his stepson. The boy was strange enough to begin with, and the general decided to send him on a long sea voyage to India in the interests of his mental health. Baudelaire stayed with the ship until it touched at Réunion in the Indian Ocean and inevitably made his way back to Paris.

It was 1842, and the lonely and unhappy young man had come of age. On his twenty-first birthday he received an inheritance from his long-dead father—an inheritance he used to turn himself into a dandy on the model of the elegant Roger de Beauvoir, romantic novelist and boulevardier. This was the only period when Baudelaire had any money at all and, brief though it may have been, he indulged his tastes for the bizarre to the limit.[2] He acquired an apartment on the Ile Saint Louis in the same building in which Beauvoir lived and furnished it in a manner more appropriate to the *fin de siècle* than to the middle of the nineteenth century. He spent a great deal of money on clothes: one day he would be seen in a sky-blue coat with silver buttons and primrose vest, and on the next he would be wearing a black velvet tunic caught in at the waist with a golden belt. He began using opium and ether and hashish—as well as alcohol—to excess.[3] And he frequented popular gathering places like the Café Procope and the Closerie des Lilas, where he delighted in shocking anyone who cared to listen to him. On one occasion he turned to a young woman at the table next to his and announced that he had a compelling desire to bite into her white flesh. "And if you will permit me," he continued, "I'll tell you how I'd like to make love to you. I'd like to take your two hands, bind them together, and then tie you up by your wrists to the ceiling of my room!"

Even Cézanne had not shocked the bourgeoisie so elaborately, and Baudelaire threw himself into the rôle of satanic dandy with enthusiasm. This outlandish period did not last very long, and by 1844 he had spent half of the seventy-five thousand francs left to him by his father. At the insistence of his family, Baudelaire's financial affairs were put in the hands of a lawyer, who gave him a small monthly allowance. From this moment on, poverty dominated his life, and for the first time he turned seriously to writing in order to supplement his income. He wrote a certain amount of perceptive art criticism on the Salon exhibitions of the 1840s, and by the end of the decade he had fallen under the spell of Edgar Allan Poe and was translating his work into French. At the same time he was writing some of the poems which were to appear ten years later as *Les Fleurs du mal*. Almost from the beginning he took a stand in favor of modern art, and in the course of his career he devoted time to the defense of such controversial figures as Manet and Thomas De Quincey and Richard Wagner, whose operas were to have an enormous influence on French poetry.

In his tormented mind he was arranging the elements of what he called "modernity." And in focusing his attention on contemporary life—and particularly on the new urban environment—he was aligning himself with realists in other branches of the arts. If indeed he can be called a

realist, it was a higher realism which he practiced: a form
of realism dealing, in his own words, with "the tragedy of
being human" and the painful experiences of the subconscious mind. Baudelaire is not so much a poet as an event
in the history of literature, a revolutionary who opened a
way into the future and found in every phase of ordinary
life reflections of beauty, even in the consideration of ugliness and decay. That higher realism found its first recognition in 1886 when Jean Moréas published the Symbolist
Manifesto in the literary supplement of *Le Figaro*. Moréas
acknowledged that the new symbolist poetry being written by Mallarmé and Jules Laforgue and Tristan Corbière
had its origins in an earlier generation of ignored and neglected poets. Rimbaud and Verlaine and especially Baudelaire, like those young painters who worked against the
grain during the Second Empire, had created a new idiom
capable of expressing the tensions and problems of modern
life—taking their images from the subconscious mind as
well as from the real world. For Baudelaire the result was
a dark and personal vision of the human condition and
the kind of pessimism unacceptable to the pleasure-seekers
of the Second Empire. He was one of the first of the nineteenth-century French poets to deal with the spiritual experiences of modern man, and the price he paid for his
clarity of vision was despair and final madness. But his
reward was to have set down with elegance, not only the
movements of a vanished era, but the essential features of
the human spirit captive in a world of indifference and
evil and crushing materialism.

In the brief compass of *Les Fleurs du mal* are to be
found all the reflections of Baudelaire's unique and unset-
tling genius. If he had written nothing else, his place in
literary history would be secure. Into these poems, as he
himself said, he poured all his thought and his heart and

his hatred. The publication of *Les Fleurs du mal* in 1857 brought him to the attention of the establishment for the first time, and he soon found himself charged with having offended public morality. He was summoned to the Palais de Justice and the dreary Sixième Chambre Correction-nelle with its dirty green wallpaper and dusty windows. There, among beggars and tramps and derelicts accused of indecent assault, he waited his turn until called at last before the same Imperial Prosecutor who had presided at Flaubert's trial six months earlier. For the outrage committed against public morals Baudelaire was fined three hundred francs and his publisher, Poulet-Malassis, two hundred. Six of the poems in *Les Fleurs du mal* were to be deleted in any future edition, since it was the judg-ment of the court that they were "obscene" and "im-moral."

Baudelaire was crushed by the decision, although Victor Hugo took the occasion to write him a letter from the Channel island of Guernsey, where he was spending his exile. "May I congratulate you?" he said. "One of the few decorations which the present régime can grant, it has be-stowed on you."

Victor Hugo's opinion was not widely shared, unless by Bohemians like Cézanne, who soon committed all the poems to memory. A damaging review in *Le Figaro* seemed to sum up the reaction of the literary establish-ment, although its author was forced to acknowledge something of Baudelaire's talent:

Never have so many brilliant qualities been squan-dered. There are moments when one has doubts of the sanity of Monsieur Baudelaire, but there are others, on the contrary, when no doubt is possible. . . . The whole volume is an asylum full of all the inanities of the human mind, of all the putrescence of the human heart.

This refrain was to have been expected: Baudelaire, like Flaubert and Zola and the Goncourts, had displeased the traditionalists by emphasizing the ugly realities of modern life. He had gone even further by emphasizing the ugly realities of the human spirit. Critics schooled in Cartesian logic could not deal with the idioms of the new sensibility, and Baudelaire was attacked for filling his poems with obscure and decadent imagery. It was also obvious that on one level he was putting forward an indictment of the Second Empire. The pessimism associated with a realistic view of modern life led many writers to engage in savage criticism of the imperial government. But Baudelaire's meaning was more general: it was not so much his desire to attack the social and political corruptions of the day as to suggest the larger issue of man's ambiguous position in a cruel and indifferent environment. Zola used many symbols to describe the materialistic civilization of the nineteenth century, but Baudelaire concentrated on one compelling image: the great city of Paris itself.

Baudelaire's Paris is a disturbing city. It is partly the city which appeared in the engravings of Charles Méryon, who died in the madhouse of Charenton in 1868 and who composed a strange picture of Paris which had nothing to do with the eagles and trumpets of the Second Empire. It was a city of horrors, both real and imagined—a city sharing the features of the Medieval Wasteland and Dante's Limbo and T. S. Eliot's London:

> Unreal City,
> Under the brown fog of a winter dawn,
> A crowd flowed over London Bridge, so many,
> I had not thought death had undone so many.[4]

For Baudelaire, as for T. S. Eliot, the modern metropolis becomes the symbol of modern civilization itself. Jules Laforgue suggests that Baudelaire was the first of the French poets "to speak of Paris like any ordinary lost soul of the capital," the first to see "the street lamps tormented by the wind." Friends often found him wandering in different sections of Paris, alone in the middle of Europe's gayest city and uttering remarks like: "I am watching an endless procession of death's heads."

Whatever the larger applications, his vision was a personal one, and he felt that in the context of the great modern city the meaning of his life—or its lack of meaning—could be explored most successfully. He had always been enchanted by Paris, and he spent many long hours walking its streets, studying its people and its buildings and its nervous rhythms. In the manner of an Impressionist painter he set down some of the chaotic images of everyday life and tried to discover in these fugitive moments of time the essentials of the human condition. After his death the rough draft of a poem was found among his papers. It is dedicated to the city of Paris, and he had planned to put it at the head of a new edition of *Les Fleurs du mal*. One line reads: *"Tu m'as donné ta boue, et j'en ai fait de l'or"* ("You gave me your filth, and I turned it into gold").

Out of the street's sad mud came gold, and one of his finest evocations of the city is to be found in *Les Fleurs du mal* in that group of poems known as the *Tableaux parisiens*. Symbolically they suggest the poverty and despair with which Zola filled the many thousand pages of *Les Rougon-Macquart,* and realistically they duplicate the Paris recorded by Daumier and Constantin Guys and the photographer Nadar. Above everything else Baudelaire had a clear sense of the meaning of the era in which he lived, and in describing certain aspects of Second Empire

Paris he underlined not only his own spiritual and emotional frustrations, but those of contemporary man as well.

Comprising a miniature dance of death, the *Tableaux parisiens* reveal the inner and outer landscapes of the modern city. For the first time the sights and sounds of an industrial metropolis were added to the subject matter of French poetry. It is the same material which Daumier and Courbet and Manet gave to the vocabulary of French painting. And Baudelaire becomes one of the earliest poets to deal with themes basic to the twentieth century: the movements of the city and the life of the poor and the disinherited. In the *Tableaux parisiens* we are taken on a tour of the capital, moving from morning to evening and from evening to dawn along the crowded streets. It is a harsh landscape which Baudelaire has chosen to paint: the mists rising over the river, the winter fogs and the autumn rains, the lighting of the gas lamps in the evening, the springtime mud and the night itself coming in on a "soft wolf tread." A procession of the hopeless and the defeated weaves through the twilight landscape—the blind and the sick, the red-haired beggar girl, innumerable old men and women, murderers and drunkards, prostitutes and ragpickers shuffling through the lost quarters of Paris.

This legion of the damned makes its way against a background of stone: bridges and theaters and hospitals, cheap hotels and graveyards, brothels and apartment houses and palaces under construction. All around are the noises of the city: the rattle of carriage wheels, the songs on a street corner, the bugles at dawn, the music of a military band and the sound of a violin trembling like a soul in pain. One disturbing image follows another: the sun draped in black, drunken revelers staggering through the first light of day, carrion on the road, gypsies and skele-

254

tons and Creole women, black cats and owls and prison bars. Over all a foul yellow mist rises through the January sleet, and the poet has laid bare the clogged heart of the city—a city quite unlike the lovely capital which Louis Napoleon and his prefect of the Seine had erected to astonish the world and herald the wonders of the Second Empire:

> Fourmillante cité, cité plein de rêves,
> Où le spectre, en plein jour, raccroche le passant.*

There is a harsh beauty to Baudelaire's vision of Paris, and he has set down a number of the realities of modern life, capturing its ambiguity and its unresolved conflicts between ecstasy and horror and—its pain.

In that disdainful city there could be found no one more hopeless or damned than the poet himself, a wanderer sentenced to live in a world that was half dream and half reality. One day he wakes from a vision of black marble palaces and fountains gushing gold and enchanted rivers with banks of jade to find himself still in a "cheap and sordid hole." From beyond the window of his shabby room come the realities of Paris—and of life itself:

> La pendule aux accents funèbres
> Sonnait brutalement midi,
> Et le ciel versait des ténèbres
> Sur le triste monde engourdi.†

---

* Ant-seething city, city full of dreams,
  Where ghosts by daylight tug the passer's sleeve.
                    Translated by ROY CAMPBELL
† Brutally the twelve strokes of noon
  Against my naked ear were hurled;
  And a grey sky was drizzling down
  Upon this sad, lethargic world.
        Translated by EDNA ST. VINCENT MILLAY

The pain of living, intensified by the brutal environment of the modern city, filled Baudelaire's personal life with sex and drugs and hallucinations. The same pain filled his poetry with images of death and exile and long voyages over water.[5] An escape into oblivion is perhaps his final solution to the neurosis of modern life, imperfect and romantic as that solution may be. He longed to sleep like a shark in some anonymous ocean wave.[6]

His originality notwithstanding, Baudelaire was far from being unique among contemporary poets in his awareness of the pain and ugliness of modern life. In fact, a great deal of the poetry written during the Second Empire had rejected the idealism and imprecision of an earlier romantic school and was moving, even more rapidly than the new painting and fiction, in the direction of realism. Two groups of poets dominate the period: the Parnassians, who used the methods of an age of science to retreat into the antique past, and those more original and experimental writers like Verlaine and Rimbaud and Mallarmé who suggested the enigmas of modern life in a new language of symbolic realism. Inevitably, the second group—those *poètes maudits* among whom Baudelaire must be counted—formed the vanguard of twentieth-century European and American poetry. However melancholy their vision may have been, time has proved its accuracy, and there is truth in Shelley's remark that poets are the unacknowledged legislators of the world.

Leconte de Lisle, considered the major figure of the Parnassian school, was as sensitive as Baudelaire to the cruelties and vulgarities of the transitional time in which they both lived. He felt as keenly the hollowness of an urban industrial civilization. "I hate this day and age," he said with characteristic pessimism, and he and his followers turned their backs upon it. Unlike Baudelaire, who also chose escape, they did not seek their inspiration in the movements of the present. Instead, they looked to the ancient days of Greece and Rome and found their imagery in the exotic lands of the East. In 1866 an editor brought the work of some thirty-five of them together in a volume called *Le Parnasse contemporain*—a roll call of Second Empire poets in reaction to romanticism. The Parnassians concentrated on perfection of form and scientifically impersonal description, and they had been influenced by Théophile Gautier's *Emaux et Camées,* a collection of serene and impassive poems published in 1852. Gautier himself was represented in the new volume, as were others who wrote in a similar vein: naturally, Leconte de Lisle, Théodore de Banville and José Maria de Heredia as well. In *Le Parnasse contemporain,* however, there were several less serene and detached poets—among them, Baudelaire and Verlaine and Mallarmé—and the two directions of contemporary poetry were to be seen at the same time and in the same place. Although the Parnassian poets used the impersonal approach of science, their art otherwise gave back no reflection of the age in which they lived and it came finally to the dead end of Art for Art's Sake.

That divorce from the compelling problems of the nineteenth century and the larger issue of life's meaning can be found in the work of one of the most elegant and accomplished of the Parnassian poets. Born in Cuba of a French mother, José Maria de Heredia represents the ultimate failure of a school which acknowledged the ugliness of the contemporary world only by retreating from it. He had written poems throughout the Second Empire, but his work was not collected until 1893, when *Les Trophées* appeared. This was a group of exquisite sonnets dealing with Greece and Rome, the Middle Ages and the Renaissance and various countries of the Orient. In the cool and sculptural perfection of his art Heredia made no commitment to the modern world and ended by working in a vacuum as complete as the one which surrounded academic Salon painters and *fin de siècle* novelists like J.-K. Huysmans.

In 1884, some ten years before Heredia's collection of sonnets appeared, Paul Verlaine published a volume of essays called *Les Poètes maudits*. It described and quoted selections from those ignored and misunderstood poets who had begun their careers under the Second Empire: Tristan Corbière, Mallarmé, Rimbaud and Verlaine himself. The symbolists were everything the Parnassians were not: personal, undisciplined, turbulent, often incomprehensible. In many cases their private lives were confused and disastrous, and they looked for their metaphors and symbols in the streets of Paris and in the wilderness of the subconscious mind. Like the Parnassian poets, they were reacting against romanticism, and they were realists after their fashion. But they carried the impulse of poetry far beyond the Parnassians and were not content simply with painting descriptive pictures. They did not reject the present, but rather threw themselves into it—and into its most disturbing areas. In the despair and uncertainty of a new civilization they found the materials of poetry and committed themselves to a diagnosis of modern life.

The symbolists achieved no recognition under the empire. Paul Verlaine began his career with the *Poèmes saturniens,* written in the impassive style of the Parnassian school and published in 1866. Nevertheless, under the surface there were notes of melancholy and the suggestions of an unquiet sensibility. His own life a nightmare, Verlaine searched for an earthly paradise and the meaning of his existence amid the noise of the cabarets and the dirt of the street, seeing always the mud from the omnibuses and the naked plane trees on the boulevard. Arthur Rimbaud, his young and perverse companion, was a precocious genius, a stranger to all conformity. While still under twenty, he composed two of the great psychological documents of the modern sensibility: *Le Bateau ivre* (1871) and *Une Saison en enfer* (1873). In the former poem he describes himself alone on a boat, tossed by hurricanes into a birdless sky, and that strange voyage becomes the symbol of his soul's confusion. It is a small step to extend Rimbaud's confusion to include the confusions of contemporary man. Perhaps the finest of the symbolist poets was Stéphane Mallarmé: he emphasized the musical aspects of poetry, taking up Baudelaire's correspondence between sight and sound and creating an entirely new language to suggest the enigmas and paradoxes of human experience. Throughout the Second Empire every kind of experiment was being made. In 1868, for example, the fragments of a prose poem were published by a young man who called himself the Comte de Lautréamont. A deep silence greeted the publication of *Les Chants de Maldoror,* a work filled with hallucinations and nightmare images, blasphemous and erotic, full of toads and vampires and grotesque animals—a work which almost fifty years later would serve as an inspiration for the surrealist poets. Under the conventional surface of the Second Empire, poetry was moving rapidly in the direction of the twentieth century. The visions of the symbolist poets were disturbing, although unhappily justified in terms of what was to come. They were the laureates of a dying civilization—a civilization perhaps still dying.

Charles Baudelaire, the forerunner of the symbolist poets, was among the first to acknowledge the turbulences running under the surface of Second Empire life. And the new poetry which began with him prefigures many of the recurring themes of modern literature: disgust with the contemporary world, a pervading *mal du siècle,* hatred of hypocrisy and materialism and a revelation of the pain of living. In pointing to the uncertainties and doubts of modern life Baudelaire and the symbolists suggest an indictment, not only of Louis Napoleon's fragile empire, but of the new directions of an industrial civilization. Throughout the nineteenth century a gallery of figures stands in mute testimony to the failures of an age: Courbet's stonebreakers, Daumier's washerwomen and third-class travelers, Flaubert's provincials, Manet's prostitutes, Zola's alcoholic workers, Baudelaire's grotesques. During the Second Empire these realistic figures served to startle and confuse a nation which believed in the virtues of money and material progress. It is not surprising that the Impressionist painters and realistic novelists and symbolist poets had to find their recognition among future generations—generations which would be faced even more tragically with the failures of progress and the ambiguities of modern civilization and the horrors of human life.

Paradox and ambiguity form the fabric of *Les Fleurs du mal* as they form the fabric of symbolist poetry and realistic fiction and, to a lesser extent, Impressionist painting. The academic artists and writers who flourished during the Second Empire did not acknowledge the overwhelming ironies of life, and it is this silence which makes them unacceptable to a twentieth-century audience. Their work was too easy, and pain and despair and doubt had no place in their vocabulary. Pain and doubt and despair, nonetheless, are the realities of life—and particularly, it would seem, the realities of modern life.

Baudelaire's poetry gains strength and authority from his recognition of the duality of contemporary man. He called *Les Fleurs du mal* the "discordant product" of the Muse of Modern Times. And disharmony, so alien to the "unspeakable jargon of the age," illuminates his poems as it illuminates the work of other innovators who experimented during the empire. For Baudelaire that disharmony resulted from the conflicts between *spleen* and *idéal,* between good and evil, between instinct and idealism. These are conflicts that have always been present in the nature of man, but conflicts made more desperate by the doubt and despair which an industrial civilization was generating. To an extraordinary degree Baudelaire's poetry reveals the spiritual experiences of modern man. And modern man's melancholy and alienation and sense of guilt have provided material for poets and painters and novelists to the present day.

Before an autumn rain dispersed the small crowd in Montparnasse Cemetery, Théodore de Banville had time to say a few words over Baudelaire's grave. "He accepted modern man in his entirety," said Banville, "with all of modern man's weaknesses and sickly grace and useless struggles."

That acceptance of modern man and his contradictions forms much of the meaning of Baudelaire's work. He was compelled to leave nothing out—seeing always the distance between dream and reality and pointing to the perpetual conflict between heaven and hell at all times present in man. His poetry is the autobiography, not of one tormented individual, but of modern man divided by the pressures of a new civilization. It is something which Emile Zola did not understand at all when he said that in a hundred years *Les Fleurs du mal* would be a literary curiosity only.

"Who among us is not a duplex man?" asked Baudelaire, and the Second Empire was a Janus-faced time of neurosis and alienation, an era of double men and double currents. There were two sides to every coin: liberty and authority, youth and age, poverty and luxury. Duality was a pervading theme: from the tormented searching of poets like Rimbaud and Baudelaire, from the indecision of politicians like Louis Napoleon who faced in two directions at the same time, from the confusion between the real and the unreal—to the slums behind the façades and the double vision of Offenbach's operettas and the *grand écart* of the cancan itself.

The destructive nature of modern life and the enormous irony of it were apparent to Baudelaire who takes his place as the laureate of a dying civilization, putting an interrogation point to the wonders of an age. It was inevitable that he should have found no recognition in his own day, since few people were willing to accept the intensity of his vision or the melancholy nature of his revelations. In a vulgar and frivolous society these revelations had to be made more palatable, and in the Second Empire there were other laureates of decay more eager to please—and rather more amusing.

CHAPTER FIFTEEN

Orpheus in Hell

THE ceremony in the church of the Madeleine was over, and it had begun to rain. The funeral cortège did not go directly to Montmartre Cemetery, however, and a detour was made to carry Jacques Offenbach's coffin down the Grands Boulevards which had been the center of his life. His glamorous star, Hortense Schneider, was in the procession, as were other survivors of more frivolous days. They walked in the October rain along the streets of an unsympathetic city. It was 1880, and the music and the laughter and the great good times seemed to have ended a thousand years ago.

By the last decades of the nineteenth century Offenbach was an anachronism, the epitome of an age gone by, for he symbolized the Second Empire as surely as Louis Napoleon or Eugénie. Even today his music will call back in an instant those vanished years, and it is an emotional evocation not found with the same intensity in the work of more durable artists like Zola and Manet, Dumas *fils* and Baudelaire. Of his contemporaries only the painter Constantin Guys succeeded in capturing as effectively the immediacy of the moment, and it is pleasant enough to rest on the surface delights of Offenbach. Through his music you will come to share the exuberance of France at the beginning of a new age—an age when everything was bright and unopened and full of hope—and you will feel something of the charm of twenty thoughtless years given over to pleasure and money and self-gratification. Few artists have been more in harmony with their time and place than the composer whom Rossini called the "Mozart of the Champs Elysées."

"Jacques Offenbach is modern," said a contemporary critic. "His music is *daemonic,* like the century we live in—the century which rushes on, full steam ahead."

A great deal, of course, depends on the definition of modernity. The years of which Offenbach was the most entertaining chronicler ended in disaster. And if he had done no more than record the superficial tempos of an era best forgotten, his work would be without meaning today. For all the surrealist trappings of the operetta, however, Offenbach was more modern than most of his contemporaries could have guessed. He saw the defects of his limited world as clearly and dispassionately as Zola or the brothers Goncourt, and, like Baudelaire, he acknowledged the century's pervading fear which no amount of tinsel and scenery could hide. Surely he did not have Baudelaire's intellectual capacity or emotional temperament, but he did have the poet's sense of the present. His music is something more than frivolous, and behind the cancans and mazurkas of *La Belle Hélène* and *La Vie parisienne* lie innumerable intimations of disaster—intimations, it must be said, which passed over the heads of the tired businessmen and gaudy harlots who made up a large part of the audience at the Bouffes Parisiens, where most of his hundred operettas first appeared.

Others have been more sensitive: after the First World

War, and for almost twenty years thereafter, a satiric and intellectual Viennese named Karl Kraus delighted in giving readings of Offenbach's operettas. At first glance it seems appropriate for Offenbach to have been appreciated in the city of Johann Strauss, where the tradition of the classical operetta was alive well into the twentieth century. But his talent for gaiety and frivolity was not what attracted Karl Kraus: he was the editor of a journal called *Die Fackel,* founded by him in 1899 and devoted to an examination of the decay of the Austro-Hungarian Empire. There are many analogies between that society and the society of the Second Empire. An aura of unreality hangs over them both, and a number of recurring themes are the same: the presence of brutal poverty at a time of national prosperity, hypocrisy and materialism in the middle class, and the fact that love had been replaced by sexuality and justice by corruption. In the first years of the twentieth century an old order was coming to an end in Vienna as surely as one had come to an end during the course of Louis Napoleon's régime. Karl Kraus thought of Vienna as an "experimental station" for world decline, and in the work of Offenbach he recognized the similar rôle played by Second Empire Paris. In the improbabilities of the operetta he saw a reflection of the improbabilities of modern life itself, and he acknowledged that conflict between reality and unreality so apparent in Offenbach. There was a desperate gaiety in his music—a gaiety which often seemed to mask some enormous fear. It has been noticed many times. "The laughter I hear in Offenbach's music," said the novelist François Mauriac in a discussion of *La Grande Duchesse de Gérolstein,* "is that of the Empress Charlotte gone mad." [1]

Jacques Offenbach was Parisian in a way which only an émigré could have been. For all his identification with

French manners and society, he saw his adopted country from the outside, and in the ghettos of his youth he had experienced realities unknown to the boulevardiers of Paris. He was born in Prussia in the city of Cologne on June 20, 1819, the son of Isaac Eberst, who was the cantor of a synagogue and had come originally from Offenbach-am-Main. The boy inherited an interest in music and at an early age showed a mastery of the violoncello. Recognizing Jacob's ability and wishing to free him from the ghetto of Cologne, his father took him to Paris in 1833 along with his brother to study music at the Conservatoire. The boy, who soon changed his name to Jacques Offenbach, studied music for a year and then supported himself by playing the cello in various theater orchestras, notably at the Opéra Comique. As a very young man and a foreigner he spent his leisure hours absorbing the splendid new city in which he found himself. These were important years in terms of the material he was unconsciously gathering for his future operettas. At once corrupt and alluring, Paris was strangely ambivalent, and that ambivalence became the leitmotiv of his mature work.

In the 1830s Paris was the domain of Louis Philippe, the citizen king, but his sober felt hat and bourgeois umbrella had by no means crushed the city's gaiety. Life along the Boulevard was more active than ever and, poor though he was, Offenbach threw himself into it with enthusiasm. To a young man from Cologne the excitements of the great city might well have confirmed the German proverb which defined happiness as living "like God in France." In those days the amusement center of Paris was along the boulevard du Temple, often called the boulevard du Crime because of its many theaters given over to dramas of mystery and suspense. The streets surrounding the theater district were crowded day and night: there was an endless procession of sword-swallowers and human skeletons, dwarfs and performing fleas, acrobats and jugglers, mountebanks and magicians and salesmen of patent medicine. The Cirque Olympique with its trained animals was in the neighborhood, and along the boulevard du Temple came organ grinders with their monkeys, little girls selling ribbons, and beggars in carefully contrived rags. All the materials for an operetta lay at hand, and the degree to which Offenbach studied the life of the Grands Boulevards and understood the colorful characters who frequented them is to be found in his satiric tour of the city, *La Vie parisienne.*

Everywhere he looked he saw a horde of frivolous men and women eager for money and pleasure. All of them found their way into his work, often as the gods and goddesses of Olympus: all those available young women, all those dandies and aging rakes who filled the Boulevard. He watched the bored aristocrats coming out of the Café Tortoni with their hats tilted over their eyes; he saw the crowd at the Bains Chinois; he was familiar with the habitués of the Café de Paris: little Major Frazer, Dr. Véron who directed the Opéra, Roger de Beauvoir in his embroidered waistcoat and that most amusing of journalists, Nestor Roqueplan. Paris was becoming a cosmopolitan city full of political refugees like the Prince Belgiojoso and moral ones like Lola Montez and Thérèse Lachman, who later achieved notoriety as La Païva. Newspapers and journals were devoted to scandalous gossip, and sex had become an increasingly profitable commodity in the theaters and along the Grands Boulevards.

Offenbach saw the elegant figures of the demimonde in their daily round of pleasure, and he knew those careless ladies from the neighborhood of the church of Notre Dame de Lorrette who walked the streets in search of cus-

tomers.[2] He was enchanted on carnival days like the Feast
of the Bœuf Gras when the city was filled with costumed
revelers: harlequins, pierrots and pierrettes, pantaloons
and punchinellos. At night there would be masked balls
at the Opéra and at theaters like the Variétés, and during
the day singers and musicians performed along the Boulevard. Bugles and trumpets and drums were heard everywhere, and the streets were choked with soldiers in garish
uniform, particularly after the beginning of the empire in
1852. Dancehalls and cafés-concerts were crowded all the
time, and the cancan was becoming more and more popular. Brought over from Algeria by Marshal Bugeaud's
soldiers, it was no longer restricted to low taverns. As time
went by, the search for pleasure grew more intense, brilliance and immorality and the love of money flourished
and in those first years of empire all Paris seemed to be in
the grip of some frantic saraband. It was a world of make-
believe, and few adjustments were necessary to translate
the improbable life of the Boulevard to the operetta stage.
The cast was ready and waiting, and Offenbach's moment
was upon him.

For almost twenty years he had been building a modest
reputation in musical circles—at first, it is true, only as a
performer. Although he had composed a number of
waltzes and ballads, he spent most of his time giving re-
citals in the salons of the faubourg Saint Germain. Looking like some mythological bird, tall and thin as a knife
blade, with the famous ribbon and glasses crowning his
large nose, Offenbach captivated his fashionable audi-
ences. He enjoyed playing the cello, but he was vaguely
dissatisfied that his life did not seem to have any particular
direction. Change was in the air, however: one day as he
sat in the Café Cardinal he was approached by Arsène
Houssaye, director of the Comédie Française. Houssaye
offered him a job conducting the orchestra at a salary of

six thousand francs a year. More important than the modest salary was the opportunity of being at the center of the light-opera world. It was 1850, and Offenbach stood on the threshold of a fabulous career—a career corresponding almost exactly to the term of the Second Empire itself. His most popular works were written between 1855 and 1867, dates commemorating those two great expositions which publicized the wealth and material accomplishments of Louis Napoleon's régime.

In the months before the opening of the Exposition of 1855 Offenbach finally lost patience waiting for the management of the Opéra Comique to accept some of his songs and brief reviews. He was tired of playing other people's music and felt that the time had come to find a showcase for his own talent. In keeping with the emphasis of the day, frivolous musicals were becoming more and more popular: Hervé (Florimond Ronger) had enjoyed great success with *La Gargouillada,* a parody of Italian opera, and there was a large audience hungry for entertainment of a similar kind. Never before or since in the history of Paris has the world of the theater assumed such importance.

On the Champs Elysées, very near the recently completed Palais de l'Industrie which was to house the Exposition of 1855, Offenbach discovered a shabby and deserted theater hidden away among the trees.[3] It was hardly more than a shed, and on rainy days water poured through the roof. He bought it nevertheless, and with the patronage of Prince Plon-Plon and Auguste de Morny—as omnipresent in the world of the theater as elsewhere—he obtained a government license to stage pantomimes with three characters.[4] Sharing the Second Empire's delight in luxury and ostentation, Offenbach spent a great deal of money which he did not have on refurbishing the theater, and by summer the work was completed. He called his sumptuous little theater the Bouffes Parisiens, and opening night was scheduled for July 5, 1855. The revue he offered the public included a musical farce which he composed, some scattered themes from Rossini, a romantic idyll and a prologue written by a young government employee named Ludovic Halévy, who was to become one of his principal librettists. The program was thin enough, but for Offenbach the years of fame had begun. Everything was happening on cue: the theater had been available, Halévy had appeared as if by magic, and in that same summer a young singer came up from Bordeaux in search of a career. Her name was Hortense Schneider, and she would be Offenbach's greatest star, making *La Belle Hélène* and *La Grande Duchesse de Gérolstein* the most successful operettas of their day.

In 1855 Paris was an international capital, and the Second Empire was at its optimistic beginning. The tempo of life was increasing daily, and money flowed into the city from all directions. On one occasion Arsène Houssaye made over eight hundred thousand francs on the Bourse—and lost it all the same week. "After the coup d'état," he said, "people started talking in millions, and everyone began to dream of his own millions." The reality, he pointed out, far exceeded the dream. Money was easily made and easily spent, and much of it went for pleasure and amusement and mental oblivion. Paris was ready for Offenbach.

During the winter he moved his company from the Champs Elysées to a larger theater in the passage Choiseul which he still called the Bouffes Parisiens. In December he put on a short operetta, *Ba-ta-clan,* with a libretto by Halévy. It was a farce about a Chinese despot who was the absolute ruler of a nation of twenty-seven people, and its success was instantaneous. Even the Olympian critic Jules Janin had to admit that the audience "laughed, clapped, shouted" as if in the presence of a miracle. In the weeks following, Offenbach's music was heard everywhere, his songs were sung in dancehalls like the Bal Mabille and someone even opened an enormous café-concert on the boulevard du Prince Eugène and named it Ba-ta-clan. The fast tempo and delirious gaiety of all his future operettas are to be found in this first popular work. "Let us waltz! Let us polka! Let us leap! Let us dance!"—so they sang in *Ba-ta-clan,* and Offenbach was beginning to set his unique stamp on Parisian life. He wrote at a pace as feverish as his music, never alone and always busy, attending to the thousand details of stage production and staying close to the Grands Boulevards, which had been his inspiration. In 1857 he composed five pantomimes and several cantatas and twenty short operettas for the Bouffes Parisiens.

At this point in his career he had written nothing but one-act operettas, and it was not until the two acts of *Orphée aux enfers* opened on October 21, 1858, that he perfected the form so intimately identified with the Second Empire. In fact, the première marks the beginning of the classical operetta, and its source was to be found in earlier works like *The Beggar's Opera,* written by John Gay and produced in London in 1728. Offenbach carried forward the tradition of Gay's satiric realism, and the type of operetta he created, in spite of outward similarities, was fundamentally different from the sentimental light opera and musical parodies staged at the Opéra Comique. Underneath the delicious surface of *Orphée aux enfers* was a message for those who cared to look for it. It was an ambiguous message; however, the audience was there to be amused, and John Gay's self-composed epitaph in Westminster Abbey could certainly be applied to Offenbach:

> Life is a jest, and all things show it;
> I thought so once, and now I know it.

That point of view was quite in keeping with the mood of Paris in the middle years of the nineteenth century, provided one was willing to overlook three quarters of the population. Surprisingly enough, *Orphée aux enfers* was by no means an immediate success. It was not until a month and a half after the opening that success came. And it came because the influential critic Jules Janin, writing in *Le Journal des Débats,* expressed his disgust with the entire production—objecting violently to Offenbach's burlesque of classical antiquity. The operetta did deal in a light-hearted manner with the legend of Orpheus and Eurydice, and it cast Jupiter and Pluto and the other gods of Olympus in a somewhat ridiculous light. Therefore Janin could only conclude that it was an attack on "holy and glorious antiquity." For a critic of his reputation, however, the antagonism he showed does not make a great deal of sense: parodies of classical mythology had been found on the French stage for over two hundred years. There was something else bothering him, and the reasons for his outrage are not too difficult to guess. He was simply reacting to Offenbach in the way others would react to Manet's *Olympia* a few years later. Perhaps unconsciously, he was shocked to find that this amusing operetta was about contemporary life and only superficially concerned with classical antiquity. It is true that on one very obvious level Offenbach's work was a criticism of Louis Napoleon's court, but there is little reason to suppose that this sort of criticism by itself would have provoked an intellectual like Janin who had applauded the similar theme of *Ba-ta-clan.* In spite of severe press laws, newspapers and journals were devoting a good deal of time to oblique attacks on the imperial régime, and political satirists like Henri Rochefort were beginning to be heard. However, if criticism were kept within the limits of triviality and restricted to the scandal sheet and the operetta stage, a certain amount of latitude was allowed. Something more serious was disturbing Jules Janin.

The blasphemy he found in *Orphée aux enfers* had become increasingly common in advanced artistic and literary—and now musical—circles. Young painters and poets and novelists were turning their attention to the failures of modern society and striking what blows they could against the established order. To do so they concentrated on the disturbing realites of contemporary life, and a traditionalist like Janin must have found such realism wildly out of place on the operetta stage. Moreover, realism in itself seemed to incorporate an attack on the fundamental principles of middle-class thought. Others had attacked the foundations of bourgeois life: Courbet, Flaubert, the Goncourts—to mention only a few. And a year before the opening of *Orphée aux enfers* Charles Baudelaire had been brought to trial and fined for publishing his dark and realistic vision of the modern world. Janin, both as a critic and as a member of the middle-class establishment, was shaken by what he had seen and heard in the surrealistic context of the Bouffes Parisiens.

His discomfort, however, provided the new operetta with badly needed publicity, and people hurried to see what all the trouble was about. The musical lasted for 228 performances, a glorious run for the time, and only exhaustion of the cast forced its closing. After one of the many revivals Louis Napoleon himself wrote a note thanking the company for the charming evening it had given him. Surely the emperor was not so somnabulent as to have overlooked the many obvious references to his new régime, and he laughed along with the others. The libretto, provided by Hector Crémieux with additional material by Halévy, was more than explicit, and Offenbach's music gaily emphasized its satirical direction. Contemporary references could not have been missed, and the audience was delighted with the many allusions to Louis Napoleon. He was easily recognized in the person of Jupiter, an autocratic ruler given to marital infidelity and plagued by a jealous wife—a tyrant who, when reminded of his sins, would say: "I have an appointment with my architect." And the evening must have come when Baron Haussmann himself sat laughing at the witticism and applauding with the others the revolt of the gods on Olympus:

> Aux armes, dieux et demidieux!
> Abattons cette tyrannie!
> Ce régime est fastidieux!
> Aux armes! Aux armes! *

As if the point needed underlining, Offenbach added a few bars of the *Marseillaise,* that republican call to arms effectively banned since 1852. This sort of thing delighted an audience which felt its sophistication in recognizing every topical allusion and showing familiarity with the argot of the Boulevard. It was harmless fun, and the imperial government did not find Offenbach's point of view subversive—perhaps because it regarded the operetta as a trivial form of entertainment not to be taken seriously, perhaps because it felt that tensions were relieved more gently at the Bouffes Parisiens than on the barricades.

By and large, however, the contemporary audience accepted the operetta at face value and took it to be Offenbach's hymn to the gaiety and excitement of a new em-

---

* To arms, gods and demigods!
  Let's overthrow this tyranny!
  This regime is oppressive!
  To arms! To arms!

pire, a tribute to the prosperous years just beginning. Considered in this light, his music is the re-creation of a lost moment in time, and there is no doubt that it was a hymn to the vitality of a new age. Nor is it surprising that his waltzes and cancans were heard everywhere and that the light infantry of the Imperial Army marched to his melodies. However, gaiety and genial criticism of Louis Napoleon aside, there was far more to *Orphée aux enfers* —and to the rest of his operettas—than a pleasant evening's entertainment. The entertainment was spectacular enough, but there is a greater depth to Offenbach than to most of his followers, who range from Johann Strauss to Franz Lehár. If he held a mirror to Second-Empire society, that mirror reflected not only its undeniable charm but its disastrous weaknesses as well. The satiric realism of text and music is directed at larger issues than the peacock court of Louis Napoleon, and Offenbach, like the avantgarde artists of the day, was attacking the foundations of contemporary life. What is deceptive, of course, is that he has done so with unsurpassed lightness and elegance. As effectively as Daumier he illustrated the hypocrisy and greed and love of ostentation which characterized the times. He looked behind the façades of empire as implacably as Zola, and, like Baudelaire, he put a question mark to the certainties of an age. These are the things by which Jules Janin was unconsciously offended.

Infidelity is a major theme of *Orphée aux enfers,* and it comes to the surface in the opening scene. Orpheus, a pompous music teacher, accuses his wife of having a lover. The theme receives fuller elaboration in the person of Jupiter, whose numerous infidelities are described, and he undertakes to seduce Eurydice by turning himself into a fly and buzzing around her head. Adultery was a diversion familiar to Offenbach's audience, which was composed to an impressive degree of courtesans and philandering bankers and dissolute dandies from the Jockey Club. The infidelities of the operetta are played against a background of stultifying hypocrisy. Offenbach and his authors replaced the traditional chorus of the classical drama with the figure of Public Opinion, who appears regularly in order to point up the theme of decorum and to insist on the importance of keeping up appearances at all costs. Appearances are particularly important to Jupiter himself, and his attitude is stated clearly enough: "Everything for decorum and through decorum."

The mask of decorum covers more than infidelity: it covers as well a deeper sensuality and a consuming interest in materialism and self-gratification. These ideas are expressed musically in the last scene of the operetta—a scene often taken as an example of Offenbach's gaiety and triviality and worship of pleasure. To the contrary, it may be considered the darker vision of a doomed society whose every restraint has been cut away. In the Babylonian splendor of the final scene Eurydice sings a hymn to Bacchus, the tempo of the music reaches frantic proportions and the minuet gives way to a wild cancan. The scene, lavishly staged with costumes by Gustave Doré, marks the first appearance of the characteristic *offenbachiade*. The gods and goddesses of Olympus, wrapped in tiger skins and wearing vine leaves in their hair, engage in a dance which goes far beyond the simple affirmation of pleasure into a realm of Dionysian excess. The *offenbachiade* is its own comment on contemporary society: a society, like the music describing it, at once too gay, too desperate, too sensual. There is too much of everything, and musically Offenbach has given us both a description and a criticism of the attitudes prevalent in the early days of the Second Empire. At least one critic has dismissed the frenzied melodies of the closing scene as "brothel music," while others have considered the scene a supreme example of wit —wit, of course, being the ability to recognize the inconsistencies and absurdities of life. And, if there are sinister undertones to *Orphée aux enfers,* they derive from the abandoned gaiety of Offenbach's music. In a curious way the music is without joy, however joyful it may appear to be on the surface.

Offenbach's first major operetta contains all the elements of his future work, and it may be considered as the revelation, in the unreal context of the Bouffes Parisiens, of some of the realities of modern life. He has taken us behind the glamour of the imperial court, behind the mask of bourgeois decorum and behind the careless pursuit of pleasure which reached such a crescendo along the Boulevard during the Second Empire. Satire must have some positive frame of reference, and Offenbach found it in the plea for reality which is a recurring theme of the operetta. "No more nectar!" cry the gods and goddesses, and Diana herself remarks that the atmosphere of Olympus is stifling with its "implacable blue sky." Offenbach makes his point clear enough by using the cancan as a form of laughter to underline the pretensions of the day. But a certain charming ambiguity remains: the cancan shares the double thrust of the age, leading at once into satiric laughter and at the same time carrying the audience and the performers into an ecstasy of sensuality and abandon.

After the success of *Orphée aux enfers* Offenbach's career moved rapidly ahead, and he entered a phase of incredible productivity. For his three most successful operettas he was fortunate in having a team of accomplished librettists: Ludovic Halévy, who had been with him from the beginning, and Henri Meilhac, a boulevard wit whose knowledge of Parisian life magnificently complemented the music. With Hortense Schneider in the leading role, *La Belle Hélène,* another parody of classical mythology, opened at the Variétés in the winter of 1864, and two years later you could have seen *La Vie parisienne* at the Bouffes. By this time Offenbach's reputation was international, he had received ovations in London and Vienna and one critic suggested that even the cannibals, when they came to dessert, would be singing *Tout tourne* from *La Vie parisienne.* Perhaps the greatest triumph of the collaboration between Offenbach, his writers and his star came during the year of the Exposition of 1867 with *La Grande Duchesse de Gérolstein,* the last joke of the empire. Crowned heads and visitors from every part of Europe laughed uproariously at this satire of an absurd German principality, even Otto von Bismarck was amused and it is only in retrospect that the operetta appears to have had such melancholy implications. However, while Offenbach surely did not anticipate the catastrophe of 1870, some feeling for the realities of the day must have dictated his choice of theme. The battle of Sadowa had been fought, and it is behind *La Grande Duchesse de Gérolstein* that François Mauriac heard the mad laughter of Carlotta of Mexico.

There is no point in denying that Offenbach's main motive was to entertain his audience. If he had done no more, he simply would have joined that company of ephemeral producers and composers and musicians who throughout the Second Empire catered to vulgarity and encouraged the mindless search for diversion. However, within the artificial structure of the operetta, Offenbach took time to consider some of the darker themes of his century—themes evident in the work of those young poets and painters and novelists who found themselves opposed to the imperial government and at odds with the direction of

contemporary life. In their own ambiguous way the operettas are quite as realistic as Zola's novels, and Offenbach's
voice must take its place among those other voices of dis-
sent which grew more strident as the empire came to its
inevitable conclusion. The failures of a new civilization
smoothed the way for disaster, and those failures are documented with monotonous regularity in the work of
avant-garde artists: materialism, hypocrisy, greed, sensuality, indifference. No one listened, of course. The world of
the Grands Boulevards—the world of carousing bankers
and vulgar courtesans, of decayed aristocrats and imitation noblemen—was a land of operetta to begin with, and
it is appropriate that Offenbach should have presented the
real failures of his era in the unreal atmosphere of the
Bouffes Parisiens and the Variétés.

The last work he wrote makes it clear enough that there
were unsuspected depths to the operettas which had entertained Europe for more than a generation. Old and ill, his
days at the center of the Paris stage behind him, Offenbach set down the final piano arrangement of *Les Contes
d'Hoffmann* the afternoon before he died. It was not performed until 1881, but Offenbach had fulfilled his ambition to write a serious opera. His desire was understandable, since Paris in the nineteenth century was the operatic
capital of Europe and had seen the premières of many
works by French composers: among others, *Faust* and
Roméo et Juliette by Charles Gounod and Meyerbeer's *Le
Prophète* and *L'Africaine*. Offenbach's opera was inspired
by the macabre stories of the German writer E. T. A.
Hoffmann, which had been adapted for the Paris stage in
1851. It is a disturbing opera, and its theme rests on the
conflict between appearance and reality. Although the set-
tings are lavish and the music is gay, Hoffmann's haunted
imagination struck a deep chord in Offenbach: fear and

death dominate the scene. In the act devoted to Olympia, the lovely mechanical doll, Offenbach re-creates some of the frivolous mood of the Second Empire. And in the second act he presents the luxurious debauchery of Venice and considers the realities of evil in the person of the courtesan Giulietta. The music is filled with panic and terror, and *Les Contes d'Hoffmann* lays bare the darkness in Offenbach out of which the earlier operettas had come.

In spite of charm and money and superficial gaiety the Second Empire was a time of fear. It marked the beginning of the journey into a new world, and the unknown was not without its nightmares. An era was coming to an end, and only a handful of artists and writers and musicians sensed the far-reaching changes which would have to be made. Rejecting an older set of values, they began to search for new ones capable of dealing with the future. 1870 marks the end, not simply of Louis Napoleon's harlequin empire, but the beginning of the end of a larger pattern of western civilization. That end was prefigured in the work of certain experimental artists whose message was ignored, among them the amusing and light-hearted Jacques Offenbach. A great deal was coming to an end: a thousand years of classical certainty, the old order of agricultural Europe and many traditional forms of government and society. New paths lay ahead, and along them could be seen the silhouettes of great industrial cities and by the side of the road the mass of the neglected poor. And so, among the careless movements of the Grands Boulevards, we find the feverish tempos and ambiguities of Offenbach, the hallucinations of Baudelaire, the elegant impersonality of Manet, the brutal realism of Zola—all attempts to deal in some new manner with the uncertainties of a transitional time.

In terms of the artistic imagination these artists were

looking far beyond Louis Napoleon's collapse. Their century would fail to deal with the problems of the modern world, nor would it succeed in coming to terms with science and industry and the harsh facts of social revolution. Some general collapse was not impossible, and at the beginning of the twentieth century Karl Kraus sensed that imminent collapse in Vienna. And Vienna was only one of the lovely and enchanting cities which would share the fate of Offenbach's Paris.

PART FIVE

THE END OF THE DAY

We are ready. We are so ready that, if the war should last two years, we would not have to buy even the button for one legging.

LEBOEUF, Minister of War, 1870

CHAPTER SIXTEEN

La Gloire

Ever since the *Marseillaise* had been banned, the unofficial anthem of the Second Empire was a song about a young knight leaving for the Crusades. The music for *Partant pour la Syrie* had been written—it seems improbable enough—by Queen Hortense, Louis Napoleon's mother. In any case, it set something of the emotional mood of the régime and gave a chivalric tone to its military exploits, rather considerable exploits when one remembered that at the beginning the emperor had promised his countrymen nothing but peace:

> Le jeune et beau Dunois
> Venait prier Marie
> Partant pour la Syrie,
> De bénir ses exploits:
> "Faites, Reine immortelle,"
> Lui dit-il en partant,
> "Que j'aime la plus belle
> "Et sois le plus vaillant." *

* On leaving for Syria,
  The young and handsome Dunois

From the distribution of the eagle standards to the army in 1852 to the great military review at Longchamp in 1867, much of the history of the Second Empire is the history of war—in Italy and the Crimea, in the Middle East and North Africa, in China and Indochina and finally in Mexico. The culmination of these adventures came in the September of 1870 at Sedan, a fortress town not far from the Belgian border.

The Second Empire began under a military dictatorship, and Louis Napoleon had appealed to the divided country as a strong man on horseback. The harshness of his dictatorship diminished as time passed, but the whole régime was cast in a military mold. Not since the days of Napoleon Bonaparte had the streets of Paris been filled with so many uniforms. Officers on leave from Châlons strolled along the Grands Boulevards, there was regimental music in the garden of the Tuileries and impressive parades were mounted on the least occasion. In keeping with Louis Napoleon's emphasis on splendor, the uniforms of officers and enlisted men alike were dazzling in their richness and variety. There were élite troops of the Cent Gardes, Zouaves in their tasseled hats, Spahis from the desert, all manner of lancers and hussars and cuirassiers, Chasseurs d'Afrique and elegant officers of the Guides in green and gold. Soon after the beginning of the Second Empire, France regained its position as the leading military power on the continent, and the campaigns of the Crimea had shown its superiority to both England and

Prayed to the Virgin Mary
To bless his undertaking:
"Grant, Immortal Queen,"
He said to her on leaving,
"That I may love the most beautiful maiden
And be the most valiant knight."

Russia. During the days of triumph only the British Navy might have presented a threat to France. That this superb military machine should have crumbled so unexpectedly before the citizen soldiers of the German states is another of the irrational aspects of the régime.

Among the appeals which Louis Napoleon exercised in his bid for power in 1848, a return to the military glories of the national past was not the least. In 1852, six months before the Senate proclaimed him emperor, he presided over an imperial ceremony on the Champ de Mars. To each of the army regiments he presented an eagle standard, a gesture derived from Roman times and duplicating the ceremony conducted by Napoleon Bonaparte in the winter of 1804. In spite of the peace promised at Bordeaux a few months later, the direction of the new empire seemed clear enough. It is a further paradox that Louis Napoleon himself saw no damaging contradictions in the attention he was lavishing on the Imperial Army.

When the Second Empire began, there had not been a general European conflict for almost forty years. However, they had not been years of inactivity for the French: in North Africa the army made use of an impressive training ground for its officers and men. That training ground had been available since 1830, when a French expeditionary force landed at Algiers, a port long familiar to the Barbary pirates. Three years previously the Turkish dey Hussein had struck the French consul with a fly whisk in a fit of Oriental temper. This trivial insult furnished a pretext for invasion, and the French laid siege to the city. During the reign of Louis Philippe more and more soldiers were sent out to North Africa in an attempt to bring order to the country by subduing the desert tribes and conquering the fierce Berbers of the Atlas Mountains. At one time or another, French military and naval forces.

were commanded by the king's sons, the Prince de Joinville and the Duc d'Aumale. And most of the leading military figures of the Second Empire served their apprenticeship in Algeria, learning under the *régime du sabre* little
that would equip them for the more sophisticated campaigns of Europe.[1] Out of the desert came Pélissier, hard,
rude, gross, with the face of a bulldog; Saint Arnaud,
master of deception and first Minister of War under
Louis Napoleon; Bazaine, former sergeant in the Foreign Legion, organizer of the withdrawal from Mexico
and despised for his surrender at Metz; Yûsuf, the bloody
condottiere; MacMahon, later Governor General of Algeria and President of the Third Republic; and Canrobert,
perhaps the only one of the African generals to have
emerged with his honor intact after the Franco-Prussian
War. Algeria was a brutal training ground, it is true, although many officers who learned their profession in the
desert could not read maps in any intelligent fashion and
were unprepared to deal with the more complicated tactics of Continental warfare.

The beginning of the pacification of Algeria came in
1847 when the rebel chieftan Abd-el-Kader surrendered at
Sidi Brahim to General Lamoricière, himself to become a
victim of the coup d'état. The first governor-general was
appointed in 1851, and six years later the subjugation of
the desert tribes of Kabylia was accomplished and the col-
onization of Algeria began. In many ways Louis Napoleon came to think of himself as the Emperor of the Arabs
as well as of the French. He had released Abd-el-Kader
from imprisonment in the château at Amboise, and in
1865 he made a triumphal journey to Algeria. Prosper
Mérimée describes the emperor riding out into the Sahara,
where some twenty thousand Arabs fired rifles in his ear
and cleaned his boots with their beards, a sign of great

288

respect. A feast followed, and Louis Napoleon ate roast oxen and ostriches and "other impossible animals." In any event, he had consolidated the work begun under the July Monarchy and laid the foundations for much of the future administration of Algeria as one of the departments of metropolitan France.

Algeria was a colonial problem and represented no particular threat to international peace so far as the French were concerned. However, the Second Empire's first war, fought in alliance with the British and the Turks against the Russians, came within two years of Louis Napoleon's famous boast: "The Empire means peace." [2] In 1853 the Russians invaded the Danubian Principalities, then under Turkish rule and later united as the kingdom of Rumania. The invasion disturbed the European powers for a number of reasons. Traditionally, France had assumed responsibility for protecting the Christians who lived under Turkish rule, and England was anxious to guard the route to India, for this reason opposing any interference with the Ottoman Empire. In addition, France and Russia had been at odds for some time over the privileges accorded Roman Catholic and Greek Orthodox clergy in the Holy Places at Jerusalem. On another level, Louis Napoleon saw in an ambiguous situation the opportunity of refurbishing French prestige by allying himself with England against Russia. Russia, even more than England, had caused the defeat of his uncle, and the present tsar had insulted the Second Empire by refusing to address Louis Napoleon according to the protocol of European royalty as *"Mon Frère."* Actually, none of these reasons justified the conflict which followed. The Crimean War made little sense in its own day and makes even less from the vantage point of the present. In any case, France and England declared war on March 26, 1854.

It was a disaster from the beginning. The British Army had not been in the field since Waterloo, and most of its generals were old and inflexible, skilled only in the intricate politics of Whitehall. Lord Raglan, the British commanding officer, had not seen service since 1815, he had never even led a company, and during the Crimean campaign he was in the habit of referring to the enemy as "the French," so adding to the general confusion. Nor were the French themselves much better prepared for large-scale warfare, adept as they may have been in the lightning raids of the North African desert. The truth is that by the time the Anglo-French expeditionary force reached the Black Sea, the Russian invasion had been repulsed by the Turks and there was even less reason for war than there had been before. Crowded into Varna, the Allies looked around in desperation for a place to engage the enemy and at last chose the remote Russian naval base at Sebastopol on the Crimean peninsula. In the September of 1854 a siege was begun, and it was carried on in agony for the better part of a year. The transportation of men and matériel from distant European ports was difficult enough without the inspired inefficiency of the War Office in London and the Ministry of War in Paris. The problems of supply were rarely solved: troops were dispatched by steamship, their horses arriving weeks later under sail; tents and blankets and winter uniforms were endlessly delayed; and medicine and surgical equipment were often nonexistent. Typhus and cholera and frostbite claimed many more men than the Russian siege guns, and the Crimean War was a monstrous exercise in waste and mismanagement and unreality—perhaps best symbolized by the charge of the British Light Brigade at Balaclava. And this was only one example of the courageous incompetence of the forces engaged in the Crimea.

The French, it must be said, were rather less disorganized than the British, and the final victory was theirs. In addition—and the fact was never widely publicized—they supplied more than twice the number of soldiers and suffered far greater casualties, both from enemy action and from disease. The French part of the campaign falls into three major phases: the Battle of the Alma, Saint Arnaud commanding; the Battles of Balaclava and Inkerman, Canrobert commanding; and the final assault on the Malakoff under Pélissier. The siege came to an end on September 8, 1855, when the British and the French mounted simultaneous attacks on the Redan and the Malakoff, two of the most formidable of the Sebastopol fortifications. The day was cold and dark and foggy, with a bitter north wind sweeping down over the Russian steppes. The British attack on the Redan was a failure, and the French prepared for their assault by making their tattered uniforms as elegant as possible. Officers drew on white gloves as if they had been on the parade ground at Saint Cyr, and fierce African troops led the attack. Finally the Zouaves planted the tricolor on the mined tower of the Malakoff, and General MacMahon uttered his immortal words: *"J'y suis, j'y reste"* ("I am here, and here I will stay"). It is one of the great moments of French military history, and through that victory Pélissier became the Duc de Malakoff and a senseless and wasteful war was over.

However, for Louis Napoleon the war was neither senseless nor wasteful. It had been the means of returning France at one stroke to the pinnacle of military and political glory. When the soldiers came back from the Crimea, one could only think of the vanished days of Napoleon Bonaparte and the Grande Armée as regimental flags flew and cannon sounded through the city and there were uniforms everywhere. As late as 1920 an old lady recalled that victory parade, as the most compelling memory of her childhood, and she would never forget the sappers of the Garde Impériale with their white aprons and great beards and gleaming axes. She said that after such a sight it was difficult to return to reality—a difficulty often encountered at the time of the Second Empire.

The French capital had been chosen as the site of the peace talks following the Crimean War, and the Congress of Paris became the most important European meeting since the Congress of Vienna in 1815. Delegates arrived from England and the continent, from Russia and the Near East. For the first time they had an opportunity to see the transformation of Paris undertaken by Louis Napoleon and his Prefect of the Seine. The splendid new city offered endless glamour and diversion, and France once again was the cynosure of all eyes. Even this good fortune was not enough: in the early morning hours of March 15, 1856, near the end of the peace conference, one hundred and one cannon salvos announced the birth of the Prince Impérial, and the new empire was assured of a succession. Louis Napoleon's gamble had been more than justified, and out of the waste and incompetence of the Crimean War he had plucked honor for himself and for France. When his son was baptized in the cathedral of Notre Dame on June 15, 1856, the tapestries on the walls embroidered with golden bees and a representative of the Pope performing the ceremony, Louis Napoleon must have felt —for he was—at the height of his power and influence and happiness. In a few short years the ridiculous adventurer had become the most important ruler on the continent; he was a respected arbiter of international problems; and after 1856, when you spoke of "the Emperor," you could only have meant Napoleon III.

Unfortunately, the prominence and influence which he

achieved so rapidly led him into the first of his many difficulties. Like all future difficulties, it arose from his sincere
desire to help France and other countries maintain their
national integrity, and surely it was a misunderstanding
of the problems of nationalism which led to his own eventual downfall. However, in 'he years which followed the
Crimean War, he was flushed with success—success as a
statesman of international reputation and success as the
commander-in-chief of the finest army in Europe. He
took an active interest in the problems of other countries,
and in 1859 he found the opportunity of helping a divided
Italy free itself from Austrian tyranny. As a young man he
had expressed sympathy for the cause of Italian nationalism and had been associated with the Carbonari in an uprising in the Romagna. In 1858 he made a secret pact at
Plombières with Cavour, the Prime Minister of Sardinia,
to support that country in the event of Austrian aggres-
sion. The opportunity to honor the pledge came in the following year when the Austrians delivered an ultimatum
to Sardinia. Louis Napoleon kept his word: on April 24,
1859, French troops marched through a cheering crowd to
the gare de Lyon and boarded trains which had been
marked in chalk: "Excursion to Italy."

In spite of the bloody battles of Magenta and Solferino,
it was a cheerful summer campaign of brief duration.
Knowing how to read maps little better than his African
generals, and relying on his training as an artillery officer
in Switzerland, the emperor managed to direct the
campaign himself and win it. Nevertheless, he had little
stomach for violence, and after one early battle he sent a
telegram to Eugénie: "It's a good beginning, but how sad
to see all the wounded and the dying." Perhaps this is part
of the reason he signed an unexpected armistice with the
Emperor Franz Josef at Villafranca on July 11, 1859. In

the matter of Italian independence the results of the war were disappointing: the Austrians retained control of Venetia and the Pope was assured of Rome and the Patrimony of St. Peter. Psychological results, however, were impressive: Austria, like Russia another of the victors of 1815, had been defeated by a new French Imperial Army, and the decisions of the Congress of Vienna were being reversed.

Louis Napoleon made the triumphant return of the soldiers from Italy the occasion for a celebration which overshadowed even the ceremonies following the end of the Crimean War. Crowned with laurel, the emperor's portrait appeared on new coins, and a general amnesty was given to all who had opposed his coup d'état. The celebrations in Paris were arranged with the theatricality which so often marked the military events of the Second Empire. On August 14, 1859, the Army of Italy, its banners torn by the shells of Magenta and Solferino, marched along the Grands Boulevards and down the rue de la Paix into the place Vendôme to pass in review before the emperor. Louis Napoleon sat in the blazing sun mounted on a magnificent English charger with his little boy astride the saddle bow in the uniform of the Garde Impériale. Miss Bicknell, an American watching the parade, noticed how handsome the emperor looked on horseback and how bronzed he was from the Italian campaign. As the soldiers passed by, spectators shouted the names of popular generals: "Canrobert!" "MacMahon!" They cheered wildly when the Zouaves appeared with flowers in their gun barrels. And they applauded the little *vivandières*—not campfollowers but nurses of a kind—tripping gaily by in uniforms patterned after the regiments they were serving. The colorful scene suggested nothing so much as an Offenbach operetta—a rather lugubrious operetta, it must

be added, since empty places were left in the ranks to indicate comrades fallen in action. Seated proudly in his saddle, Louis Napoleon saw the finest army in Europe march
before him, he looked at regimental banners proclaiming
the victories in Italy and the Crimea, and he must have
felt a strong kinship with his long-dead uncle. The wits
on the Boulevard would have nothing to laugh about
today.

During the middle years of the régime the Imperial
Army was spread all over the world and French soldiers
and sailors and Legionnaires were laying the foundations
of an immense colonial empire. Under Louis Napoleon
there was a standing army of nearly half a million men:
70,000 were committed to Algeria; 30,000 to defend the
Pope at Rome; and the rest scattered everywhere, bringing
French laws and customs to a variety of Asians and Afri-
cans and Pacific islanders. It was the beginning of the
mission civilisatrice which reached such proportions
under the Third Republic.[3] By 1854 a brilliant captain of
engineers named Louis Faidherbe was bringing order to
Senegal and creating what would become French West
Africa. There were imperial troops and colonial administrators in Tahiti, Somaliland, New Caledonia and Mada-
gascar. An expeditionary force had been sent to Syria, and
the French had joined with the British in the Second
Opium War and burned the Summer Palace at Peking.
There was a colony in Cochin China, ceded by the King
of Annam in 1862, and the capital at Saigon had been
built on the model of French cities. At the same time
Cambodia became a protectorate, and France was sending
men and money and machinery to every part of the world.
Perhaps the most important new sphere of influence was
at the Isthmus of Suez, where Ferdinand de Lesseps was
completing his great canal and assuring French promi-

nence in the Mediterranean for years to come.

Prosperity at home and a growing empire and the power of the military complex over which he had control made Louis Napoleon overconfident and led him into the worst political blunder of his career: the War of Intervention in Mexico. In an adventure thousands of miles from France he lost his enormous prestige as well as the support of many of those who believed in him. He was not the first invader to have been defeated by Mexico, but he was very nearly the last. Even while a prisoner in the fortress at Ham, he had shown interest in the problems of the New World, and under the influence of the Saint-Simonians he had considered the possibility of building an inter-ocean canal through Central America. At the same time he developed a vague plan for the creation of a Catholic empire in the western hemisphere to counteract the influence of the United States. When he married Eugénie, her interest in such a project was made inevitable by her Spanish background, and around her there grew up a coterie of Mexican exiles anxious to gain control of the country. In the winter of 1861 Mexico was in the throes of a continuing revolution which had followed its freedom from Spanish rule. The insurgents were led by the Indian Benito Juárez. When he took over the presidency and ousted the conservative Catholic Miramón, he repudiated all foreign debts. France and Spain and Great Britain took the occasion to land troops at Veracruz in order to protect European financial interests. Louis Napoleon saw this intervention as the chance for which he had been waiting. And the moment did seem particularly ripe: the United States had been engaged in a destructive civil war since the spring of 1861, when the Confederacy had attacked Fort Sumter and seceded from the Union. Under the circumstances it seemed unlikely that the Union government would be worrying about its neighbor south of the Rio Grande, and Louis Napoleon moved quickly. When the token British and Spanish occupation forces left Mexico, he did not order a similar withdrawal, but rather sent in more soldiers in an attempt to pacify the country and gain control of it.

The French suffered their first defeat in the Battle of Cinco de Mayo at Puebla in 1862. Obviously, some larger commitment was necessary: in the following year thirty thousand troops took ship at Toulon and Marseille, and two battalions of the Foreign Legion marched out of the great barracks at Sidi Bell-Abbès, singing a song of farewell to the empress. Under the command of General Forey the army landed at Veracruz, captured Puebla and swept north to Mexico City. The capital had been abandoned by Juárez, and the French occupied the city on June 10, 1863. A soldier writing home to his mother described General Forey at the head of his troops:

> What a man, what a peacock! He strutted around for at least six hours. That's perfectly all right for a pretty girl to do, since she's a pleasure to look at, but it is grotesquely ridiculous to see a fat old general of 63 doing the same thing. The entry into Mexico City looked like the promenade of the Boeuf Gras during carnival time.

This sort of theatricality dominated the Mexican adventure as it dominated all the military exploits of the Second Empire, and Forey's conduct was quite in keeping with a general tone of unreality. One basic contradiction was striking: Louis Napoleon looked upon himself as a liberator, holding out to the Mexican people the gift of a unified nation and a monarchy under French protection. In line with that policy, the army of occupation established an interim government made up of conservative Mexicans. It was soon persuaded to offer the crown of a new Catholic empire to the Austrian Archduke Maximilian, brother of the Emperor Franz Josef, former Governor-General of Lombardy and Venetia, and Louis Napoleon's personal choice for the office. Leaving the tranquillity of his castle at Trieste, Maximilian arrived in Mexico City with his wife, Charlotte, and accepted the crown on June 12, 1864.

Perhaps there has never been a ruler chosen with less attention to reality. At once liberal and autocratic, he was as out of place in the palace of Chapultepec as in the dusty plazas of the Mexican villages. An idealist, tall and blond and entirely alien to the country in which he now found himself, he faced Benito Juárez and a hostile population. Above everything else, Juárez was a realist able to see behind the splendor of French uniforms and the glamour of a Europeanized court. The adventure was doomed, and he was content to wait impassively for its conclusion. The end was inevitable because of Louis Napoleon's misunderstanding of political reality in the western hemisphere. He had assumed the American Civil War would be won by the Confederate States, and he did not appreciate the fact that the Mexican people, however much they wanted a Mexican nation, did not want a king or an emperor or a foreign ruler. Nevertheless, surrounded by French bayonets, Maximilian I of Mexico began his reign with high seriousness, attempting to create order out of disorder and to impose his own standards on a land of quicksilver which forever eluded him.

In the spring of 1865 General Robert E. Lee surrendered his Army of Northern Virginia at Appomattox Court House, and the American Civil War was virtually over. The Union government was now free to turn its attention to matters of international importance, and the tragedy in

Mexico had come to its last act. The United States sent harsh notes to France pointing out the provisions of the Monroe Doctrine, and General Sheridan's cavalry rode back and forth along the Texas border. There was a rumor that forty or fifty thousand Union troops were being assembled in the area, and in France the middle class and the country villagers were unsympathetic toward another hopeless cause. Louis Napoleon had little choice but to withdraw his support from Maximilian, although he offered the unhappy emperor a chance of escaping with French convoys now beginning to move south to the port of Veracruz along a corridor protected from Mexican guerrillas. Honorable to the end, Maximilian refused, and by February of 1867 Achille Bazaine, carrying the baton of a marshal of France, led the last of his troops out of Mexico City in a well-conceived and orderly withdrawal. The adventure, having proved nothing, was over at an enormous cost in blood and gold, and Maximilian was left to his fate. Word of his execution before a firing squad at Querétaro on June 19, 1867, was relayed to France, arriving some ten days later as Louis Napoleon and Eugénie were distributing prizes at the Paris Exposition of that year. The cloud was a dark one, and a greater empire than Maximilian's was coming to an end.

A serious misunderstanding of political reality had caused the French disaster in Mexico, and the blame must be Louis Napoleon's alone. However, if the prestige of the emperor himself was seriously diminished by the events in Mexico, the prestige of the military was not. The Imperial Army had suffered no defeat—Bazaine, in fact, had effectively scattered the rebel forces—and it had been withdrawn only through political expediency. In France people still listened for echoes of the Grande Armée, the streets of Paris were full of uniforms and the French soldier was regarded as the finest in Europe, if not in the world. Only a few days before Maximilian's execution a fantastic military review had been held in Paris at the racetrack of Longchamp, observed with some admiration by Tsar Alexander and King Wilhelm of Prussia. Even from the unhappy experience in Mexico there had come one immortal moment and a compelling example of the glory of French arms.

On April 30, 1863, during the second siege of Puebla, a handful of Legionnaires fought almost to the last man against an overwhelming force of Mexicans. On the highway to Puebla the Third Company of the First Battalion of the Foreign Legion, under the command of Captain Danjou, was attacked by enemy cavalry and retreated to an empty hacienda near Camerone (Camarón). For nine hours Captain Danjou (a wooden hand replacing the one he had lost in the Crimea), two officers and fifty-nine Legionnaires withstood repeated attacks by some two thousand Mexicans. The scene was reminiscent of the events at the Alamo a quarter of a century earlier. By the end of the day only three Legionnaires were left standing, and even in the face of bayonets they refused to give up their weapons. The Mexican commander spared them. "These are not men," he said. "These are demons."

Still celebrated each year by the Foreign Legion, the Battle of Camerone is indicative of the long tradition of military honor and glory and service which reached something of a culmination during the Second Empire. In other times and in other places these concepts have seemed out of date, but in the age of Louis Napoleon—as in the age of Napoleon Bonaparte—they surrounded the Imperial Army with an aura of glamour which even later defeat could not entirely negate. There was no army in the world with the same dash and brilliance of style. Typical

of the attitudes of the day, both military and civilian, were
the words of the marching song of the Guides, the most
illustrious cavalry regiment in the Garde Impériale:

> Cavaliers intrépides,
> Sans reproche et sans peur,
> Toujours seront les guides
> Au chemin de l'honneur.*

That concept of military honor, however unrealistic it
may have been in terms of the era in which they lived and
the enemies whom they faced, inspired junior officers as
they led their men from the Alma to Mexico City, from
the Sahara to Sedan—officers who ranged from simple
professionals like Captain Danjou to romantic figures like
the Marquis de Galliffet.

Gaston Alexandre Auguste, Marquis de Galliffet and
Prince de Martignes, was an officer as unrealistic, as courageous and as destructive as the times out of which he came
and as the empire to which he gave allegiance. His elegant
person symbolizes, as few others can, the nature of *la
gloire* which provided the military establishment of the
Second Empire with its strength—and its weakness. Born
in 1830, Galliffet belonged to a rich and ancient family
and was destined to live at the center of the military and
social life of his day. After graduating from the cavalry
school at Saumur, he joined a fashionable regiment of hussars in 1848. During the course of his career he served in
most of the campaigns of the Second Empire: he was at
the siege of Sebastopol (his cousin sent out a great fur-
lined cloak in which the seamstresses had hidden notes of

---

* Intrepid horsemen,
  Above reproach and without fear,
  The Guides will always be
  On the path of honor.

encouragement); he fought in the Italian campaign of
1859; he led desert raids in North Africa; he was severely
wounded at Puebla in 1863, crawling back to his own
lines and holding a képi over the gaping wound in his
stomach. By 1867 he was the colonel in command of the
Third Chasseurs d'Afrique, and during the Franco-
Prussian War he would lead one of the most glorious and
useless cavalry charges since Balaclava. After the Commune of Paris his Arab horsemen would be responsible
for unnecessary brutality, and in the last year of the century he would be named Minister of War, thriving as
glamorously under the Third Republic as under the Second Empire.

His career was remarkable in every way, although his
bravery and panache were far from being unique. It was
simply that Galliffet did it all a little better than anyone
else. As well known along the Boulevard as in the officers'
mess, he was one of those insolent young men who surrounded the Duc de Gramont-Caderousse, and he had
married the daughter of the wealthy banker Laffitte. The
Marquise de Galliffet was one of the beauties of the imperial court, and she and her husband were welcomed in
every fashionable circle. Galliffet attended the famous
party at the Hôtel d'Albe in the spring of 1860 dressed as a
rooster; he knew the ladies of the demimonde; he was at
home with duels and affairs and masked balls; he and his
elegant friends amused themselves by throwing gold na-
poleons from the windows of the Café Anglais. And during the exposition year of 1867 he could often be seen in
the box at the Variétés, where the Prince of Wales went
nightly to admire Hortense Schneider in *La Grande
Duchesse de Gérolstein*. In many ways a figure from the
operatta stage himself, Galliffet was cynical and egotistical
and convinced that everything was permitted to one of his
caste. Nevertheless, in an age of materialism and greed

and hypocrisy, he was an honorable soldier and the personification of the young and handsome Dunois holding up his sword to be blessed by the Virgin Mary.

There was in Galliffet and in the whole military establishment of the Second Empire much that was flamboyant and unreal. Something of this atmosphere can be found in a forgotten novel published in 1867 by an English writer who called herself Ouida. *Under Two Flags* is the romantic story of an Englishman who served with the French in North Africa. The novel is full of the beat of drums and the sound of moving squadrons; it glorifies the tricolor flying over desert forts and the simple gravestones in the sand; it records the cosmopolitan life of Algiers, whose white boulevards were crowded with Bedouins and bearded sheiks, French staff officers in glittering uniforms, jet-black Sudanese, demimondaines in the latest Paris gowns, Moorish women hidden behind the folds of the *yashmak* and any number of Zouaves and Turcos and Legionnaires. Ouida's novel is filled with desperate battles in the desert, and here a Chasseur d'Afrique describes the death of another trooper after one such encounter:

"Then we broke from the ranks, and we rushed to the place where the chargers and men were piled like so many slaughtered sheep. *Rire-pour-tout* laughed such a gay, ringing laugh as the desert never had heard. '*Vive la France!*' he cried. 'And now bring me my toss of brandy.' Then down headlong out of his stirrups he reeled and fell under his horse; and when we lifted him up there were two broken sword blades buried in him, and the blood was pouring fast as water out of thirty wounds and more."

Over-romantic and bathetic and preposterous—all this is true enough. However, in a curious way Ouida was almost a realist, and there is more than an element of truth in her description of an era when bravura was a military virtue. It was not all fiction: others had cried *"Vive la France!"* and fallen, not only in the sands of the Sahara, but on the frozen ground before the Malakoff, by the gates of Puebla and the bridge at Palikao, in the rice paddies of Cochin China and the plains of Lombardy. Flamboyance and bravura contributed as much to the victories of the Imperial Army as they did to its eventual defeat. Surely it is difficult to remain impassive and realistic when the imagery is so compelling. Consider, for example, an afternoon in spring with Louis Napoleon and Eugénie reviewing the troops at Longchamp: the lines of infantry and cavalry moving past; the bayonets gleaming in the sunlight; the shakos and the turbans and the fur hats; the plumes and the banners and the flags; the trumpets and the *tambours;* the sound of marching men and the beat of horses' hoofs; and the regimental bands playing *Partant pour la Syrie.*

Behind the martial music there may have been, as Offenbach suggested, the echoes of a nursery rhyme. It was undeniably splendid, however, and the paradox is a hard one to resolve. Even in *La Grande Duchesse de Gérolstein,* a satire against the military and its imbecilities, Hortense Schneider could stand on the stage of the Variétés, perhaps looking up to where the dashing Marquis de Galliffet sat with the Prince of Wales, and sing with all her heart and with the entire approval of the audience: *"Ah, que j'aime les militaires!"*

CHAPTER SEVENTEEN

The Last Spring

AT ELEVEN O'CLOCK on the New Year's Day of 1870 there was a family luncheon at the Tuileries attended by Prince Plon-Plon and his Italian wife, Clotilde, Prince and Princess Murat, Princess Mathilde and other imperial relatives. The emperor's old friend and physician, Dr. Conneau, was on hand as were members of the palace staff: the *Grand Chambellan,* the *Grand Maréchal,* the Master of Ceremonies and the Prince Impérial's tutor. There were many dignitaries present: Persigny, of course, M. Drouyn de Lhuys, General Bourbaki of the Maison Militaire and another distinguished soldier: Marshal MacMahon, Duc de Magenta and Governor-General of Algeria. During the course of the day a number of visitors came by to pay their respects: among them, Baron Haussmann, Prefect of Police Piétri, the Comte de Nieuwerkerke and M. Schneider, who was president of the Legislature and the head of Le Creusot. The favorite ladies of the court were very much in evidence: Princess Metternich, the Marquise de Galliffet, the Duchesse de Cadore and Marshal Pélissier's young Spanish wife.

It was a genial and relaxed occasion, and later in the

afternoon Louis Napoleon himself addressed members of the Diplomatic Corps. "It is my hope that the year which is now beginning," he said, "will further cement our mutual interest in peace and civilization."

The day ended on this optimistic note, and a secure future seemed to lie ahead. There were clouds on the horizon, of course, but there did not appear to be any particular cause for alarm. The last months of 1869 had been most encouraging: in November Eugénie had presided over the ceremonies opening the Suez Canal, and through them French prestige had gained new luster. 1870 began under the same happy auspices, and life in Paris was as entertaining and glamorous as ever. It did happen that the first party of the winter season scheduled at the Tuileries was canceled because of a riot in one of the working-class districts and the food for the buffet was distributed to a regiment of Turcos, but before long the tempo began again. Soon there were parties everywhere: a reception at the Russian Embassy, a ball at the Ministry of Finance, the Marquise Roccagiovine gave a concert and Princess Mathilde had a dance, to which she invited the Prince Impérial, now a boy of fourteen. During the winter months there was ice-skating in the Bois, and at night gentlemen wore clever little lanterns in their buttonholes. When spring came, a group of Americans introduced roller-skating to the capital—everyone thought it no more than a passing fancy—and there was a party at the Ministry of War, with gay military tents in the garden, to celebrate Leboeuf's promotion to Marshal of France. Life in Louis Napoleon's capital was much the same as it had been throughout the years of empire—if anything, rather more sophisticated and rather more luxurious. Naturally, *Tout Paris* looked forward to the great event of the season: the running of the Grand Prix at Longchamp.

The race track in the Bois de Boulogne had been the scene of many of the splendid theatrics of empire, both military and otherwise, and this great sporting event was no exception. The track itself had been inaugurated in 1857 through the efforts of the Duc de Morny, and the Grand Prix de Paris established six years later. It quickly became one of Europe's leading races and attracted competitors from England as well as from the rest of the continent. On June 12, 1870, hundreds of sportsmen and spectators hurried toward Longchamp from every direction. They came by railroad and *bateau mouche* and in a variety of carriages. The avenue de l'Impératrice leading into the Bois was crowded with landaus and calèches, and there were unusual numbers of coachmen in white silk stockings and powdered wigs. Everyone of any importance in the social and political life of Paris was there, and the stands were full of beautifully dressed women. This season it seemed that blue was the dominant color, Tyrolean straw hats were popular and one young lady created something of a sensation in a taffeta skirt printed to resemble a tiger skin. Shading themselves from the sun under swan-feather umbrellas you might have seen the Comtesse Walewska and Mme. Rimsky-Korsakoff, Princess Metternich and the Marquise de Galliffet, among many others well known at court and in the palaces of the faubourg Saint Germain.

All the great sportsmen of the day were on hand: the members of the Jockey Club with their president, the Vicomte Paul Daru; the Comte Henri Delamare; the Comte d'Osmond, who had lost his left hand in a hunting accident; Mr. Mackenzie Grieves with his monocle and old-fashioned riding coat; Montguyon, the Duc de Morny's intimate friend; and the Barons Alphonse and Gustave de Rothschild. There were English bookmakers taking bets, and the Prince Impérial could be seen with his equerry and a group of young sportsmen. The course itself was three thousand meters long, and twelve three-year-olds had been entered in the race, including two English horses, Pandora and Prince of Wales. The purse was a substantial 141,700 francs, and in addition a silver trophy had been contributed by the emperor. Everyone was impatient for the race to begin.

Now the horses were away, and soon a loud cry came up from the stands: "Sornette! Sornette!" A French horse was in the lead, but spectators consulting the program found that Sornette was something of a mystery, its owner listed as a certain Major Fridolin whom no one seemed to know. As a matter of fact, there were three owners: M. Charles Laffitte, the son of the well-known banker; Baron Nivière; and Khalil Bey, an Oriental exotic with English manners who often played billiards with his friends on horseback. His flat in the rue Taitbout was the scene of many a sumptuous party, and he ended in the great tradition of the Boulevard by going through all of his money. Today, however, was a lucky day, and his Sornette was the winner. In fact, the first four horses were French, and all through the stands one could hear the popping of champagne corks as the victory was celebrated with enthusiasm. On that June day—with the sun bright on polished saddles and racing silks, with the green grass and the superb horses, with beautiful women and aristocratic sportsmen and cavalry officers everywhere—on that June day only a lunatic would have suggested that this was to be the last ceremony of the empire. In the following month a disastrous war would begin, and one can only remember what Hermann Bahr said about Imperial Vienna in the last days of the Habsburgs: "I mistook the dying afterglow for the first flush of dawn."

The imminent collapse of a secure and prosperous world of pleasure and elegance, however, had been anticipated in a number of different ways during the past year. In June of 1869, in the summer before Sornette won the Grand Prix at Longchamp, Offenbach's librettist Ludovic Halévy attended a performance of Gounod's *Faust,* although he saw very little of the opera. In the last few weeks elections had taken place, putting a group of anti-establishment figures into the limelight: among them, Henri Rochefort, whose satirical writings had so insulted the imperial family, and Léon Gambetta, the lawyer who had defended Delescluze at the Baudin trial. Gambetta, in fact, had been elected to a seat in the Assemblée Nationale, and the mood along the Boulevard was definitely revolutionary. Night after night mobs of workmen swarmed through the streets, and the cavalry was out in force. Some explosion was inevitable, and it came during Halévy's evening at the opera. In the theater they were singing the Soldiers' Chorus, and the music was almost drowned out by the shouts of the crowd and the clatter of horses' hoofs in the street outside. Halévy hurried to a window backstage, and below him he could see that a mêlée had begun: hats and helmets were flying through the air, sabers were flashing and horsemen being pulled from their saddles. The sight was a disturbing one, and Halévy returned to his seat in a somber state of mind. What impressed him then was the scene inside the Opéra: the boxes and stalls filled with elegantly dressed women and sparkling diamonds and military uniforms and on the stage the interior of a palace with sixty beautiful girls dancing the last-act ballet. As a writer Halévy was fascinated by the contrast between this dazzling scene and the nightmare in the Boulevard outside. Which was the illusion and which the reality? He had come face to face with one of the compelling paradoxes of the Second Empire, and he recognized the ugly mood which was staining its last days.

A similar feeling of doom prompted him to join with Henri Meilhac in writing *Froufrou,* a play which opened at the Gymnase in the fall of 1869. It was not a musical but rather a dark comedy of manners, something quite unexpected from the authors of *La Belle Hélène* and *La Grande Duchesse de Gérolstein.* On the surface it was the story of an unfaithful wife, a subject popular at the time and to be found in plays by Dumas *fils* and Emile Augier as well. The plot is simple enough: a spoiled and frivolous woman escapes from her dull marriage and goes to Venice with a lover. While there, she suffers a collapse and returns dying to her family. However, with the play Halévy and Meilhac suggest some of the realities of the Second Empire and symbolically anticipate its destruction. The month after she returned from the opening of the Suez Canal Eugénie went with her husband to see a performance of *Froufrou.* It was reported that she cried so desperately that the rouge ran down her face and she dared not show herself after the final curtain. In an apparently conventional play about adultery two writers of comedy had exposed a painful nerve and considered some of the disturbing currents running beneath the surface of contemporary life. Along with Baudelaire and Offenbach and the Goncourts they were afraid, and in their fear they showed an artistic understanding of the meaning of their era.

As the last months of the régime began, more and more nerves came to be exposed and more and more unpleasant realities brought to light. Only a few days after Louis Napoleon's optimistic New Year message a scandal broke out which pointed to further cracks in the edifice. On January

10, 1870, Prince Pierre Bonaparte, the emperor's cousin and a troublemaker unwelcome at the Tuileries, shot and killed a man named Victor Noir who worked for Henri Rochefort's inflammatory journal, *La Marseillaise*. Victor Noir had come as a second to arrange the details of a duel in which Prince Pierre was to take part following a controversy with a well-known radical newspaper. Pierre Bonaparte had a long record of violence: he had fought for Bolívar in South America and, among other irregularities, there was a report that he had killed a papal agent in Italy in the 1830s. While president of the Second Republic, Louis Napoleon tried to redeem his cousin by giving him a post with the Foreign Legion in Algeria. Pierre soon left without leave and was subsequently cashiered. He was given a small income by the emperor but otherwise kept at arm's length. The murder of Victor Noir surprised no one who knew the disreputable prince, and the incident would have passed without notice had his name not been Bonaparte. The satirist Rochefort seized on the event and magnified it to the proportions of a national tragedy. On the day after the murder *La Marseillaise* appeared with its front page bordered in black, and Rochefort printed an unmistakable call to revolution:

> For eighteen years now France has been held in the bloodied hands of these cut-throats, who, not content to shoot down Republicans in the streets, draw them into dirty traps in order to slit their throats in private. Frenchmen, have you not had quite enough of it?

The government lost no time in suppressing the newspaper, and Prince Pierre was already behind bars in the Conciergerie. However, it was rumored that Louis Napoleon himself was very near collapse. Victor Noir's funeral on January 12 became the occasion for a revolutionary demonstration, and a crowd of over a hundred thousand people gathered in Neuilly to accompany the casket to the cemetery. A large detachment of troops was waiting to put down any violence, but the day passed without incident. Rochefort's revolution had failed, although walking behind Victor Noir's coffin were men like Delescluze and Raoul Rigault who fourteen months later would lead the successful uprising known as the Commune of Paris. Pierre Bonaparte was put on trial, and in March he was acquitted—apparently with justice. He was sentenced to pay damages to the dead man's family, and the incident seemed to be closed.

However, by this time the social atmosphere in Paris and in the provinces was deteriorating rapidly. There had been a number of violent strikes, and it was growing more apparent every day that material progress had been limited to the middle and upper classes alone. In spite of the emperor's efforts, the working man still had little security, conditions at home and in the factory were generally impossible and his wages had hardly kept pace with inflation. For the past several years there had been periodic revolts at Lyon and other industrial cities, and blood was beginning to flow. Thirteen workmen were killed by government troops at La Ricamarie in June of 1869, and fourteen more were dead at the Aubin mines in October. At the beginning of 1870 over twelve thousand steel workers struck at the steel mills of Le Creusot, and there were many ugly incidents. Urgent messages were relayed from provincial city halls in various parts of the country to the Ministry of the Interior and the Ministry of War in Paris to send more soldiers. The dissatisfaction of the nation at large was shown in the elections of 1869, when a shift of only half a million votes would have given power to the opponents of the régime. Paris and all the large cities voted against Louis Napoleon, and only the rural vote saved him. Ten years earlier the situation had been quite the reverse, and confidence in the government had been expressed by over five million affirmative votes. Nevertheless, in creating the Liberal Empire under Emile Ollivier, Louis Napoleon managed to divide the opposition and so save his régime.

As a matter of fact, in the first months of 1870 it became apparent that the imperial government was regaining its strength. Prosperity was still growing, and peace in Europe seemed certain for many years to come. Even as late as the end of June, only a few weeks before the French declaration of war, Emile Ollivier could address the Assemblée Nationale in soothing terms. "In whatever direction we look abroad," he said, "we find no pressing problems. There has never been a time in history when the prospects of peace in Europe have been better." The tensions following the Austrian defeat at Sadowa in 1866 had been dissipated, and only a handful of negative thinkers suspected that some future coalition of the new North German Confederation and the other German states would result in a threat to European harmony and unsettle the existing balance of power.

In some ways the omens of disaster prevalent in the last days of the empire were more apparent than real. They derived from the musings of literary men and the theatrics of practiced revolutionaries. Surely a few strikes, a few riots in the street did not mark the end of an era. Even an incident like Victor Noir's murder could be smoothed over, once it became clear that Louis Napoleon himself was in no way involved. The grievances of miners and textile workers could be dealt with, and an intelligent foreign policy and a strong army could contain the menace of Prussia. The Second Empire was a substantial fact, and there was little that could not be corrected by a ruler as advanced in his social thinking as Louis Napoleon. Among private papers found in the Tuileries after the fall of the empire was a note in his own hand:

What we wish for:
Progress in every form;
Dignity in foreign affairs;
The well-being of farmers and industrial workers.

Under such a broad and modern policy, carried out within the new context of a constitutional monarchy, everything could be resolved in time. It required no more than a firm hand on the helm. Unhappily, that firm hand was lacking, for by 1869 Louis Napoleon had come to the end of his strength.

Many years later an Englishman recalled that as a boy he had attended a ceremony that year in the garden of the Tuileries to see the young Prince Impérial drill a company of fellow cadets. The prince performed his role admirably, and Eugénie was standing by, straight and lovely in a black-and-white bonnet and a zebra-striped dress. The young Englishman, however, soon noticed another figure among the spectators:

On a bench overlooking the gravel sat a very tired old gentleman, rather hunched together, and looking decidedly ill. I do not think I should have recognized him but for his spiky moustache. He was anything but terrifying in a tall hat and a rather loosely-fitting frock coat.

The tired old gentleman was Napoleon III, and all the optimism and courage with which he had started the Second Empire had deserted him completely. Along with his strength had gone his illusions. For a long time now his health had been deteriorating in an alarming fashion, and he looked far older than his years. He smoked cigarettes incessantly and had weakened his constitution with an unusual sexual appetite. More significant was the fact that he was suffering from a painful gallstone "as big as a pigeon's egg." Even as long ago as 1859, when he was little more than fifty, the British ambassador, Lord Cowley, had reported back to London that the emperor looked much older "than his birth certificate would indicate." The same observation was made by the emperor's old friend and personal physician, Dr. Conneau, who arranged for a consultation with the English surgeon, Sir William Ferguson. In order not to alarm the emperor, the examination was largely a visual one, and Sir William established a diagnosis—obvious to the least footman in the Tuileries—that Louis Napoleon was suffering from "general fatigue" and "an excess of nervous tension."

In 1864, during military maneuvers at the camp of Châlons in the autumn, Louis Napoleon was seized with violent pains one night, and the presence of a gallstone was first suspected. His condition continued to grow worse, and particularly after 1866, the year of Sadowa, he was a different man. One day in those years Marshal Canrobert saw him at Saint Cloud. "He could hardly rise from his chair," said Canrobert, "and his drawn features betrayed both mental anguish and physical pain." In fact, during one of the festivals at Saint Cloud the noise of the revelers so disturbed his sleep that he was forced to move to Villeneuve, the little retreat where he and Eugénie had spent their honeymoon. As the result of intense pain, his character had darkened, and he was living in a shadow world of medication. He was given tranquilizers with an opium base for his pain, and at night he regularly took sleeping drafts. In the tense days after Sadowa he would wake

from a drugged sleep and ask to speak to General de Saint
Arnaud—a fellow conspirator who had been dead since
the Crimean War. When appearing in public, the emperor often put on make-up to disguise his physical condition, although every sort of rumor was abroad in the capital and those at court were well aware of the truth.

His physical decline intensified a corresponding mental
decline, and his vitality was practically gone. During the
Exposition of 1867 Otto von Bismarck dismissed him as a
mediocrity—an *"incapacité méconnue"*—and General
von Moltke noticed the dead look in his eyes. Surely these
observations helped justify the Prussian militarists in their
decision to force him into an unwanted war. It was true
enough that his grip on the reins of government was
slackening: the establishment of the Liberal Empire in itself had weakened his autocratic position, and his illness
obliged him to give Eugénie more and more of a rôle in
affairs of state until at the end she actually was appointed
regent. In the last months of the empire he seemed willing
to drift with the tide of events instead of turning them to
his own purposes as he had done in the past. Indeed, by
the summer of 1870 he had approved a plan of abdication
which would put the Prince Impérial on the throne in 1874
when he reached the legal age of eighteen. Then the sick
man would be relieved of the fatigues of office and free to
pass his time in retirement at Biarritz and elsewhere. That
decision had been almost inevitable: on June 19, 1870, the
emperor had finally agreed to an extensive physical examination conducted by a brilliant young doctor named Germain Sée. The diagnosis of a gallstone was confirmed, and
less than a month later a group of consultants arrived at
Saint Cloud to consider the surgical intervention which
Dr. Sée strongly recommended. The older doctors were
afraid of the risks involved—in the previous year Marshal

Niel had died following a similar operation—and they decided to wait and see what the future might bring. And so it happened that Louis Napoleon went off to his last war, hardly able to mount a horse.

"England is an empire," said the nineteenth-century historian Jules Michelet, "Germany is a country and a race, but France is one person." The Sun King and General de Gaulle come to mind, and the fact that Louis Napoleon was so completely the Second Empire explains in part why the nation collapsed unexpectedly in 1870. Louis Napoleon had a splendid gift of improvisation which carried him from Strasbourg to Boulogne to the imperial throne—and a position as the most important ruler on the continent and the leader of a rich and progressive country adjusting to a new industrial civilization and approaching the twentieth century with confidence. Once his health was gone, everything was gone. And, as so often in its history, France suffered from the deficiencies of personal rule. At the end of the Second Empire there was no one else to take over the burdens of government, for Louis Napoleon had surrounded himself with old friends of doubtful intelligence, and there were certain actual incompetents who stayed with him to the end. The decisions had always been his to make, and he no longer had the strength to make them. The painful illness from which he suffered accentuated all the defects of his personality and pointed up its contradictory elements: Don Quixote and Machiavelli in the same person, courage and timidity side by side, charm and rudeness in a single breath, and conservatism at odds with a liberal point of view unique among contemporary rulers. In any case, he never lost a fatalistic sense of humor and a sad lucidity of mind. When Emile Ollivier finally summoned up the courage to tell him that his faculties were declining, he said with a melancholy smile: "That is consistent with all the reports I have received."

However much the disintegration of his health had begun to symbolize the collapse of the nation, there was a surprise in store for those who thought that he was finished. On May 8, 1870, a plebiscite was held to approve the creation of the Liberal Empire and the beginnings of parliamentary government. The results astounded even the emperor's most enthusiastic and unthinking followers. His policies were approved by an overwhelming majority of the electorate: 7,358,000 to 1,571,000. Louis Napoleon was delighted, and the first thing he did after the results had been tabulated was to show them to his son. This vote of confidence meant that the Prince Impérial was assured of succession, and the emperor had put more and more of his future into the boy's hands. Surely the outcome of the plebiscite seemed to mark the end of republican aspirations. Léon Gambetta, seeing the promise of a democracy fade before his eyes, remarked sadly: "The empire is stronger than ever before."

It was true. Had Louis Napoleon died at this moment, his régime might well have come down to us as one of the most successful and prosperous—as well as most splendid —in French history.[1] What failures there had been, disasters such as Mexico, had occurred thousands of miles away from home. On the other hand, the successes were to be seen on all sides: the railroads and factories and great boulevards, the hospitals and bridges, the magnificent army and the financial prosperity and the social program years ahead of its time.

However, by 1870 the French were bored again, as bored as they had been when Lamartine diagnosed the condition under the July Monarchy. The perceptive British ambassador Lord Lyons described it more fully:

"There is no glitter at home or abroad to divert public attention, and the French have been a good many years without the excitement of a change." In the past Louis Napoleon had supplied the necessary bread and circuses with a lavish hand. But now—weak, uncertain, in pain, physically and mentally exhausted—he had lost control. It came to pass that his countrymen, more as a result of their own arrogance and boredom than of his incompetence, allowed themselves to be tricked into declaring a war for which they were not prepared. In spite of the emotionalism surrounding the defeat at Sedan, there is every indication that Louis Napoleon did not destroy France. Tragically, he was too weak to prevent his country from destroying itself in one final access of unreality.

CHAPTER EIGHTEEN

The Mousetrap

THE die had been cast on July 3, 1866, at Sadowa, a village some seventy miles east of Prague on the Bohemian plain. There the Seven Weeks War came to an end with Prussia unexpectedly defeating the Austrian Empire and forcing a change in the balance of power on the continent. Half a million men were engaged in this final battle, known to the Germans as the battle of Königgrätz, and the victory allowed Bismarck to realize his ambition of elevating Prussia to the leadership of the German-speaking world. The victory took Europe by surprise, although some of the French generals were well aware of its implications. "Be as rude as you like about this army of lawyers and oculists," said Bourbaki, commandant of the Garde Impériale, "but it will get to Vienna just as soon as it likes."

The Prussians did not choose to go to Vienna. It was enough that they had broken the power of the Austrian Empire, and Bismarck was content with a political victory. Moreover, the war gave the Prussian Army a training ground such as the Third Reich would find in Spain and Poland many years later. In the brief campaign the

Prussian General Staff had an opportunity of analyzing its mistakes and tabulating the weaknesses and virtues of its army. The battle of Sadowa demonstrated the superiority of the Dreyse needle-gun, a breech-loader which allowed the Prussians to fire with greater speed than the enemy, but the battle also showed the inefficiency of their artillery. Soon after Sadowa a reform was undertaken by the Inspector General, and at the beginning of the Franco-Prussian War the army was completely equipped with field guns made of steel by the Krupp Works at Essen. In contrast, the French were still using bronze cannon which had seen service at Sebastopol and Magenta. As important as the military reorganization which followed the battle of Sadowa was the fact that a North German Confederation had been formed—an event marking the beginning of a coalition of states under Prussian control which eventually became a new German Empire. Three times in less than a hundred years that coalition was to destroy European harmony and disarrange a balance of power based on French supremacy on the continent. The consequences of Sadowa were far-reaching, and some of them were immediately understood in Paris.

Soon after the disturbing summer of 1866 Louis Napoleon sent a trusted officer to serve as military attaché in Berlin: Lieutenant Colonel Eugène de Stoffel. It was his responsibility to supply the emperor with confidential reports on the state of the Prussian Army and the psychological mood of the General Staff. The reports were detailed and gloomy, and their essence is to be found in an often-quoted remark. "Prussia is not a country which has an army," he wrote in the winter of 1870. "Prussia is an army which has a country."

It is easy to oversimplify and imagine that in the years which preceded the Franco-Prussian War Bismarck's generals had at their disposal a magnificent military machine while the French Imperial Army was weak and confused and hopelessly outdated. The reality is rather more complicated: in the opening movements of the war both armies made unbelievable blunders, and the Prussians were far less confident of victory than the French. In the final analysis, however, they made fewer mistakes, they learned to profit from the mistakes they did make and they employed all the new tools of industry and science. On a symbolic level some conflict between the two countries had become inevitable. Like the First World War, the Franco-Prussian War of 1870 was the verification of something which had already happened. It confirmed the clash of two irreconcilable points of view—one with roots in a vanished age and the other taking into account the industrial and social and military changes of the nineteenth century. The war reflects that same conflict between the old and the new so apparent in every phase of Second Empire social and political life and evident in a continuing intellectual battle between realism and romanticism.

There is little question that the French were prepared for war—after a fashion. It is simply that they were prepared for the wrong war and ready to retrace their footsteps to Italy and Mexico and the Crimea. They were by no means prepared for the first of the modern European wars: a war in which railroads and technology carried the day; in which steel cannon cut down hussars and cuirassiers heavy with silk and gold braid; in which unromantic citizen soldiers faced a glamorous professional army—a French army with ideas nourished by the memory of Napoleon Bonaparte and skills limited to desert raids and medieval tactics of Solferino and Magenta. The Landwehr had no magnificent uniform, but its soldiers were supported by the steel guns of Krupp. The Franco-Prussian

War marks the triumph of science and realism, however much it warms the blood to think of the arrogant Marquis de Galliffet riding at the head of his Third Chasseurs d'Afrique against the methodical lawyers and oculists of the German infantry.

The condition of the French Imperial Army in 1870 could have been appreciated most fully by paying a visit to the great military camp at Châlons-sur-Marne. A hundred miles to the east of Paris, the camp was the showcase of the Imperial Army and a hymn to the glories of the past. In the garrison town of Mourmelon there were inns like Au Zouave Galant and streets like the rue Canrobert, and brilliant uniforms shone everywhere. Officers filled their tents with elaborate furniture, while enlisted men occupied off-duty hours making sculptured lions and decorating the grounds. Like so much else in the Second Empire, appearances were of the first importance. One day during maneuvers a young colonel was congratulated by his commanding officer for having led a brilliant cavalry charge against a detachment of infantry. The young colonel could not resist saying that the situation might have been different had there been real bullets—as there soon would be.

"Well, then," said the general, "what would you have done?"

"I'd have gotten the hell out of here, sir!"

And of all the unrealistic incidents which had taken place at Châlons none can surpass the day in 1863 when the young Prince Impérial pinned the grand cross of the Légion d'Honneur on the visiting Prussian Minister of War, General von Roon.

In the peaceful years which followed the withdrawal from Mexico the Imperial Army grew soft and complacent on garrison duty, content to polish gold buttons and

prepare for dazzling reviews. In the matter of organization—or possible reorganization—it relied on the imprecise means which had carried it from one doubtful victory
to the next: Le Système D. It was a system well known in
other areas of French life. *"On se débrouillera toujours,"*
they said and still say. "We'll muddle through somehow."

Guided by this popular philosophy, the Imperial Army
had muddled through the confusions of the Crimean War
when men and weapons and supplies arrived on different
timetables. It had survived the inadequacies of the Italian
campaign when there were no bandages and not enough
ammunition. Actually, all the wars of the Second Empire
had been mismanaged, and in addition a number of
promising young officers had been killed in Mexico. Older
officers—whatever their dash or glamour may have been
in the past—were not of the first rank: not Pélissier or
MacMahon in the Crimea, not Cousin-Montaubon in
China, not Forey or Bazaine in Mexico. Inefficiency and
the lack of military brilliance, however, were obscured by
splendid uniforms and embroidered battle flags, by golden
eagles and resounding titles: Comte de Palikao, Duc de
Magenta, Duc de Malakoff.

With the stark fact of Sadowa and the example of Prussian military reorganization before their eyes, Louis Napoleon and some of his generals demonstrated far more realism than might have been expected. In the year after the
defeat of Austria, General Trochu published (under a
pseudonym) a book which outlined the glaring deficiencies of the Imperial Army and, among other revolutionary
observations, pointed out that cavalry had little place in
modern warfare. *L'Armée française en 1867* ran through
sixteen editions in the first few weeks of publication, although it was apparently overlooked by the staff officers at
the Ministry of War. Well aware of the state into which a

magnificent army had fallen through mismanagement and incompetence, Louis Napoleon proposed a number of major reforms. Most of these recommendations were conveniently lost in the labyrinth of the military establishment. In particular he had been interested in an excellent new breech-loading rifle developed in one of the government arsenals by an employee named Chassepot. At the emperor's insistence and over the objection of generals such as Randon, the *chassepot,* as the weapon came to be called, was put into production in 1866. By the outbreak of the Franco-Prussian War there were a million of them available, and in every way they were superior to the Prussian needle-gun, with an effective range a thousand yards greater. Nevertheless, with the exception of this weapon and the overrated *mitrailleuse,* the emperor was thwarted in his efforts at reform.[1] He had wanted a general staff on the Prussian model and an expansion of the system of reserves. After all, the Prussians held an entire nation in the reserve of the Landwehr, and no one could escape serving. In France, largely dominated by middle-class interests, it was still easy enough to buy a substitute when you were called up. The lack of sufficient reserves was disturbing to Louis Napoleon, since Colonel Stoffel's reports from Berlin indicated that the Prussian General Staff was working out a detailed plan for the rapid mobilization of the Landwehr—a plan involving the creation of precise railroad schedules and the establishment of convenient supply depots near the French border and elsewhere. In the face of these obvious preparations for war, the French military still could not take a nation of beer drinkers with any seriousness and continued to rely on Le Système D, a gay method of improvisation which ultimately depended on the bravery of the French soldier.

An inevitable conflict, based on national personality and

international politics, was drawing near, and in the summer of 1870 a trivial argument drove France into declaring war on Prussia. The war was scarcely welcome to Louis Napoleon and to the King of Prussia, but the prospects of it were greeted with enthusiasm by Bismarck and his generals as well as by the French people. In 1868 a military junta had dethroned Queen Isabella of Spain, and the regent Marshal Prim had been looking around for a king to replace her. Finally the choice fell on Prince Leopold of Hohenzollern-Sigmaringen. The choice seemed innocuous enough, and should the French object to having a cousin of Wilhelm of Prussia at their southern border, it could be pointed out that the blood of the Murats and the Beauharnais also flowed in Leopold's veins.

Obsessed with memories of the first Napoleon and convinced of their nation's rôle as the arbiter of European affairs, the French objected violently. A decision had been taken without consulting them, and public opinion, reflected in the Paris press, demanded the immediate withdrawal of Leopold's name as a candidate for the Spanish throne. Intoxicated with the Napoleonic Legend, newspapers spoke grandly of "a question of prestige" and "the honor of France." By July 12, 1870, the King of Prussia, wanting no trouble and at a loss to understand the violent objections, finally agreed to have Prince Leopold's name withdrawn. There the matter should have ended, but by this time the French had become illogically aggressive. The Comte Benedetti, French ambassador to Berlin, pursued Wilhelm to the spa at Ems near Coblenz and demanded a further concession: the assurance that Leopold would *never again* seek the throne of Spain. This arrogance was too much for the King of Prussia, who dismissed Benedetti in irritation, saying that the issue had been decided and that he was unable to make any guarantees about the future.

A report of the interview was sent by telegram to Bismarck in Berlin, arriving as he was at dinner with Generals von Roon and von Moltke. The three of them were disappointed that the argument between France and Prussia was being resolved without a declaration of war. Their disappointment was understandable: the generals were anxious to test the formidable army they had created, and Bismarck was quite as eager for war, although with different motives. The chief minister saw a war with France as a means of bringing the remaining German states together to form one nation dominated by Prussia. Now the opportunity seemed to be slipping from his hands. He studied the telegram from Ems with care and at last came to the conclusion that a little editing would turn the report of the king's interview with Benedetti into an insult to Prussia as well as to France. He altered the tone of the telegram and released its new contents to a leading Berlin newspaper, the *Norddeutsche Zeitung,* and to all Prussian representatives abroad.

As he suspected, the notorious Ems Telegram aroused strong chauvinistic feelings in both countries. When the report was published in Berlin, people ran through the streets shouting *"Nach Paris!"* And the next day, overcome by the same general madness, Frenchmen in Paris were crying out *"A Berlin!"* and *"Vive la guerre!"* and for the first time in eighteen years permission was given to sing the *Marseillaise.* Paradoxically, the most enthusiastic proponents of war were the Parisian workers, who crowded the Boulevard to demonstrate their support of the Second Empire. On July 14, 1870, the Duc de Gramont—classified by Bismarck as the stupidest man in Europe—announced in his capacity as Minister of Foreign Affairs

that the French would be across the Rhine in two weeks.
There was no reason to disbelieve him, and at this point
even the Prussian generals might have agreed. The reputation of the Imperial Army was enormous.

On the day after the Duc de Gramont's boast the
French government proposed a declaration of war, and it
was formally presented to the Prussians on July 19, 1870.
Unbelievably, the Second Empire had blundered into war
with a nation at arms. More incredible was the fact that
France had been the aggressor and even Bismarck's cun-
ning had been superfluous.

Louis Napoleon had never been more of a prisoner of
his romantic name than at this moment. He knew exactly
how unprepared the nation was, and he would have
agreed with Emile Zola's later analysis of the tragedy of
the Franco-Prussian War:

> We were broken by the method of a people less brave
> and more ponderous than ourselves, we were crushed
> by masses maneuvered with logic, we were routed by
> the application of science to the art of war.

With his grasp of the present and his feeling for the future, Louis Napoleon was well aware of the reality of the
situation. The irony was that he had come to power on the
strength of the Napoleonic Legend and, no matter what
his better judgment might be, he could not deny it now.
Public opinion was too strong, and no one seemed to care
that the Prussians had half a million men ready and waiting and could raise that figure to a million almost over-
night. These harsh facts did not penetrate the editorial
offices of newspapers in Paris, where journals like *Le Pays*
and *Le National* defined the peace which Louis Napoleon
publicly urged as shameful and demeaning to the glory of
France. A strange collective insanity was blossoming

along the Boulevard: one night the editor of *Le Constitu-tionnel,* which was against the war, was hissed in the street as people tore up copies of his newspaper and threw the pieces into his face. He fled into the Café Riche, where the playwright Victorien Sardou chided him for his stub-bornness in the face of public opinion. "Believe me," said Sardou, "we will go through Prussia like a knife through butter."

No one could have appreciated this unreal cliché more than Louis Napoleon himself. However, he had com-mitted himself a long time ago to the dictates of popular approval. Now the price would have to be paid: he would be forced to watch the destruction of the modern govern-ment and the prosperous nation he had created and go down in defeat with only the tattered rags of the Napole-onic Legend around him. Not only was he committed to honoring his country's desire for war, but his name com-mitted him to leading it into battle. On June 23, 1870, he gave a speech indicating that he would follow the will of the people, and a few days later he appointed Eugénie re-gent and prepared to leave for the front at the head of his troops. The same day he issued a proclamation to the Im-perial Army notable for its lack of theatrics and its silence on the subject of *La Gloire.* "The war which is begin-ning," he said, "will be long and painful."

At ten o'clock on the morning of July 28, 1870, he ap-peared at the small railroad station at the edge of the park of Saint Cloud ready to leave for war. Earlier he had at-tended mass and received communion from the Arch-bishop of Paris. The imperial train was waiting, Eugénie was there with a final admonition for him to do his duty, and Louis Napoleon—sick and pale and drawn in spite of the make-up which covered his face—stepped on board with his young son. The Prince Impérial, fourteen years old, looked small and frightened; he was being taken to war at his mother's insistence and against the advice of the generals. Those who witnessed this melancholy departure could only think of a funeral cortège, and surely the emperor in no way suggested a Napoleon leaving for war. Only a few days earlier Princess Mathilde had told him how very ill he looked. "It's true," he had said after a glance at the mirror. "I'm not exactly the picture of health."

Nevertheless, he took the train from Saint Cloud and arrived at seven o'clock the same evening at Metz in the northeast corner of France. Here he was to take command of eight army corps—some 220,000 men—spread along a hundred-mile salient behind the Saar, from the Luxembourg border to the Swiss border. The immediate plan was to invade the southern German states, and his forces were optimistically called the Army of the Rhine.

As if celebrating some sinister carnival, the town of Metz was in complete chaos, and everyone seemed to have lost his head. The morning after he arrived Louis Napoleon sent a message back to the empress: "Things here are not as far along as I had hoped." It was a remarkable understatement, for the French mobilization had begun in a condition of disorder which would have surprised the most pessimistic observer. Troops were arriving by train from Paris, drunk and without discipline; tents and cooking equipment and ammunition often did not arrive at all; there was no money for the paymaster; and the only maps issued were of the German side of the frontier. It seemed rather pointless for the Zouaves to have trained a parrot to say *A Berlin!* when hundreds of officers could not find the regiments to which they had been assigned and thousands of Gardes Mobiles stood around waiting to share a handful of antique rifles, Model 1842. Trains were late and overcrowded, and no adequate arrangements had been made for supply depots. Confusion followed upon confusion, and it was in the nature of a miracle that on August 2, 1870, elements of the Imperial Army managed to penetrate a few miles beyond the border and capture the town of Saarbrücken. It was a small victory—and the last one.

Four days later the French suffered the twin defeats of Fröschwiller and Forbach, and MacMahon's army was driven back to Lorraine in disorder. These defeats and the ones which followed made it clear that a new age of military technology had dawned: time and again the long-range Prussian artillery decimated the imperial cavalry and outdistanced the antique French guns. The end was beginning, and the invasion of Germany had turned into the invasion of France as Prussian and Saxon and Bavarian troops poured across the frontier. In Paris they found it impossible to believe the news coming in from the front —oddly enough, the General Staff in Berlin was as amazed—and Frenchmen would have preferred the optimistic picture painted by the Prince Impérial. *"Chère Maman,"* he telegraphed his mother in the middle of August, "I am very well and so is Papa; everything is getting better and better."

The last act had begun. By now Louis Napoleon had turned his command over to Marshal Bazaine, who proceeded to lead more than a hundred thousand men into a trap at Metz, where he was surrounded and besieged and eventually captured. The emperor joined Marshal MacMahon in a demoralized retreat back to Châlons. Even then the fate of the Second Empire might have been avoided, had Louis Napoleon been strong enough to insist on his plan of returning with MacMahon's army to the defense of Paris. But frantic telegrams arrived from the capital, where Eugénie and the generals at the Ministry of War were calling for the relief of Bazaine at Metz, convinced that Louis Napoleon's return would precipitate a revolution. Pain and melancholy had consumed him, and the emperor was in no condition to object. Here at Châlons in the last week of August he had all but abdicated. In fact, everyone at Châlons seemed to have abdicated: officers wandered around in dirty uniforms, drunken soldiers reeled across the parade grounds and every day contradictory orders arrived from Paris. The will to fight had gone and discipline was nonexistent. The situation became so desperate that at last the Gardes Mobiles, who had been sent to bolster MacMahon's army, were gathered up from the bars and brothels and sent back to Paris as completely useless. The rapid demoralization of the army was symbolic of the spiritual decay of a nation which for too long had given itself over to pleasure and unreality.

By the end of August Marshal MacMahon had managed to put the Army of Châlons into some semblance of order, and he set out to relieve Bazaine at Metz. Louis Napoleon followed in the wake of the army like a phantom, all his strength and authority gone. The Germans watched the progress of this dispirited relief column with interest, and the Uhlans of Moltke's Second Army circled the line of march like wolves. The way to Metz was blocked, and in desperation MacMahon sought to regroup his forces and inject some new fire into his men. To this end he assembled his army in the fortress town of Sedan a few miles from the Belgian border. It was a military decision of outstanding incompetence, since the town was entirely surrounded by hills and was in every sense an untenable position—a fact which did not escape the Prussians. Looking over his maps, General von Moltke exulted: "Now we

332

have them in a mousetrap." And General Ducrot, soon to take over command of the Army of Châlons, put it rather more succinctly: he said that the French were sitting at the bottom of a chamberpot *"et nous y serons emmerdés."* Then he wrapped his great cloak around him and sat by the campfire of the Zouaves and waited calmly for the morning of September 1, 1870, to begin.

High on a wooded hill above Frénois, south of the Meuse and not far from Sedan, a group of horsemen sat and looked down at the destruction of the French Imperial Army. The King of Prussia was there; Generals von Roon and von Moltke and other staff officers; Bismarck and members of the Foreign Office; Colonel Walker, an observer from the British Army; General Sheridan of the United States Cavalry; and Mr. W. H. Russell, the famous correspondent of *The Times* of London. Sitting in the saddle like the rulers of some Mongol empire were the German princes in their gorgeous uniforms—Leopold of Bavaria, William of Württemberg, Duke Frederick of Schleswig-Holstein, the Duke of Saxe-Coburg and the Grand Duke of Mecklenburg-Strelitz. Below them the Uhlans and Death's Head Hussars rode through the hills surrounding Sedan as Prussian and Saxon and Bavarian guns cut the French Army to pieces.

In a final attempt to escape from the mousetrap the French tried their last and most useless weapon: General Margueritte's cavalry. A thundering charge came down along the plain of Floing like an avalanche, and clouds of dust rose in the hot sultry air. But, as had happened so often in the brief campaign of the Franco-Prussian War, the gallantry and flashing sabers of the cavalry were no match for well-armed infantrymen. When the charge came to an end, the bodies of horses and riders were piled high in front of the German lines. Undaunted, the survivors rode back to regroup. Margueritte had been hit in the face by a bullet, and Ducrot asked the Marquis de Galliffet, now a general, if he would lead a second charge. Galliffet's answer was in the great French tradition. "As often as you like, *mon général,*" he said, "so long as there's one of us left."

The odds were overwhelming, and even the bravery of the French soldier counted for little against the cool professionalism of a modern army. A few hours after Galliffet's heroic and pointless charge at Floing, Louis Napoleon regained his composure sufficiently to perform an act of courage which, in the contradictory way of everything connected with the Second Empire, served only to earn him a despised name in French history.[2] He had spent the morning in the vicinity of Bazeilles, where the first fighting of the day had begun and where Marshal MacMahon had been wounded. It was agony for the emperor to ride—for two days now he had been passing blood—but he rode out among his troops with a cheerful countenance helped to some extent by the make-up he wore. As he galloped across the battlefield, he tried to give heart to his soldiers as well as to find death for himself. Again and again he took unnecessary chances, but the comfort of death was denied him. It was his fate to see the tragedy through to the end. And the end had come at last: by early afternoon the Imperial Army was finished and faced inevitable defeat. During the whole engagement the chain of command had been confusing and contradictory. Early in the day MacMahon had been wounded and replaced by Ducrot, and then General de Wimpffen had arrived from Paris. In any case, none of them had been able to reverse the pattern of events. General Margueritte's cavalry was virtually destroyed and the long-range German guns had made an inferno of Sedan. The town was choked with supply wagons and disorganized troops, shells were exploding mercilessly in the crowded streets and men were being trampled to death as they tried to reach the closing gates.

Louis Napoleon knew then that he had no right to sacrifice even one more soldier in the interests of his prestige and the glory of his empire. In his mind there was no alternative, and at three o'clock on the afternoon of September 1, 1870, the white flag of surrender was raised. However, isolated fighting continued, and later in the day General Reille, an officer of the Imperial Household, crossed to the German lines with a message from the Emperor of the French to the King of Prussia:

> Monsieur mon frère,
> N'ayant pas pu mourir au milieu de mes troupes, il ne me reste qu'à remettre mon epée entre les main de Votre Majesté. Je suis de Votre Majesté le bon frère.
> Napoleon *

Some time after the official surrender took place on the following day a correspondent for the *Daily News* of London made his way into Sedan and described the aftermath of defeat: French soldiers lying drunk in the streets with burned houses and dead bodies on every side of them. Even now the Germans had begun to round up prisoners. During the course of the battle they had captured some twenty thousand men, and after the capitulation there were eighty thousand more, along with six thousand horses and 419 guns.

On the morning of September 3, 1870, the remnants of the Army of Châlons, guarded by Prussian cavalrymen,

---

* "My Brother, Not having been able to die with my soldiers, I have no alternative but to turn my sword over to Your Majesty. I am Your Majesty's devoted brother. Napoleon."

began the march toward the temporary internment camp at Iges on the Meuse—which the French came to call *le camp de la misère*—before being sent by railroad car deep into Germany. A heavy rain was falling, and some of the defeated soldiers looked up from the muddy ground long enough to see Louis Napoleon driving by in a carriage on his way to captivity at Schloss Wilhelmshöhe above Cassel. The silent and haggard men looked at him with indifference, although a few managed to shout obscenities. Wearing a uniform without insignia, the emperor sat huddled in the corner of his seat, looking at the French countryside for the last time. Behind him clattered the carriages and supply wagons of the Imperial Household, and the entourage, complete with postillions in powdered wigs, was escorted by a detachment of Death's Head Hussars. The rain poured down over their black capes, and the imperial convoy vanished.

On the previous evening in Paris a rumor had gone like wildfire through the newspaper offices and clubs, along the corridors of the Palais Bourbon and up and down the Grands Boulevards: the Imperial Army had surrendered at Sedan and the emperor himself was a prisoner. Few people in the capital found it possible to believe the rumor, and it was not until the following day that the truth began to be accepted. At four-thirty on that Saturday afternoon the Director of Posts and Telegraphs personally delivered Louis Napoleon's final message to Eugénie and all the rumors of defeat were confirmed. If in the beginning Parisians had refused to believe the news, they moved now with incredible speed to eradicate all traces of what had become in an instant the most hated régime in French history.

The last day of the empire was Sunday, September 4, 1870. By evening, without violence and without bloodshed, the leading actors of the imperial masquerade had disappeared, the scenery itself was being dismantled and a joyful revolution had taken place. The day began at seven in the morning when the empress-regent called the ministers of the government together at the palace of the Tuileries. All of them were tired and pale and disheartened, and Eugénie was wearing a black cashmere dress which she had not changed for days. She was making a last desperate attempt to save the régime, and her Spanish courage had never been more evident. But one disturbing report after another was coming in from the Prefect of Police. The official announcement of the surrender at Sedan had finally been made, and a large crowd was gathering in the place de la Concorde. Some in the crowd were moving across the river to the Palais Bourbon, where the Assemblée Nationale was in session, and others were gathering in front of the iron gates which closed off the garden of the Tuileries. Cries of "Down with the empire!" and *"Vive la République!"* were heard everywhere, and the mob was growing unmanageable. The Zouaves of the Garde Impériale were hard put to prevent the crowd from breaking through the gates of the Tuileries, and on the other side of the palace the place du Carrousel was black with people. By early afternoon the Tuileries was virtually surrounded, and the chanting grew louder and louder: "Down with the empire!" *"Vive la République!"*

It was clear that the time had come for Eugénie herself to take flight. There was almost no one left in the palace, where the shutters were drawn and summer slipcovers still shrouded the furniture. The only friends who remained with the empress were the Italian ambassador and Prince Metternich and her reader, Mme. Lebreton. The decision to leave the palace was quickly made, and the empress had time only to pack a small case and gather up her jewel

337

box. Every exit from the palace was blocked by the mob in the streets outside, and the only way to escape was through the Louvre. The small band of fugitives hurried through the Galerie de Diane and the Pavillon de Flore and along the Grand Gallery of the Louvre itself. When they reached the street and stood facing the church of Saint Germain l'Auxerrois, a group of workmen in blue blouses ran past shouting: "Down with Badinguet! Down with the Spaniard!" They took no notice of Eugénie, and Prince Metternich managed to hail a passing cab. The empress and Mme. Lebreton stepped inside and drove away in search of a temporary refuge. They tried several addresses and were finally welcomed in the house of an American dentist on the avenue Malakoff. Dr. Evans had long tended the imperial family, and he arranged to take Eugénie to Deauville, where they found a small yacht sailing for England. On Monday, the day of their escape from Paris, as they were driving along the Route Impériale, the great highway following the Left Bank of the Seine, Eugénie turned to the doctor and said: "In no country in the world is the step between the sublime and the ridiculous so short as in this."

By three o'clock on the incredible Sunday afternoon of September 4, 1870, Eugénie's personal flag had been taken down from the Tuileries and the servants had already begun to loot clothes and silver and jewels. The Second Empire was no longer in existence, and at six o'clock in the afternoon Léon Gambetta, the new Minister of the Interior, proclaimed a Republic at the Hôtel de Ville. Members of the Garde Nationale began removing the brass eagles from their shakos, and along the rue de Rivoli they were singing the *Marseillaise*. Drunken soldiers and workmen were everywhere, and Edmond de Goncourt saw that the gilt N's on the gates of the Tuileries were being covered with old newspapers. Wreaths of flowers appeared where imperial eagles had been, and all through the night Parisians overturned statues and destroyed whatever other reminders of the Second Empire they could. It was not long before even the street names had been changed and you would have had difficulty finding the avenue de l'Impératrice and the avenue de la Reine Hortense and the rue de Morny. Almost within hours every memory of Napoleon III had been erased, and it seemed impossible to believe that this was the man whom the French people had called to power and maintained in power for twenty years. The night of September 4, 1870, was a night of freedom: a carnival spirit reigned in Paris, and people amused themselves by singing obscene songs about the fallen empire to the tune of *Partant pour la Syrie.*

The carnival spirit did not seem entirely justified in terms of the melancholy events which followed: a winter siege of Paris by the Germans and the subsequent uprising of the Commune in which more Frenchmen were executed than during the Reign of Terror. Through it all the hatred of Louis Napoleon grew, and at last in the spring of 1871 they destroyed his palace of the Tuileries. The citizen-generals of the Commune put it to the torch, and in the fire and explosion vanished three centuries of French history. Along with the memory of kings and emperors were consumed the last small relics of the Second Empire: the crinolines, the Sèvres vases, the Winterhalter portraits, the Scottish costumes of the Prince Impérial, Eugénie's mauve parasol with the ostrich trimming—all gone forever.

Out of the flames of that great fire which burned for three days rose a new France, and before long it became the modern nation for which Louis Napoleon had been preparing his countrymen. The final paradox of the Second Empire is the most overwhelming one of all: those amusing and disastrous years mark not an end—but a beginning. For some time the walls of the Tuileries remained standing, and there were heaps of stone in the cour du Carrousel.[3] Those wandering among the ruins still could see the old sign which had been fastened to the gate of the imperial garden: THE PUBLIC IS NOT ADMITTED. And below these words some wit of the Boulevard had scrawled in blue crayon an acknowledgment of modern France: YES—ONCE IN A WHILE.

NOTES

CHAPTER 1   The Garden of the Tuileries

1. Edmond de Goncourt (1822–1896) and Jules de Goncourt (1830–1870) were novelists and men of letters. In 1851 they began to keep their famous *Journal des Goncourt,* a rich commentary on all aspects of French life and letters.

2. At the rate of exchange in the middle of the nineteenth century there were five francs to the dollar and twenty-five francs to the pound.

CHAPTER 2   An Evening at the Theater

1. In French the hydrangea is *l'hortensia.*

2. Félix Bacciochi, during the empire the Superintendent of Imperial Theaters, was best known as Louis Napoleon's *"maître du plaisir"* and the organizer of his many sexual adventures. Victor Fialin, self-appointed Comte de Persigny, was a former soldier and journalist and the emperor's most loyal friend.

3. It is perhaps of interest to recall that after the Commune of 1871 the Third Republic was responsible for executing 20,000 people, making prisoners of twice that number and deporting 7,500 to New Caledonia.

4. At this period in history a far greater number of Frenchmen than Englishmen had the right to vote, while four out of five Englishmen had no vote at all.

5. The Saint-Simonian social philosophy was developed by the Comte de Saint Simon and carried on after his death in 1825 by a number of disciples, the most prominent being Prosper Enfantin. The Saint-Simonians believed that hope for the future lay in the spirit of association, and that government should be organized with finance and industry on the same level as art and science. It

is a philosophy clearly associated with the growth of nineteenth-century industry and finance.

6. *"L'Empire, c'est la paix,"* said Louis Napoleon: "the empire means peace."

7. Louis Napoleon was proclaimed Emperor of the French by a decree of the Senate on November 7, 1852, though the official début of the Second Empire was December 2, 1852. Napoleon Bonaparte's son, "L'Aiglon," although he never reigned, was considered to have been Napoleon II.

CHAPTER 3   Imperial Saraband

1. The British Ambassador, Lord Cowley, reported that before the proclamation of empire at the Hôtel de Ville the soldiers of the Garde Nationale danced the cancan to keep warm.

2. Elizabeth Anne Howard was later given an estate and the title of Comtesse de Beauregard as well as some five million francs—largely money she had lent Louis Napoleon in pre-imperial days.

3. Prince Napoléon-Joseph-Charles-Paul (1821–1891), nicknamed Plon-Plon, was the son of King Jérôme and the brother of Princess Mathilde.

4. Mathilde (1820–1904), the daughter of Jérôme Bonaparte, former King of Westphalia, was the sister of Plon-Plon. During the Second Empire, and after, she conducted a famous salon in the rue de Courcelles.

5. The following is an example of one of the popular verses of the moment:

> Montijo, more beautiful than wise,
> Heaps vows upon the emperor.
> This evening, if he finds a maidenhead,
> It will mean that she had two of them.

6. The *Grand Écuyer* was the principal equerry, and the *Grand Veneur* was in charge of the imperial hunt. Each office carried with it an impressive salary.

7. The Villa Eugénie now forms part of a luxury hotel in Biarritz called the Hôtel du Palais.

CHAPTER 4 Hall of Mirrors

1. Zola's cycle of twenty novels, *Les Rougon-Macquart,* was written between 1871 and 1893 and contains, among other social documents, *Nana, Germinal* and *La Bête humaine.*
2. Rigolboche (Marguerite Badel) was a music-hall actress popular in Paris during the middle of the nineteenth century. She acted and danced most often at the Délassements Comiques.
3. The Duchesse de Persigny was well known for her promiscuity. Once, when her husband was ambassador in London, she could not be found. An aide asked: "Have you looked everywhere? Under the chairs and table? Under the secretaries?"
4. Alexandre Dumas *fils* (1824–1895) was the son of the famous author of *Le Comte de Monte-Cristo* and *Les Trois Mousquetaires.* Dumas *fils* became one of the most successful dramatists of the Second Empire, and perhaps his most famous work is *Camille* (*La Dame aux camélias*).
5. Many important figures of the Second Empire were to die of syphilis: among them, Jules de Goncourt, Manet, Dumas *fils* and Baudelaire.
6. The Hôtel de Païva at 25 avenue des Champs Elysées is now and has been for many years the Travellers Club. Except for the furniture, the house remains as it was during the Second Empire.
7. The Frères Provençaux was a restaurant well known for its private dining rooms and rich clientele. It was in the galerie de Beaujolais in the arcade of the Palais Royal.

CHAPTER 5 The Splendid City

1. The wall of the Farmer Generals, broken by sixty gates, circled Paris on the present second ring of boulevards. Built between 1784 and 1791, it was also called the *octroi* wall because toll booths collected customs duty on goods being brought into the city.
2. When Haussmann came to renovate the Ile de la Cité, the area contained almost a hundred streets and alleys. Some 25,000 residents were evicted, and the hundred streets became sixteen.
3. By the spring of 1969 Les Halles, outdated and creating a monumental traffic jam in the middle of Paris, had been moved to Orly. Traditionalists are horrified at the move, but surely Louis Napoleon would have approved of progress in the interests of efficiency.

4. The population of Paris almost doubled in the course of the Second Empire. In 1860 seven new *arrondissements* were added to the city by including the area between the demolished wall of the Fermiers Généraux and the outer ring of fortifications erected during the July Monarchy. Population figures: 1851 (1,053,300); 1856 (1,174,300); 1861 (1,696,000); 1866 (1,825,300); 1872 (1,851,800).

5. Jacob-Emile and Isaac Péreire were Jewish financiers and Saint-Simonians intimately connected with the business life of the early Second Empire. They founded the Crédit Mobilier, a vast holding and investment company which through public subscriptions promoted railroads and shipping and urban development.

6. At the contemporary rate of exchange this was $500,000,000. In view of the results it may appear relatively modest, but the entire national budget at the time was only $400,000,000. The cost was indeed astronomical.

7. Zola's novel *Le Ventre de Paris* (1873) features Les Halles as chief protagonist and contains many lush descriptions of food. Most famous is the hymn to cheese, the *symphonie des fromages*.

CHAPTER 6   The Other Paris

1. Louis Napoleon's seizure of Orléans property was popularly known as *"le premier vol de l'aigle"*—a pun on *le vol*, meaning both "flight" and "theft."

2. Soulouque was the Emperor Faustin I of Haiti, the archetype of the brutal Caribbean tyrant. He came to power at almost the same time as Louis Napoleon and, like him, created an imperial court. Clever journalists like Rochefort delighted in comparing Soulouque's regime with the Second Empire.

CHAPTER 7   The Great Fair

1. This breech-loading rifle was the invention of Antoine Chassepot, who worked at the Châtellerault arsenal. It was first used by French troops at Mentana and officially adopted by the army in 1866.

2. The waitress was speaking in the lower-class argot of one of the "red" *arrondissements* created during the Second Empire.

3. As one jealous friend said, *"C'est le passage des Princes, cette femme-là."*

4. The Malakoff was a fort which formed one of the central defenses of Sebastopol during the Crimean War. It was taken by General MacMahon and his Zouaves on September 8, 1855. Magenta and Solferino were battles fought during the Austro-Sardinian Campaign of 1859.

Chapter 8   The Bombs of Orsini

1. Louis Blanqui (1805–1881) was an early *carbonaro,* and his political activities earned him prison terms at Belle Ile and in Corsica and North Africa. Charles Delescluze (1809–1871) had been exiled after the coup d'état, but returned to France during the amnesty of 1859. He played a prominent role in the Commune of 1871.

2. Cayenne was in French Guiana and included the notorious prison colony of Devil's Island. Lambessa was in French Algeria.

3. During his years of exile at Jersey and Guernsey (he did not return to Paris until after the fall of the Second Empire) Hugo produced a number of violently critical books and poems and pamphlets, among them the *Histoire d'une crime,* a more than biased study of the coup d'état.

4. The government was supported with the following narrowing margins: 1857 (4,800,000); 1863 (3,300,000); and 1869 (1,083,000).

Chapter 9   The Pragmatists

1. This motto was at the base of the statue of Ferdinand de Lesseps which used to stand at the entrance of the Suez Canal at Port Said. The statue was blown up by Egyptian nationalists in 1956.

2. At the heart of Pasteur's scientific genius was the conclusion that chemical compounds capable of deflecting polarized light—compounds, in other words, made up of asymmetric molecules—indicate the presence of life.

3. $40,000,000 at the going rate of exchange; in the end the canal was to cost in the neighborhood of $100,000,000, much of the money coming from the Egyptian government.

Notes

CHAPTER 10 Syllabus of Errors

1. An extended description of children working in the coal mines of the north can be found in Zola's novel *Germinal*.

2. During the Second Empire the great arcades on the east and west of the Stock Exchange were areas where securities were traded constantly. These arcades made up the Coulisse, which Zola has described in *L'Argent*.

3. The *Syllabus Errorum* along with another encyclical, *Quanta Cura,* was issued on December 8, 1864. In them Pius IX condemned what he considered depraved modern opinions which corrupted society as well as the individual.

4. Achille Fould (1800–1867) was one of a family of Jewish bankers and acted as Minister of Finance during Louis Napoleon's presidency of the Second Republic from 1849 to 1852 and again under the empire from 1861 to 1867.

5. Eugène Schneider, later the presiding officer of the Corps Législatif, was head of the great iron and steel works of Le Creusot, one of the great French armament combines and the scene of a bloody strike in 1870.

CHAPTER 11 The Establishment

1. The Salon was the official yearly exhibition of the academic painters approved by the Ecole des Beaux Arts.

2. There is a famous anecdote about a well-known courtesan who met a friend on the Boulevard and said she had to hurry home to finish reading Renan's *Vie de Jésus,* since she was anxious to find out how the story ended.

3. Both Flaubert and Baudelaire were put on trial, not so much for having offended morality—the substance of the charges—as for having defied the established order.

4. Perhaps the only significant examples of modern design made by Second Empire architects were Labrouste's reading room at the Bibliothèque Impériale and Baltard's design for the pavilions of Les Halles.

5. These are padded ottomans and small sofas.

6. The Salon des Refusés, proposed by Louis Napoleon in 1863, was not the triumph of modern art which many people have supposed. Rather, it simply confirmed the public view that modern art was worthless.

346

7. Other examples of the *roman policier* by Gaboriau: *Le Crime d'Orcival* (1867), *Le Dossier No. 113* (1867) and *Monsieur Lecoq* (1869). Lecoq was the precursor of Sherlock Holmes.

8. The reference is to the novel about a poor servant girl by the Goncourts and Manet's painting *Olympia*.

CHAPTER 13   The Scientific Eye

1. Naturalism is simply an extension of realism with an emphasis on fact, no matter how sordid, and photographic accuracy in descriptive passages.

2. The first exhibition of the Impressionists took place in Nadar's photographic studio on April 15, 1874, and included paintings by Degas, Cézanne, Monet, Renoir, Pissarro and Sisley. Most of the viewers regarded the work as "appalling," "stupid" and "hideous."

3. Professor Magendie, Bernard's teacher, had said: "Like the ragpickers, I collect everything I can find."

4. These articles have been published in book form as *Causeries du lundi* and *Nouveaux lundis*.

5. Among Michelet's work on natural history we find *L'Oiseau* (1856), *L'Insecte* (1858), *La Mer* (1861) and *La Montagne* (1868).

CHAPTER 14   Flowers of Evil

1. The *grisette* was an available young woman, by no means a prostitute, who believed in "free love and Courbet," as one of them once said. An archetype is Mimi in Henri Murger's *Scènes de la vie de Bohème,* published in serial form in 1848 and dramatized the following year.

2. On a visit to Catulle Mendès near the end of his life, Baudelaire sat down with pen and paper and estimated that his entire literary career had earned him exactly 15,892 francs and 60 centimes—a little over $3,000 at the then rate of exchange.

3. He later lived in a building on the quai d'Anjou where the notorious Club des Haschischins met in the apartment of the painter Boissard.

4. From T. S. Eliot, *The Waste Land,* 1922.

5. "Death, old captain, the time has come: raise the anchor!"
6. *"Et dormir dans l'oubli comme un requin dans l'onde."*

CHAPTER 15   Orpheus in Hell

1. *La Grande Duchesse de Gérolstein,* composed by Offenbach and presented at the Théâtre des Variétés during the year of the Exposition of 1867. During the same year word was received from Mexico that the Emperor Maximilian had been executed. His wife was the Empress Charlotte or Carlotta.

2. Nestor Roqueplan first defined these ladies of easy virtue as *lorettes,* since they lived in cheap lodgings near the church of Notre Dame de Lorette.

3. The Palais de l'Industrie was near the pont des Invalides on the present site of the Grand Palais and the Petit Palais.

4. Morny had an abiding interest in the theater—and in actresses. Later, under the name of Saint Rémy, he wrote a libretto for which Offenbach composed the music: *M. Choufleuri restera chez lui le—*

CHAPTER 16   La Gloire

1. The brutality of French troops in the desert was well known. General Lamoricière was feared for his *razzias,* lightning raids on desert tribes.

2. *"L'Empire, c'est la paix"*: an excerpt from the famous speech given by Louis Napoleon in Bordeaux in the fall of 1852. From exile Victor Hugo wrote: *"L'Empire, c'est la peur."*

3. Louis Napoleon said that the French had come to Algeria not to oppress and exploit the people but "to bring them the benefits of civilization."

CHAPTER 17   The Last Spring

1. The day after the proclamation of the Republic, Louis Pasteur, admittedly pro-Bonaparte, wrote a letter to Marshal Vaillant: "In spite of the vain and stupid clamors of the street . . . the emperor can look forward with confidence to the judgment of the

future. His reign will remain one of the most glorious in our history."

Chapter 18   The Mousetrap

1. The *mitrailleuse* was a primitive machine gun, cumbersome and unwieldy.

2. On his deathbed (January 9, 1873) in exile in England, almost his last words were to his old friend Dr. Conneau: "We weren't cowards at Sedan, were we, Henri?"

3. Tons of the scorched remains of the Tuileries were bought by the Corsican Duke Pozzo di Borgo, whose family had feuded with the Bonapartes for years. With them he built a château looking out over the gulf of Ajaccio, where the first Napoleon was born.

BIBLIOGRAPHY

UNLESS otherwise indicated, the following books were published in Paris, and the publisher's name is in parenthesis:

Adam, Madame Juliette, *Mes Sentiments et nos idées avant 1870* (Alphonse Lemerre), 1905.

Allem, Maurice, *La Vie quotidienne sous le Second Empire* (Hachette), 1948.

D'Ambès, Baron (pseudonym), *Intimate Memoirs of Napoleon III*, 2 vols., London (Stanley Paul), n.d.

Amiel, Henri-Frédéric, *Fragments d'un journal intime*, 2 vols. (Stock), 1927.

André-Maurois, Simone, *Miss Howard* (Gallimard), 1956.

Arnaud, René, *Le 2 décembre* (Hachette), 1967.

Aubry, Octave, *The Second Empire*, New York (J. B. Lippincott), 1940.

Aumoine, Pierre, and Charles Dangeau, *La France a cent ans* (Fayard), 1965.

Bac, Ferdinand, *Intimités du Second Empire*, 3 vols. (Hachette), 1931.

Baldick, Robert, *The Siege of Paris*, London (Batsford), 1964.

Barbier, J.-B., *Silences sur le Second Empire* (Librairie française), 1962.

Barbier, Pierre, and France Vernillat, *Histoire de France par les chansons*, 8 vols. (Gallimard), 1956–1961.

Baudelaire, Charles, *The Flowers of Evil*, ed. Marthial and Jackson Mathews, New York (New Directions), 1962.

Bell Smith Abroad, New York (J. C. Derby), 1855.

Bellessort, André, *La Société française sous Napoléon III* (Perrin), 1932.

Bertaut, Jules, *Le Boulevard* (Jules Tallandier), 1957.

Bessand-Massenet, P., *Air et manières de Paris* (Grasset), 1937.

Bicknell, Anna L., *Life in the Tuileries under the Second Empire*, New York (Century), 1895.

Bibliography

Billy, André, *The Goncourt Brothers*, New York (Horizon Press), 1960.

Blanchard, Marcel, *Le Second Empire* (Armand Colin), 1950.

Bleton, Pierre, *La Vie sociale sous le Second Empire* (Les Editions ouvrières), 1963.

Boulenger, Marcel, *Le Duc de Morny* (Hachette), 1925.

Brada (Contessa di Puliga), *Souvenirs d'une petite Second Empire* (Calmann-Lévy), 1920.

Brogan, D. W., *The French Nation*, New York (Harper), 1957.

Burchell, S. C., *Building the Suez Canal*, New York (American Heritage), 1966.

Burnand, Robert, *Napoléon III et les siens* (Hachette), 1948.

Castelot, André, *La Féerie impériale* (Perrin), 1962.

——, *The Turbulent City: Paris 1783 to 1871*, New York (Harper & Row), 1962.

Castex, P.-G., and P. Surer, *Manuel des études littéraires françaises* (Hachette), 1966.

Cesena, Amédée de, *Le Nouveau Paris* (Garnier Frères), 1864.

Christ, Yvan, *L'Art au xixe siècle: Du Second Empire à la fin du siècle* (Flammarion), 1962.

Mémoires de Monsieur Claude, chef de la police de sûreté sous le Second Empire, 3 vols. (Rouff), 1881.

Collins, Irene, *The Age of Progress*, London (Arnold), 1964.

Corti, Count Egon Caesar, *Maximilian and Charlotte of Mexico*, 2 vols., New York (Knopf), 1928.

Crespelle, J.-P., *Le Maîtres de la Belle Epoque* (Hachette), 1966.

Cuny, Hilaire, *Louis Pasteur*, New York (Fawcett), 1967.

D.P. (Denis Poulot), *Le Sublime ou le Travailleur comme il est en 1870 et ce qu'il peut être* (Librairie Internationale), 1872.

The War Correspondence of the Daily News, London, 1871.

Dansette, Adrien, *Les Amours de Napoléon III* (Arthème Fayard), 1938.

Decaux, Alain, *Offenbach roi du Second Empire* (Pierre Amiot), 1958.

Delord, Taxile, *Histoire du Second Empire*, 6 vols. (Germer Baillière), 1869–1875.

Delvau, Alfred, *Dictionnaire de la langue verte* (E. Dentu), 1867.

Deschanel, Paul, *Gambetta* (Hachette), 1919.

Desternes, Suzanne, and Henriette Chandet, *Napoléon III: Homme du xxe siècle* (Hachette), 1961.

Dictionnaire de Paris (Librairie Larousse), 1964.

Dino, Duchesse de, *Chronique de 1831 à 1862* (Plon), 1909–1910.

Dolléans, Edouard, *Histoire du mouvement ouvrier*, 2 vols. (Armand Colin), 1936.

Dubos, René, *Louis Pasteur,* Boston (Little, Brown), 1950.

Du Camp, Maxime, *Paris: Ses Organes, ses fonctions et sa vie,* 6 vols. (Hachette), 1869–1875.

——, *Souvenirs d'un demi-siècle,* 2 vols. (Hachette), 1949.

Dumesnil, René, *Le Réalisme et le Naturalisme* (del Duca), 1965.

Duveau, Georges, *La Vie ouvrière en France sous le Second Empire* (Gallimard), 1946.

Ehrlich, Blake, *Paris on the Seine,* New York (Atheneum), 1962.

Evans, Thomas W., *The Second French Empire,* New York (Appleton), 1905.

L'Exposition universelle de 1867, 2 vols. (Commission Impériale), 1867.

Feuillet, Mme. Octave, *Quelques années de ma vie* (C. Lévy), 1894.

Ffrench, Yvonne, *Ouïda: A Study in Ostentation,* New York (Appleton-Century), 1938.

Field, Frank, *The Last Days of Mankind,* New York (St. Martin), 1967.

Fieldhouse, D. K., *The Colonial Empires,* New York (Delacorte), 1967.

Fleury, Comte, and Louis Sonolet, *La Société du Second Empire,* 4 vols. (Albin Michel), n.d.

Fowlie, Wallace, *Rimbaud,* New York (New Directions), 1946.

——, *Mallarmé,* Chicago (University of Chicago), 1953.

Ginisty, Paul, and M. Quatrelles L'Epine, *Chronique parisienne des six derniers mois d'empire* (Lafitte), 1912.

Goncourt, Edmond and Jules de, *Journal,* 22 vols., Monaco (Imprimerie Nationale), 1956–1958.

Gooch, Brison D. (ed.), *Napoleonic Ideas,* New York (Harper), 1967.

Gooch, G. P., *The Second Empire,* London (Longmans), 1960.

Gorce, Pierre de la, *Histoire du Second Empire,* 7 vols. (Plon), 1929.

Gramont, Sanche de, *The French,* New York (Putnam), 1969.

The Reminiscences and Recollections of Captain Gronow, London (Bodley Head), 1964.

Guedalla, Philip, *The Second Empire,* New York (Putnam), 1922.

Guérard, Albert, *Napoleon III,* Cambridge, Mass. (Harvard University Press), 1943.

Guide Historique des rues de Paris (Hachette), 1965.

Halphen, Louis, and Roger Doucet, *Histoire de la société française* (F. Nathan), 1953.

Hanotaux, Gabriel, *Histoire de la nation française,* 15 vols. (Plon-Nourrit), 1920–1929.

Hauser, Arnold, *The Social History of Art,* 4 vols., New York (Vintage), 1958.

Haussmann, Baron, *Mémoires,* 3 vols. (Victor-Havard), 1890–1893.

Hemmings, F. W. J., *Emile Zola,* Oxford (Clarendon Press), 1953.

Henriot, Emile, *Réalistes et naturalistes* (Albin Michel), 1954.

Héron de Villefosse, René, *Histoire de Paris,* 2 vols. (Editions Littéraires et artistiques), 1946.

Hibbert, Christopher, *Garibaldi and His Enemies,* Boston (Little, Brown), 1966.

Hillairet, Jacques, *Dictionnaire historique des rues de Paris,* 2 vols., 1963.

——, *Le Palais des Tuileries* (Les Editions de Minuit), 1965.

Holme, C. Geoffrey (ed.), *The Painter of Victorian Life: A Study of Constantin Guys,* London (The Studio), 1930.

Horne, Alistair, *The Fall of Paris,* New York (St. Martin), 1965.

Houssaye, Arsène, *Les Confessions,* 4 vols. (Dentu), 1885.

Howard, Michael, *The Franco-Prussian War,* New York (Macmillan), 1962.

Imbert de Saint-Amand, *Napoléon III et sa cour* (Dentu), n.d.

Jacques-Charles, *Cent Ans de Music-Hall,* 1956.

Julien, Charles-André, *Histoire de l'Algérie contemporaine* (Presses Universitaires de-France), 1964.

Jullian, Philippe, *Edward and the Edwardians,* New York (Viking), 1967.

Kenyon, Frederic G. (ed.), *The Letters of Elizabeth Barrett Browning,* 2 vols., New York (Macmillan), 1897.

Kirwan, Daniel Joseph, *Palace and Hovel,* London (Abelard-Schuman), 1963.

Kracauer, S., *Orpheus in Paris,* New York (Knopf), 1938.

Kurtz, Harold, *The Empress Eugénie,* Boston (Houghton Mifflin), 1964.

Labracherie, Pierre, *Napoléon III et son temps* (Julliard), 1967.

Larousse, Pierre, *Grand Dictionnaire universel du xixe siècle* (Larousse et Boyer), 1866–1878.

Lavedan, Pierre, *Histoire de l'urbanisme,* 3 vols. (H. Laurens), 1952–1956.

Laver, James, *Manners and Morals in the Age of Optimism,* New York (Harper & Row), 1966.

Lenôtre, G. (Louis Léon Théodore Gosselin), *Les Tuileries* (Fermin-Didot), 1933.

——, *En France jadis* (Bernard Grasset), 1938.

Le Play, M. F., *Les Ouvriers européens* (Imprimerie Impériale), 1855.

"Le Petit Homme rouge," *Court Life of the French Second Empire*, New York, 1908.

Leroy, Alfred, *La Civilisation française du xix* siècle* (Casterman), 1963.

Leymarie, Jean, *French Painting: The Nineteenth Century*, Geneva, 1962.

Loliée, Frédéric, *La Fête impériale* (Félix Juven), n.d.

——, *Rêve d'empereur* (Emile-Paul), 1913.

Longford, Elizabeth, *Victoria R.I.*, London (Weidenfeld & Nicolson), 1964.

Ludwig, Emil, *Bismarck*, London (George Allen & Unwin), 1927.

Malmesbury, Earl of, *Memoirs of an Ex-Minister*, London (Longmans, Green), 1885.

Marlowe, John, *World Ditch*, New York (Macmillan), 1964.

Martino, Pierre, *Le Roman réaliste sous le Second Empire* (Hachette), 1913.

Maurois, André, *The Titans*, New York (Harper), 1957.

Mercier, Jacques and Dominique, *Napoléon III quitte la scène* (Albin Michel), 1967.

Mérimée, Prosper, *Lettres à une inconnue*, 2 vols. (Michel Lévy), 1874.

——, *Lettres à M. Panizzi*, (Calmann Lévy), 1881.

Metternich, Princess Pauline de, *The Days That Are No More*, New York (Dutton), n.d.

——, *Souvenirs* (Plon), 1922.

Meyer, Arthur, *Ce que mes yeux ont vu* (Plon), 1912.

Morazé, Charles, *Les Bourgeois conquérants* (Armand Colin), 1957.

Morton, Frederick, *The Rothschilds*, New York (Atheneum), 1962.

Moss, Arthur, and Evalyn Marvel, *The Legend of the Latin Quarter*, New York (Beechhurst Press), 1946.

Nadaud, Martin, *Les Mémoires de Léonard, ancien garçon maçon* (Librairie universelle de France), 1948.

Namier, Sir Lewis, *Vanished Supremacies*, New York (Harper Torchbooks), 1963.

Newton, Lord, *Lord Lyons: A Record of British Diplomacy*, 2 vols., London (Longmans), 1913.

Orsi, Count, *Recollections of the Last Half-Century*, London (Longmans), 1881.

Ouida (Louise de la Ramée), *Under Two Flags*, New York (Burt), n.d.

Packe, Michael St. John, *Orsini*, Boston (Little, Brown), 1957.

Paléologue, Maurice, *The Tragic Empress,* New York (Harper), 1928.

Papiers et correspondance de la famille impériale, 3 vols. (Imprimerie Nationale), 1870–1872.

Paris Guide, 2 vols. (Librairie Internationale), 1867.

Pearl, Cyril, *The Girl with the Swansdown Seat,* New York (Bobbs-Merrill), 1955.

Pelissier, Roger, *The Awakening of China,* New York (Putnam), 1967.

Pemberton, W. Baring, *Battles of the Crimean War,* London (Batsford), 1962.

Perruchot, Henri, *Manet,* New York (World), 1962.

——, *Cézanne,* New York (Grosset & Dunlap), 1963.

Pflaum, Rosalynd, *The Emperor's Talisman,* New York (Meredith), 1968.

Pinkney, David H., *Napoleon III and the Rebuilding of Paris,* Princeton (Princeton University Press), 1958.

Ponente, Nello, *The Structures of the Modern World,* Geneva (Skira), 1965.

Poniatowski, Prince, *D'un siècle à l'autre* (Presses de la Cité), 1948.

Richardson, Joanna, *Princess Mathilde,* New York (Scribner), 1969.

Roqueplan, Nestor, *Parisine* (J. Hetzel), n.d.

Roux, Georges, *Napoléon III* (Flammarion), 1969.

Sala, George Augustus, *Paris Herself Again,* 2 vols., London (Remington), 1879.

Saunders, Edith, *The Age of Worth,* Bloomington (Indiana University Press), 1955.

Seaman, L. C. B., *From Vienna to Versailles,* New York (Harper Colophon Press), 1963.

Sée, Henri, *Histoire économique de la France,* 2 vols. (A. Colin), 1939–1951.

Segretain, André, *Souvenirs d'un officer du génie* (Hachette), 1962.

Sencourt, Robert, *The Life of the Empress Eugénie,* New York (Scribner), 1931.

——, *Napoleon III: The Modern Emperor,* New York (Appleton-Century), 1933.

Senior, Nassau William, *Conversations with Distinguished Persons,* 2 vols., London (Hurst & Blackett), 1880.

Simpson, F. A., *Louis Napoleon and the Recovery of France,* London (Longmans), 1923.

Skinner, Cornelia Otis, *Madame Sarah,* Boston (Houghton Mifflin), 1967.

Sonolet, Louis, *La Vie parisienne sous le Second Empire* (Payot), 1929.

Starkie, Enid, *Baudelaire,* New York (New Directions), 1958.

Taine, H., *Frederic Thomas Graindorge* (Hachette), 1959.

Thompson, J. M., *Louis Napoleon and the Second Empire,* New York (Norton), 1967.

Thornton, A. P., *Doctrines of Imperialism,* New York (Wiley), 1965.

Turnell, Martin, *Baudelaire,* Norfolk, Conn. (New Directions), n.d.

Twain, Mark, *The Innocents Aboard,* New York (Heritage Press), 1962.

Veuillot, Louis, *Les Odeurs de Paris* (Palmé), 1867.

Victoria, Queen, *Leaves from a Journal,* New York (Farrar, Straus & Cudahy), 1961.

Viel Castel, Comte Horace de, *Mémoires,* 6 vols., Berne (Haller), 1883–1884.

Villemot, Auguste, *La Vie à Paris* (Michel Lévy), 1858.

Wadley, Nicholas, *Manet,* London (Paul Hamlyn), 1967.

Wellesley, Henry Richard Charles, *Secrets of the Second Empire,* New York (Harper), 1929.

Wellman, Rita, *Victoria Royal,* New York (Scribner), 1939.

Williams, Roger L., *Gaslight and Shadow,* New York, (Macmillan), 1957.

——, *Henri Rochefort,* New York (Scribner), 1966.

——, *The French Revolution of 1870–1871,* New York (Norton), 1969.

Wolf, John B., *France: 1814–1919,* New York (Harper Torchbooks), 1963.

Zola, Emile, *Les Rougon-Macquart* (Bibliothèque de la Pléiade), 1961.

INDEX

Index

358

ACKNOWLEDGEMENTS

The author and publishers thank the following for the use of material for the illustrations: BULLOZ 3: Sorrieu: La République Universelle Triomphe (Carnavalet Museum). 5: Vue Générale de Saint Cloud (also The Mansell Collection). 6: Manifestation des femmes aux houillères du Creusot. 12: Bataille de Solferino (Versailles). 13: Orsini's attempt at assassination (Carnavalet Museum).

THE GERNSHEIM COLLECTION 9: Hortense Schneider, photographed in 1870. 10: Duc de Morny, photographed by Disdéri. 24: Baudelaire, photographed by Etienne Carjat. 25: Viollet-le-Duc, photographed by Nadar. 30: Edmond de Goncourt, photographed by Nadar.

GIRAUDON 14: Baudin at the barricades (Carnavalet Museum).

THE MANSELL COLLECTION 1: Napoleon III photographed by Disdéri. 18: Excursion in the Paris sewers. 17: Demolition of a portion of the Quartier Latin. From a drawing by M. Thorigny. 27: Verlaine.

THE MARY EVANS PICTURE LIBRARY 29: Dumas *fils*.

THE METROPOLITAN MUSEUM OF ART (HARRIS BRISBANE DICK FUND, 1941) 2: Eugénie. Lithograph by Alphonse Noël after the portrait by Winterhalter.

THE NATIONAL GALLERY 7: Manet's *La Musique aux Tuileries*. 23: Part of Manet's Execution of Maximilian. 26: Cézanne: self portrait (also The Mansell Collection).

THE RADIO TIMES HULTON PICTURE LIBRARY 8: Princess Pauline Metternich, painting by Winterhalter. 11: Offenbach on his 'cello surrounded by his creations, cartoon by André Gill. 15: Paris, 1867, from the original official design. 31: Jules de Goncourt.

RENCONTRE: COLLECTION BIBLIOVISUELLE 28: Manet's portrait of Zola.

ROGER-VIOLLET 20: Opening of the Paris Exhibition, 1867. 22: Digging the Suez Canal.

S. C. BURCHELL

S. C. Burchell, born in New York City, attended
Yale University as a graduate and undergraduate
and taught English there for several years. During
World War II he served with the Eighth Air Force
in England and has lived for long periods in Italy,
Spain and France. His major field of interest is
European history of the nineteenth and early twentieth centuries. This is his third published book. He
has written articles on historical subjects for magazines, notably *Horizon*. He lives in Southern California.

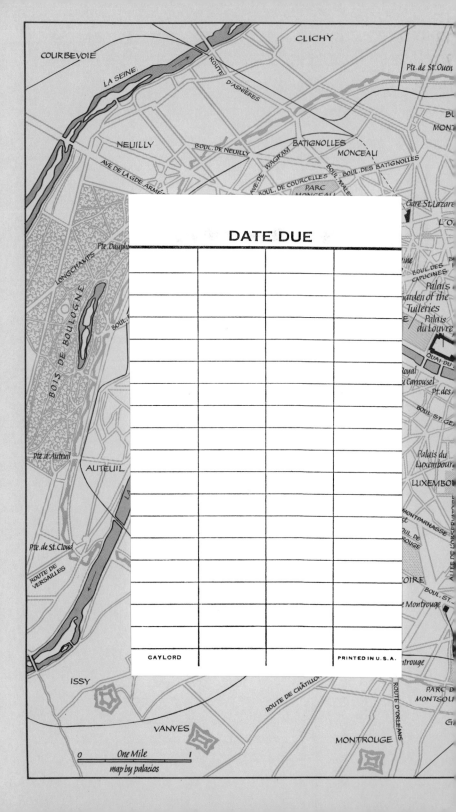